P9-EDB-525

Women in the Labor Force

STUDIES IN POPULATION

Under The Editorship of: H. H. WINSBOROUGH

Department of Sociology
University of Wisconsin
Madison, Wisconsin

Samuel H. Preston, Nathan Keyfitz, and Robert Schoen. **Causes of Death: *Life Tables for National Populations.***

Otis Dudley Duncan, David L. Featherman, and Beverly Duncan. **Socioeconomic Background and Achievement.**

James A. Sweet. **Women in the Labor Force.**

In preparation

Tertius Chandler and Gerald Fox. **3000 Years of Urban Growth.**

Women in the Labor Force

JAMES A. SWEET

Center for Demography and Ecology
Department of Sociology
University of Wisconsin
Madison, Wisconsin

SEMINAR PRESS New York and London
A Subsidiary of Harcourt Brace Jovanovich, Publishers

SEMINAR PRESS, INC.
111 Fifth Avenue, New York, New York 10003

United Kingdom Edition published by
SEMINAR PRESS LIMITED
24/28 Oval Road, London NW1

Library of Congress Catalog Card Number: 72-7704

PRINTED IN THE UNITED STATES OF AMERICA

Contents

Preface

This study is in the tradition of the cross-sectional demographic studies. We cannot, with cross-sectional data of the sort available from a census, reach any firm conclusions about the *causal* relationship between employment and fertility. However, we do have a set of data relating past or completed fertility to date to present employment. And from these data we can examine one side of the question—How does the presence of children in the family constrain the employment of married women. Clearly we cannot investigate questions relating to the role of employment desires and expectations in the process of reaching decisions about having additional children, nor can we say anything about the selectivity of women in the various cross section family statuses with respect to their "propensity" for employment independent of their family situation. These are questions that remain for other investigators with other data and other methods.

In Chapter 2 we discuss the data and methods utilized in the remainder of the study. Included is a description of the sample, a discussion of alternative employment variables, a description of the various independent variables, and a discussion of their substantive meaning and limitations.

Chapter 3 is a descriptive chapter utilizing mainly published census data. In it I document differentials in various dimensions of labor force activity in relation to family composition and age of the woman. White–nonwhite differentials are presented and discussed.

In Chapter 4 we present the results of a multivariate analysis of employment status in relation to the family status variables, education, family economic pressure, and age. In addition, we examine the effects of various aspects of marital and fertility history—such as age at marriage, number of times married, and length of the first birth interval—on current employment. The chapter concludes with a multivariate analysis of the conditional probability of working full time, given that the woman is employed.

In Chapter 5 we are concerned with interactions between the economic characteristics and the family life cycle in their effects on current employment. The life cycle employment patterns implicit in a synthetic cohort obtained from a single cross section are compared among education levels and among various levels of "income adequacy." An alternative analysis in which the responsiveness of employment to the economic characteristics is compared among women at various stages in the family life cycle.

One innovation in Chapter 5 is the investigation of the pattern of employment of married women with no children under age 18. This category is quite heterogenous, consisting of recently married women who have not yet had children, women who marry but remain childless, and those who have had children who have all grown up and left home. In order to take this heterogeneity into account, we divide our sample of women with no children under 18 by age, and report results of a multivariate analysis of the employment.

Chapters 6 and 7 deal with the pattern of earnings of married women and their contribution to total family income. Chapter 6 deals with the earnings of white women, while Chapter 7 compares the earnings of black and white wives.

Introduction

The importance of women in the labor force of the United States in the mid-twentieth century is widely appreciated. Women today constitute more than a third of the labor force; two women in five are employed. The numerical importance of women in the labor force has increased dramatically between the beginning of World War II and the present time. (See Durand, 1948, and Bancroft, 1958, for long-run trends. Long, 1944 and 1958, discusses recent experience.) In 1940 the percentage of labor force participation of women was 25.8; by 1960 it had risen to 34.5. The rate continued to rise through the 1960s, reaching a level of over 40% in 1970. The increase has been most pronounced in the case of married women, especially those with children. In 1940, 13.8% of the husband-present women were in the labor force. By 1960 this percentage had risen to 30.6. The percentages for women with children under 10 in the 2 years were 7.8 and 21.0[1]

During the period since the Great Depression, the United States government has collected and published many data on the labor force and the

[1]The 1940 data are found in U.S. Bureau of the Census (1943), *The labor force; employment and family characteristics of women*. Table 2. The 1960 data are from the U.S. Bureau of the Census (1964), *Employment status and work experience*, PC(2) 6A, Table 4. The 1960 data for women with children under 10 are from special tabulations that were prepared from the 1/1000 census sample tape. The 1960 rates for wives with children under 10 are somewhat understated because they are employment rates, rather than labor force participation rates.

labor force activity of women.[2] Many sample surveys undertaken by academic research workers have also included questions on labor force activity. Despite this wealth of data, there have been only a few good detailed studies of the determinants and consequences of the participation of women, particularly wives and mothers, in the labor force.[3]

Much of the recent work on the employment of wives has been done by economists, with a primary focus on labor supply. These studies have generally focused attention on the effects of wage rates, family economic need, and the local demand for labor on the employment probabilities of married women (Long, 1944, 1958; Mincer, 1962; Cain, 1966; Bowen and Finegan, 1969, Chap. 4; Schoenberg and Douglas, 1937). From a theoretical perspective, the labor force decision is regarded as one aspect of consumer choice. Given their tastes for market work, "leisure," and consumption of various goods and services, and the relative prices of "leisure" and other consumption items, women allocate their time among market work, "leisure," and housework.[4]

In addition to the work of economists concerned with labor supply, social scientists have been concerned with the employment of married women from a number of other perspectives.

1. A number of scholars have considered, largely in a speculative manner, the conditions in society that have changed in such a way as to permit the widespread employment of married women (Klein, 1965b, Chap. 5; Smuts, 1959; Nye and Hoffman, 1963, Chap. 3; Durand, 1948, Chap. 5; Oppenheimer, 1966, 1970; Lebergott, 1964, Chap. 2; Baker, 1964).

2. There has been a concern with the relationship between fertility and employment. Little in the way of conclusive study has been done here, because the isolation of causal connections is so difficult. This literature will be reviewed later in this chapter.

[2] In addition to the censuses of 1940, 1950, and 1960, the government has conducted a monthly sample survey of households since the mid-1940s. These data were published in Current Population Reports, Series P-50, P-57, and P-59, until 1959; in the *Monthly Report on the Labor Force* from 1959 to 1966; and in *Employment and Earnings and Monthly Report on the Labor Force* since 1966. In addition, *Special Labor Force Reports* have been published by the Bureau of Labor Statistics from time to time since 1960. The many statistical publications of the Bureau of Labor Statistics and Bureau of the Census contain descriptions of the data collection procedures and concepts used in the labor force statistics. Ducoff and Hagood (1957) discuss the history of the work force measurement in the United States and the particularly difficult conceptual and measurement problems involved in it.

[3] The literature up to the mid-1950s is summarized in Evelyn Kitagawa, "The Family as a Unit in the Work Force: A Review of the Literature," an unpublished document prepared for the Social Science Research Council Committee on Labor Market Research, 1956.

[4] This conceptual model will be discussed in more detail later in this chapter.

3. Social psychologists have considered the way in which the fact that the mother is working influences the psychological and social development of her children. A number of studies of this sort have been attempted, but none, as far as I have been able to tell, have isolated any definite effects. The lack of effects is usually regarded as a result of difficulties in measuring social psychological variables (summarized in Nye and Hoffman, 1963).

4. Some economists, particularly James Morgan, have been concerned with female labor force participation as it influences family economic welfare (Morgan, David, Cohen, and Brazer, 1962, especially Chaps. 9–11; Morgan, 1965; Morgan, Sirageldin, and Baerwaldt, 1966, especially Chaps. 3 and 4). There appears to be an increasing concern with the employment of wives and women in discussions of poverty policy.

5. Finally, various family sociologists and social psychologists have been interested in the ways in which work by the wife influences the marital relationship (summarized in Nye and Hoffman, 1963, Part 3; Orden and Bradburn, 1969).

The approach of this study was conceived after reading reports of the Social Science Research Council Committee on Labor Market Research. In those reports the Committee argued for the study of the labor force in terms of family units rather than individuals, and for simultaneous consideration of demographic and economic characteristics.

In a Social Science Research Council report entitled "Proposal for a Study of Labor Force Participation in Terms of Family Units," the Committee on Labor Market Research noted:

> Most of the information we have about the labor force, its size, composition, and dynamics, relates to the individual worker. The basic sources of our information, the Population Census, the Current Population Survey, the Bureau of Labor Statistics series on employment and payrolls, the Unemployment Compensation statistics, and the Old Age and Survivors' Insurance Reports, are collected about individual participants in labor force activities. Yet despite the great changes which have occurred in the economic role and functions of the family, it is still true that the family remains an important economic unit. For example, it is widely recognized that the family remains the basic consumer unit, especially for such items as housing and consumer durables. It has been realized for some time that the family is also an important unit in respect to the size and composition of the labor force. This assumption is at least implicit in the various studies which have attempted to deal with variations in the labor force participation of women, of the young, or the old, that is, with secondary workers. Such studies, however, largely because of the unavailability of the basic requisite data, have been discrete and segmental in character and have not been able to deal with many of the crucial factors which undoubtedly play some role in the determination of how many, and which, members of the family seek and find employment.
>
> It is proposed, therefore, to study the labor force in terms of its family unit

> composition to gain a better understanding of the way in which the composition of and changes in the labor force are affected by the characteristics of and changes in families. . . . More specifically, it is proposed to study the effects on the labor force participation of family members of variations in the demographic characteristics of families, on one hand, and variations in the economic position of families on the other [Quoted in Kitagawa, 1956].

Today, well over a decade after this proposal, there have been only a few studies of employment of wives from the point of view of their family position. There has been no detailed attempt to consider the joint influences of the demographic and economic characteristics of families on the employment of wives.

This is a study of the labor force activity of wives in the United States in 1960 as it was influenced by the composition of their families. In spite of the rapid increase in recent years of the rate of labor force participation of mothers of young children, the presence of children in the family and variations in their ages continue to produce wide differentials in rates of participation. One major goal of this study is to describe these differentials in detail. The second major objective is to compare the effects of the family composition variables on the employment of wives among various socioeconomic categories. An attempt will be made from these comparisons to infer probable causal connections. Finally, we will describe the earnings of married women in an attempt to assess the economic significance of the employment of married women.

There are at least three aspects of the family which are relevant to the study of the employment of wives in the United States in the mid-twentieth century.

(1) The family is an economic unit both in that it supplies labor to the more strictly economic units of society and is a consuming unit.
(2) The family is a reproductive and socializing unit of society.
(3) The family is composed of at least two individuals seeking their individual satisfactions.

Work by the wife has an economic dimension in that it provides the family with resources, permitting a higher consumption level than would be possible in its absence. It has a connection with the family as a reproductive and socializing institution in that the demands of the mother role and of the worker role may interfere with one another. A large part of this conflict involves the allocation of the scarce resource, time. Finally, the fact that the family is composed of psychologically distinct individuals is relevant to the study of the employment of wives insofar as work is a source of personal satisfaction. This may be the satisfaction of a career, the satisfaction of social participation, or independence, or any one of a dozen other satisfactions that have been suggested in the literature (see, for example, Hoffman, 1963). I will not attempt at this point to specify these satisfactions precisely, except to point out that work evidently provides satisfactions of various sorts to many working wives, quite apart from the economic remuneration.

The focus of this study, family composition and work, involves us squarely within the first two of these aspects of the family. Previous studies of and theorizing on the determinants of the probability of the employment of wives have stressed either the economic or the reproductive and socializing dimensions. No one has dealt adequately with the two dimensions simultaneously. The third dimension has been introduced here because the various studies undertaken from the reproductive–socializing perspective have posited various sorts of propensities or desires to work or to participate in societal units outside of the family. These propensities, it is argued, lead to an attempt to control fertility.

In this chapter I will summarize the existing thought on the determinants of the employment of wives, paying particular attention to the economic and the family composition factors. I will then describe the embryonic attempts of some sociologists to look at the dynamics of the relationship between work and fertility.

Factors Influencing the Employment of Wives: A Review of the Literature

There have been a number of classifications of the factors influencing the employment of wives. Hoffman (1963: 23ff) has suggested the major categories of "motivations" and "facilitators." She subdivides the former into monetary motivations, motivations relating to the housewife and mother roles, and personality factors. She notes that these subdivisions may not be mutually exclusive, and that a given factor may overlap categories. Facilitators are subdivided into demands of the housewife and mother roles, attitudes of the community and of the family members toward work, and employment probabilities.

Sobol (1963, Chap. 3), in a study of the determinants of the commitment to work or future work plans, classifies these determinants under three major headings:

1. Enabling Conditions (family status)
    a. Number of children now
    b. Ages of children
    c. Future child expectations
    d. Current pregnancy
2. Facilitating Conditions
    a. Education

b. Previous work experience, prior to and since marriage
3. Precipitating Conditions
a. Financial factors
i. husband's income
ii. wife's income
b. Attitudinal factors
i. life satisfaction
ii. need for accomplishment or occupation of time

Morgan and his Survey Research Center colleagues (Morgan *et al.*, 1966: 44ff) suggest a threefold distinction among "constraints," "pressures," and "more discretionary motives." Constraints include having children at home and physical inability to work. Pressures are economic motivations to work. Variables in these two categories are used by these authors as controls in order to examine the effects of the "more discretionary motives."

Regardless of the classificatory scheme, all students of this problem include very similar lists of the variables influencing employment. Rather than evaluating the classificatory schemes that are available, or proposing an additional one, I will list and discuss a number of characteristics which have been found to be associated with employment of wives.

Economic Pressure

Repeatedly, differentials in rates of employment of wives have been observed by income of husband. Table 1-1 shows the percentage employed by income of husband and age of wife for the total and nonwhite populations of husband-present women. These data are from the 1960 census. For the total population, 10–15% of the wives under the age of 18 work, regardless of the income level of the husband. In each older age group, a relatively constant proportion is at work for all husband's income levels up to $4000 per year. Above that amount, the proportion drops off sharply as income rises. For women 35–44, for example, about 40% of the wives of men with incomes of less than $4000 are at work; this proportion then drops off quite steadily to a level of 17% of wives whose husbands make $10,000 or more a year. The nonwhite wives have quite a different pattern. At each age level, the probability of the wife's employment is relatively uninfluenced by husband's income. This is particularly clear if the extreme intervals of less than $1000 and $10,000 or more are ignored.

A number of sample surveys have asked wives why they are working, why they had been working, or why they recently started working. Invariably, considerably more than half of the women respond in economic terms. The working wives in the 1955 Growth of American Families study sample (Sobol, 1963: 44ff), for example, were asked:

TABLE 1-1

Percent of Husband-Present Women Age 14–54 Who Are Employed, by Husband's Income in 1959, Age, and Color: United States, 1960[a]

Husband's income in 1959	Age of wife					
	Under 18	18–24	25–34	35–44	45–54	Total 14–54
All wives						
None	11.1	31.5	33.8	42.0	42.5	39.4
$1–999	11.0	30.6	31.0	37.4	37.9	34.8
$1000–1999	13.7	31.0	32.1	37.6	37.7	34.5
$2000–2999	13.8	30.0	32.3	43.2	39.7	35.3
$3000–3999	14.2	29.7	31.7	40.6	41.1	35.8
$4000–4999	13.9	27.9	30.0	39.8	40.6	34.9
$5000–5999	15.7	24.3	26.0	37.1	38.9	32.3
$6000–6999	16.7	21.5	21.8	33.4	37.0	29.2
$7000–9999	13.3	18.2	16.6	27.7	32.9	24.8
$10,000 or more	—[b]	17.7	12.2	17.3	21.8	17.5
Nonwhite wives						
None	—[b]	25.6	36.1	42.8	42.4	39.3
$1–999	11.2	22.4	29.7	37.8	38.4	33.8
$1000–1999	16.1	25.6	36.4	44.2	43.9	38.3
$2000–2999	12.4	26.8	37.2	47.4	47.0	40.2
$3000–3999	—[b]	26.7	36.2	44.8	44.8	39.1
$4000–4999	—[b]	28.2	35.3	44.8	41.3	39.0
$5000–5999	—[b]	27.4	36.2	44.7	40.9	39.4
$6000–6999	—[b]	30.0	34.7	43.6	43.0	39.2
$7000–9999	—[b]	28.5	31.9	41.9	45.7	38.2
$10,000 or more	—[b]	—[b]	26.0	36.3	34.3	32.7

[a]From U.S. Bureau of the Census (1964). *Persons by family characteristics*, **PC(2) 4B**, Tables 10a and 11.

[b]Base less than 2500.

> Women have different reasons for working after marriage. Some work because they like to or want a career, some work because it helps to get extra things for the family, some because the family needs income. How is it in your case?

Table 1-2 summarizes the distribution of first reasons given by the sample of women. Nearly four-fifths of the women gave reasons that are predominantly economic ("chronic and temporary financial problems," "need to acquire assets," and "work in family business"). There is a steep decline in the proportion reporting working to meet chronic or temporary financial problems as husband's income rises. Wives with husbands earning less than $3000 are somewhat less likely to report working to acquire assets, while

TABLE 1-2

Percentage Distribution of First Reasons for Working Given by Employed, Husband-Present Women Age 18–39, by 1954 Income of Husband: United States, 1955[a]

		Reason for working					
Husband's income	*N*	Chronic or temporary financial problems	Need to acquire assets	Need to accomplish outside the home	Need to occupy time or meet people	In family business	Total
Less than $3000	178	58	27	10	3	1	100
$3000–4999	154	41	42	12	2	2	100
$5000–6999	225	35	42	12	8	3	100
$7000 or more	95	17	36	18	19	10	100
Total	672	41	37	12	7	3	100

[a]Taken from Marion G. Sobol (1963), Commitment to work, in F. I. Nye and L. W. Hoffman, *The Employed Mother in America*, p. 58.

there is no appreciable difference between the income levels above $3000. Working in the family business or to occupy time or to meet people are given as reasons disproportionately by women with husbands earning $5000 or more.

A somewhat different sort of question was asked in a supplement to the February 1964 *Current Population Survey* (U.S. Department of Labor, 1965, No. 53). Women who took jobs in 1963 were classified according to the reason given as most important for doing so. Table 1-3 is reproduced from the report of the survey. For the total population of married women, 66% took jobs for what can be described as economic reasons: "financial necessity" (42%), "to earn extra money" (17%), "husband lost job or was unable to work" (7%), and "change of family status" (less than 1%). Nineteen percent took jobs for reasons of "personal satisfaction." The remaining 16% gave reasons that were not really answers to the question ("were offered a job" or "finished school"), or reasons that were not in any of these major categories.

Personal satisfaction is a more important reason for women with no young children (24%), women with some college education (22%), and women whose husbands earn $100 or more per week (26%). Among women with husbands earning less than $60 per week, the proportion giving economic reasons was 77%, and that for mothers of young children was 73%.

Clearly, economic factors are important in influencing the employment of wives. Economic factors, however, are numerous and complexly associated with employment. Economic *pressure* is a complicated matter related to

TABLE 1-3

Most Important Reason Married Women Took Jobs in 1963, by Age, Educational Attainment, Presence and Age of Children, and Income of Husband (Percentage Distribution)[a]

	Married women		Financial necessity	Earn extra money	Husband lost job[b]	Personal satisfaction[c]	Finished school or training	Offered job[d]	Other
	(Thousands)	Percentage							
Total	734	100	41.6	16.9	6.8	18.9	1.5	9.9	4.3
Age									
18–24	125	100	38.2	22.8	4.1	13.8	7.3	4.9	8.9
25–34	240	100	45.0	17.2	6.7	20.6	—	9.2	1.2
35–44	225	100	44.9	15.6	2.2	20.4	—	12.9	4.0
45–64	144	100	34.0	13.2	16.7	18.1	1.4	10.4	6.3
Presence and age of children									
Some under 6	319	100	48.1	16.2	8.0	12.1	—	10.8	4.7
6–17 only	254	100	39.6	16.8	4.8	24.4	—	8.2	4.4
None under 18	161	100	32.1	17.6	8.2	23.9	6.9	8.2	3.1
Education									
<12 years	306	100	45.2	16.8	7.3	17.5	.7	8.9	3.7
12 years	428	100	39.2	16.3	6.6	19.4	2.4	10.9	5.2
13 or more	148	100	31.3	15.6	4.8	21.8	2.7	15.0	8.8
Weekly income of husband[e]									
< $60	142	100	59.4	4.5	13.5	3.8	3.0	9.8	6.0
$60–99	212	100	50.3	20.1	7.5	14.1	1.0	4.5	2.5
$100 or more	380	100	31.1	21.6	3.6	25.5	2.5	11.8	4.0

[a]From Rosenfeld and Perrella, Why women start and stop working: A study in mobility. *Monthly Labor Review*, September 1965, p. 1078, Table 1.

[b]Includes husbands who were unable to work.

[c]Includes such reasons as: just decided to work; have something to do; gain satisfaction; and interested in particular line of work.

[d]Includes offered a job by friend, relative or former employer, or help needed in family business.

[e]Usual weekly income of husband at time wife took job.

current income, but not only a function of current income. A given current family income implies a different level of economic pressure depending on the number of family members; the existence of debt[5]; transfers of money outside the household, such as alimony or support of aged relatives, the amount of assets, and many other uses of income that are not directly related to current consumption of the members of the household. In addition, economic pressure has a subjective element. Hoffman (1963: 23–26) suggests that "income satisfaction" and "perceived financial need" have an impact on the probability of the employment of wives. She also suggests that mobility aspirations and income relative to those of members of various reference groups also may exert an influence. Clearly, consumption standards may vary from family to family, influencing the perceived adequacy of family income.

The stability of the family's income (excluding wife's income), and not merely its current level, may also be relevant. If the husband has experienced recent unemployment, his wife's participation is more probable than if his employment has been stable. In addition, if Friedman's distinction between permanent income and transitory income[6] has any merit with respect to employment decisions of wives, we would expect wives to work in higher proportions in situations where the transitory component of the husband's income is negative, in order to make the family's consumption commensurate with its permanent income. For example, this means that we would expect the wife of a young man whose education level is high, and whose income can be expected to increase as he proceeds through his career, to be more likely to be in the labor force than the wife of a man of the same age with the same current income who is not likely to have such a career pattern. Similarly, we would expect the wife of a man whose current income is depressed by any temporary factor to be more likely to be in the labor force than the wife of a man with a stable income at the same level. The accustomed or anticipated consumption level influences the actual current consumption level independently of the current income. But if current income can be increased by the wife entering the labor force, it is easier to maintain the consumption level.

Empirically, Mincer (1960) has found that, within age, education, and

[5]Rosett (1958) considered debt and asset holdings as explanatory variables. Rosett's dependent variable was the ratio of wife's earnings to husband's earnings and his other independent variables are inadequate for various reasons, making his results rather uninterpretable. As far as I know, there are no other studies including the effects of these aspects of family economic position on employment of wives.

[6]Friedman's formulation is found in *A Theory of the Consumption Function* (1957). A related discussion can be found in Deusenberry (1949). An application of these ideas to the employment of wives is in Mincer (1962) and Cain (1966).

child status categories, the probability of the wife working is greater if the husband worked less than full time, full year. A large portion of the income lost to un- or underemployment of husbands is made up by the work of wives. Thus, Mincer concludes that wife's employment is responsive to declines in transitory income. Mincer further reports that the correlations between labor force participation and weeks worked by husband, partialing out the effect of husband's income, are negative within age–education–child status groups. He interprets this finding:

> Consider a group of families standardized by age and education whose heads worked different numbers of weeks, yet with the same head's income over the year. If labor force rates of wives were related to current levels of husband's income, we would expect no correlation between weeks worked by husband and labor force participation of wife. We would expect correlation to be positive only if labor force activities of wife were inversely related only to permanent income [p. 576].

Cain found that a measure of transitory income, computed as a residual by subtracting husband's predicted income from his total income, had a smaller negative effect on wife's employment than did the predicted (permanent) income. The predicted income was based on education, age, region, and occupational status (Cain, 1966: 93–94). The empirical evidence on the relative strengths of the permanent and transitory components of income is mixed.

Employability and Earning Potential

One important determinant of the possibility of employment of a person is his ability and willingness to perform tasks for which there is a demand. The wife with an occupational skill is more likely to find work if she seeks it. She is also more likely to seek it than is a woman lacking such a skill. The more generalized the skill, the more likely she will be to find work. If it is a specialized skill, the shorter the supply relative to the demand, the more likely she will be to find work.

Willingness to perform tasks for which there is a market demand is also probably important. A woman may have the minimal skills and characteristics required for work as an operative, but only be willing to take an office position. One factor influencing the high rate of employment of black women, despite the discrimination and generally inferior work skills, may be their greater willingness to work in such occupations as domestic service and operatives in such undesirable places as laundries.

After employability is determined, earning potential influences the probability of working. The more money a woman can earn by working, the more likely she is to work, all other things the same. Earning potential is difficult to measure adequately. The wage rate of women who are currently working or who have worked in the recent past is a satisfactory measure, but there is no similar measure for women who have not worked for some time or who have never worked. Morgan and others use education as an indicator of earning potential (Morgan *et al.*, 1962: 108). Cain (1966: 92) uses a more refined measure, the median earnings of the woman's current occupation if she has one, of her most recent occupation if she has ever worked, or the median earnings of her educational level if she has never worked.

Regarding the use of education as a proxy for earning potential, it has been suggested that education is correlated with features of available employment opportunities other than earning potential (Bowen and Finegan, 1966). Education is positively correlated, for example, with access to pleasant, clean, nonmanual occupations. Education level also should be positively correlated with the opportunity to find expression of various

TABLE 1-4

Labor Force Participation Rates by Age, Education, and Color for Husband-Present Women: United States, 1960[a]

	Age					
Years of school completed	18–24	25–29	30–34	35–44	45–54	25 and over
All wives						
None	19.8	14.3	22.3	23.7	15.3	13.6
Elementary 1–4	19.2	21.9	25.9	31.3	19.2	21.0
Elementary 5–7	20.2	23.5	29.4	33.3	20.2	24.8
Elementary 8	20.9	24.5	29.0	34.1	22.2	26.6
High School 1–3	23.4	26.2	30.5	37.7	26.5	32.3
High School 4	34.3	26.2	28.3	36.8	29.3	32.8
College 1–3	39.4	28.6	27.7	36.8	33.8	34.3
College 4	56.7	34.7	27.7	38.3	41.0	38.1
College 5 or more	65.9	49.7	42.3	54.2	57.3	54.4
Nonwhite wives						
None	35.6	18.9	34.1	31.8	35.6	24.5
Elementary 1–4	40.9	32.1	37.4	43.0	40.9	33.2
Elementary 5–7	44.0	32.6	40.4	42.7	44.0	37.9
Elementary 8	45.6	31.6	39.8	47.6	45.6	40.6
High School 1–3	49.2	35.0	40.2	49.4	49.2	42.9
High School 4	54.0	40.1	44.5	52.6	54.0	46.5
College 1–3	57.9	48.1	50.4	56.0	57.9	51.8
College 4	82.4	63.8	66.6	73.5	82.4	69.1
College 5 or more	—[b]	72.4	73.4	80.3	89.3	79.1

[a]From U.S. Bureau of the Census (1964). *Educational attainment*, PC(2) 5B, Table 5.
[b]Base less than 2500.

psychological needs for which women seek work (need for self-expression, need for power, etc.). Thus, it is far from a satisfactory proxy for earning potential alone.

Earning potential and employability, I should also point out, are results of both personal characteristics and characteristics of the labor market area within which the person resides. I shall discuss this briefly in a later paragraph.

Whatever the reason, education does have a positive effect on the employment of wives in the United States. Table 1-4 shows the percentage in the labor force by education for all husband-present women over the age of 24, and for nonwhite wives of the same ages. There is a very steep positive gradient in the proportion in the labor force by education for both the total and the nonwhite populations. The effect of education is understated in these comparisons, which do not take family economic pressure into account, since education is inversely correlated with economic pressure and economic pressure is positively correlated with employment. The same sort of understatement is present in our previous data on the effects of husband's income on employment of wives.

The percentage never having worked, by education and age, is presented for both the total population and the nonwhite population in Table 1-5. The base population in this table is the total female population, and not just the married, husband-present female population. In each age group, the pro-

TABLE 1-5

Percentage of the Female Population Aged 20–54 Who Have Never Worked, by Age, Color, and Educational Attainment: United States, 1960[a]

Years of school completed	Age				
	20–24	25–34	35–44	45–54	Total 20–54
All women					
0–8	39.3	28.3	24.8	24.3	26.3
9–11	23.9	15.4	14.0	15.8	16.3
12	9.5	8.0	9.0	12.4	9.3
13–15	9.0	6.1	6.7	8.8	7.5
16 and over	3.5	3.6	4.8	5.7	4.5
Nonwhite women					
0–8	35.1	23.0	16.7	15.2	19.1
9–11	29.7	18.5	12.1	12.6	18.0
12	20.5	13.8	10.5	11.4	14.2
13–15	23.1	10.3	7.9	8.1	12.9
16 and over	7.1	4.1	3.6	2.8	4.0

[a] From U.S. Bureau of the Census (1964). *Labor reserve*, PC(2) 6C, Table 3.

portion declines very sharply as education increases. Fully a quarter of the women with only a grade school education or less have never worked. About 15% of the women who attended but did not complete high school, a tenth of the high school graduates who did not go to college, and 7 and 4%, respectively, of the women who attended and graduated from college have never worked. A similar pattern is found for nonwhite women. The fact that never working is more closely correlated with education than it is with any other variable associated with current employment, such as age, child status, and income, further suggests that the association of education with work experience is probably to a large extent a reflection of differences in employability. Most women have been in a situation at some point in their lives when their current family status or income level would have made working likely.

The research of economists has focused on the effects of income and earning potential on employment of wives. Economists are interested in labor supply. They have viewed the labor supply process as involving a choice between leisure and supplying work to the market. A rise in the wage rate at which a person is working has two effects: The "substitution effect" produces more work because it raises the cost of leisure relative to work, whereas the "income effect" leads to an increase on the purchase of all goods, including leisure. The latter thus results in less work. This simple model is appropriate only for an individual. When the unit of analysis becomes an individual within a family spending unit, there are additional variables that can change. For example, a change in the husband's wage rate or the entry of another family member into the labor force may have an income effect on the amount of work performed by the wife.

Mincer (1962) has suggested that a third alternative, in addition to market work and leisure, must be considered when the labor force activity of wives is being analyzed. This is work at home. Many of the tasks which a woman may do at home can be purchased in the market, e.g., food preparation, laundry service, and house cleaning. The care of children, when they are present in the household, during the time they are not in school, is a service that also can be purchased in the market. The conceptual problem of the economist is thus complicated by the need to consider additional sets of tastes, demands, and relative prices.

Without getting further involved in the nuances of economic theory, the first task of the economist in his analysis of labor supply has been to estimate the magnitude of the income and substitution effects. Empirical findings with regard to the effects of potential wage rate (or some proxy for it) and differences in husband's income on the employment of wives are interpreted in this manner.

Mincer (1962) and, more recently, Cain (1966) have estimated the elasticity of employment with respect to income and the potential wage rate. Their approach is to analyze differential employment rates of various subpopulations or different probabilities of employment of women in order to test the adequacy of the economic theory and to estimate the elasticity parameters.

Cain, in his *Married Women in the Labor Force: An Economic Analysis*, sets forth the following "conceptual model":

M	the amount of work supplied by a wife to the market is a function of:
Y_f	the potential income of the family in the absence of the wife's earnings;
W_m	the market wage rate of the wife determined by her market skills and the market demand for them;
W_h	a home wage of the wife determined by her home skills and the family demand for those skills (family demand is determined by the family's income and tastes for home goods);
O_m	market wage rate of other family members;
O_h	home wage rate of other family members;
T_m	the wife's taste for market work relative to home work and leisure.

Empirically, Cain restricts the application of the model to families with no other adults than the husband and wife. He takes the presence of children to be a "proxy" for the demand for home goods and skills of the wife in home work (W_h). He also suggests that the presence of children, particularly young children, reduces earning potential (Cain, 1966: 84). Why this should be the case is not adequately explained.

He applies the model to two levels of data, using first labor force participation rates of metropolitan areas (Cain, 1966: 44–89), following the lead of Douglas (1934); see also Schoenberg and Douglas (1937), Long (1958: 54–81), and, more recently, Mincer (1962), and Bowen and Finegan (1965). I shall not review this here. He then switches to individual women as units, using data from the 1955 Growth of American Families (GAF) study and the 1960 1/1000 census sample.

Cain selected the women who were not currently pregnant and not residing on farms from the original GAF sample of white, married women aged 18–39. With these 2035 cases, he performs a regression analysis. His dependent variable takes a value of 1 if the woman is employed full time, .5 if she is employed part time, and 0 if she is not employed. The independent variables of most interest are:

1. The earning capacity of the wife, as defined above.
2. The husband's predicted or permanent income, which is based on his education, age, region of residence, and occupational socio-economic status score. This is a measure used in the GAF study of fertility.

3. The husband's transitory income, which is the difference between the actual income and the expected or permanent income. Also included are the number of children in the family, the presence of children under 6, age, education, and income trend.

A regression coefficient of .109 was obtained for the wife's earning potential, −.040 on the permanent income measure, and −.020 on the transitory income variable. (All of these variables are measured in thousands of dollars.) Thus the wife's earning potential has a greater effect per dollar change than the husband's income variable. This is consistent with the findings reported by Cain and by Mincer using the metropolitan area data. The permanent income component has a larger effect than the transitory component. Cain attributes this anomalous result to probable measurement error in the residual transitory component.

When the same analysis was performed on the sample of women with one or more children under the age of 6, the regression coefficients on all three variables were reduced in absolute magnitude. (The coefficients were .044, −.023, and −.014, respectively.) However, because the mean rate of employment is lower for women with children under age 6, the elasticity (at the mean) of their employment with respect to earning potential is greater, despite the somewhat lower regression coefficient, than for all women. This, then, makes the results consistent with the theoretical conclusion reached by using the presence of children as a proxy for low taste for market work. The theoretical argument is ambiguous. Cain does not discuss why the elasticity measure is more relevant than the slope.

Family Situation

Family composition has been conceived of as largely a constraining influence on the work of wives, in that family responsibilities take time and have a higher priority than other uses of time. Thus, women with children are less likely to work than women with no children, and women with many children are less likely to work than those with few children. Similarly, younger children require more care than older children, thus depressing the probability of the employment of their mothers. School-age children are in school during much of the working day, and thus the mother is responsible for their care for a smaller proportion of the time. Special arrangements for their care in order that the mother may work may be necessary for only an hour or so after school hours and during the summer months.

It has been widely supposed that there is a sharp jump in the probability of employment when the youngest child reaches school age. Social psychologists have contended that this is both a time when the woman is freed from the responsibility of full-time child care as well as a period of psychological stress for many women.

> It is possible that the greater the joys of mothering for a woman, the more empty the days when the children are all in school. Even women who were satisfied with the housewife role before there were children may not be content to return to it. They have been used to a fuller and, in many ways, a richer day, and the housecleaning tasks may seem less important and more boring than ever.
>
> There is yet another reason why this time would by psychologically appropriate for women to return to work. The period when there are preschool children at home can have many frustrating moments for the mother. In addition to the unrewarding work activities . . . the mother's freedom is often considerably restricted . . . . Whatever the reasons, the youngest child's entering school can provide a release for many of the frustrations of the preceding years, and outside employment may be one expression of this release. This motivation is, in a sense, the opposite of the one discussed earlier and would characterize a different group of women. The former involves the notion that the early years of mothering are gratifying and the later years represent relative dissatisfaction. This one, on the other hand, suggests that the early years are frustrating and the later years allow for the release of these suppressed tension [Hoffman, 1963: 29–30].

There is some limited amount of data on the time spent on housework by mothers with different sized families. A French study reports that childless women spend a total of 61 hours per week on housework. Women with one, two, and three children spend 79, 89, and 100 hours per week on housework, respectively (Stoetzel, 1948: 47–62). Morgan and his colleagues (Morgan *et al.*, 1966, Chap. 8) report that the overall amount of housework done per year by both husband and wife together in American families is greater when the youngest child is 4 or under than when over 4 (2881 hours compared to 2259 hours, in 1964). When there are children under 4, the total number of people in the family influences the number of hours of housework performed by the husband and wife. When there is only one child under the age of 4, the total hours of housework is 2378, while when there are other persons in the household (presumably other children), the average is 3029 hours worked. Unfortunately no data are included to show the effect of both employment status of wife and family composition on housework of the wife. We would expect that the number of children in a family, as well as their ages, would be associated with the amount of housework. Mothers of several children or younger children would be less likely to feel that they have time to spend in employment outside the home.

The amount of housework, however, is apparently not fixed. Hoffman (1963: 26–28) reports that women adjust the allocation of time to housework in several ways when they work. They perform tasks less thoroughly or less often. An example of a task for which this is possible is cleaning house. They also report that they work more efficiently when they have a job outside the home. Some tasks are unnecessary and can be eliminated entirely, such as ironing certain things. Finally, there is evidence that working wives purchase goods and services that they would otherwise make or perform themselves. Examples are laundry services, prepared foods, and restaurant meals. In addition, working wives are more likely, *ceteris paribus*, to have more labor-saving equipment than their nonworking counterparts.

According to Robinson and Converse's (1966) preliminary time-use tabulations, employed married women with children worked an average of 6 hours per day on weekdays. The data shown in Table 1-6 indicate how the allocation of the remaining 18 hours per day differs between employed and nonemployed mothers.

Employed mothers spend considerably less time each weekday on food preparation, house cleaning, and laundry. They spend about the same amount of time sleeping and on "personal care." Child care as a primary

TABLE 1-6

Time Use[a] by Urban Married Women with Children[b]

	Weekdays		Sunday	
	Employed	Not employed	Employed	Not employed
Work related	6.0	.1	.6	.0
Housework	**3.6**	**5.4**	**3.8**	**3.4**
Food preparation	1.1	1.6	1.2	1.6
Cleaning house	1.5	2.2	1.4	1.3
Laundry, mending	.7	1.2	.6	.1
Other house upkeep	.2	.4	.5	.4
Personal care	**9.6**	**10.3**	**11.8**	**10.7**
Sleep	7.3	7.5	8.3	7.8
Eating	1.0	1.3	.9	1.2
Resting	.2	.3	.6	.5
Other	1.1	1.2	1.9	1.2
Child care	.7	1.4	.6	1.1
Organizations, education	.1	.5	.4	1.1
Mass media	1.1	2.0	2.6	2.9
Leisure	1.5	2.5	3.5	3.5
Other	1.4	1.6	.7	1.1
Total	24.0	24.0	24.0	24.0

[a]Mean number of hours per day spent in the activity. Columns do not add precisely because of rounding.

[b]From John P. Robinson and Philip Converse, "66 Basic Tables of Time Budget Data for the United States," Survey Research Center, University of Michigan, 1966. These preliminary figures are used with the permission of John P. Robinson. A more extended set of figures and analysis is in preparation.

activity consumes only .7 hours less per day of "mass media" contact, and an additional hour of "leisure" activities, and .4 hours per day in organizational participation.

These comparisons are very crude. We must await the publication of more detailed analysis of these data in order to understand fully the effect of maternal employment on time allocation. A particularly vexing problem is that family composition affects both time allocation and employment.

Several pertinent questions remained unanswered.

1. To what extent do other family members spend additional time on these household tasks in families in which the wife is employed?
2. To what extent are these tasks performed by purchasing services in the market? For example, to what extent do families in which the wife works buy laundry services or prepared foods rather than provide them at home?
3. To what extent is the difference in time allocation between employed and nonemployed mothers a result of the selectivity into the labor force of women who are more efficient in the performance of household tasks or whose minimum standards of performance are lower? Or similarly, the lower organizational participation of employed women may either reflect the fact that working women have less time for organizational activities or women with a lesser propensity for organizational activities have more time for work.

Another family composition factor of interest is the presence of other adults in the household, along with young children. Such adults may serve as baby-sitters, freeing the mother to work. Alternatively, they may work, obviating the need for the mother's work for the economic welfare of the family. Whether they work or not they can share the housekeeping tasks. A recent report from Current Population Survey (Waldman, 1967: 33) data shows that the presence of a nonemployed female relative raises the probability of employment of mothers of children under the age of 6 by 7% (see Table 1-7). The peculiar thing is that the presence of employed female relatives, in the absence of nonemployed female relatives, raises the probability of working 8%. Quite possibly there are socioeconomic variables confounding this relationship.

The upper panel of Table 1-7 shows that there are related females over the age of 18 in only 12.8% of all husband–wife families. They are present in 18.5% of the husband–wife families with children aged 6–17 but no children under 6, and in only 5.9% of such families with children under the age of 6. Thus, whatever the effect of the presence of related adult females, its contribution to the explanation of the total variance will be small.

The presence of other relatives, if they are elderly, may decrease the probability of a wife working, since the relative may require care just as a

TABLE 1-7

Labor Force Participation Rates of Wives by Presence of Female Relatives Age 18 and Over, and Presence and Age of Children: United States, March 1966[a]

			One or more female relatives		
Presence and age of children	All husband–wife families	No female relatives	Total	All in labor force	One or more not in labor force
Percentage distribution of families					
Total	100.0	87.2	12.8	5.6	7.2
No children under 18	100.0	85.9	14.1	6.3	7.8
Children 6–17 only	100.0	81.5	18.5	8.2	10.3
Children under 6	100.0	94.1	5.9	2.2	3.7
Percentage of wives in labor force					
Total	35.4	34.5	42.1	40.9	42.9
No children under 18	38.4	37.7	43.2	41.5	44.6
Children 6–17 only	43.7	43.5	44.6	42.9	46.1
Children under 6	24.2	23.6	31.0	32.3	30.3

[a]From Elizabeth Waldman, Marital and family characteristics of workers, March, 1966. *Monthly Labor Review*, April 1967, Table 2.

child does. We shall examine the effect of the presence of persons over the age of 64, as well as that of other relatives, with the data from the 1/1000 sample.

Not only the number of children and age of the youngest child, but also their age distribution, may influence the probability of work by the mother. Young children require considerable care, but older children, if they are also present, can provide the care. They can also assist their mother with the housework.

A 1965 report on *Child care arrangements of the nation's working mothers* (U.S. Dept. of Health, Education, and Welfare, 1965; see also Lajewski, 1959) indicates that the children are cared for predominantly by relatives, and at home. Table 1-8 shows that 47% of the children under the age of 6 are taken care of in the home, including 32% in their own home by a relative. An additional 15% are taken care of by a relative outside the home, and 15% more by the mother while working. Most of this latter category of women probably work at home or in a family business. Access to relatives either at home or nearby, the possibility of arranging work so that the mother and father are not at home at the same time, and work by the mother at home or somewhere she can take care of the child while she is working are the three major ways of arranging work and child care for pre-

TABLE 1-8

Primary Child Care Arrangements for Children of Working Mothers, by Age of Children: United States, 1965 (Distributions of Children)[a]

	Under 3	3–5	Under 6	6–11	12–13	Total under 14
Care in child's own home	**46**	**48**	**47**	**47**	**38**	**46**
Father	14	15	15	15	14	15
Other relative						
Under 16	2	3	2	6	5	5
16–64	13	13	13	13	13	13
65 and over	3	3	3	4	3	4
Nonrelative who only looked after child	8	8	8	4	2	5
Nonrelative with other duties	7	6	7	4	2	5
Care in someone else's home	**33**	**27**	**30**	**11**	**5**	**15**
Relative	17	12	15	4	3	8
Nonrelative	16	15	15	6	2	8
Other arrangements	**21**	**25**	**23**	**43**	**57**	**39**
Group care	4	7	6	1	—	2
Looked after self	—	—	1	8	20	8
Mother looked after child while working	15	16	15	12	11	13
Mother worked only during school hours	—	2	1	21	24	15
Other	2	0	1	1	1	1
Number of children	1580	2198	3778	6100	2413	12291

[a]From United States Department of Health, Education and Welfare, Children's Bureau, and United States Department of Labor, Women's Bureau, *Child care arrangements of the nation's working mothers, 1965: A preliminary report*, 1965, Tables 3 and 4.

school-age children. Thirty-six percent of the preschool-age children are cared for by nonrelatives: 15% in the child's own home, 15% in someone's else's home, and 6% in some organized form of group care such as nursery schools.

The 1960 Survey Research Center study of income and welfare in the United States collected data on arrangements for child care while mothers were working and also on the costs of such care. The results regarding costs of child care have never before been reported. There are not enough cases to permit a detailed analysis of costs of child care by age of child, whether and how the person taking care of the child was related to the head of the family, how long the mother worked, whether the baby-sitter lived in the household, how many children there were, income of the mother, or other variables that might contribute to our understanding of the ways in which child care arrangements are made, and the costs of such care. The units of the analysis here are mothers, not children. There are 173 mothers within our universe (husband-present, nonfarm, under 60) who reported that someone other than the school took care of one or more children in order that they might work. Thirty-one percent of these mothers reported that a nonrelative cared for their children. Of these nonrelated baby-sitters, 94% were paid. The average amount paid to paid baby-sitters was about $35 per month. The remaining 69% of the mothers reported that relatives cared for their children. Of the related baby-sitters, 45% were paid and the remainder were not. The paid relatives received an average of about $58 per month. Thus the mothers who arranged child care in order to work were divided in approximate thirds—one-third paid a nonrelative, one-third paid a relative, and another third received free child care services from a relative.

One additional factor which may have an influence on the probability of employment of wives is the support or expected support of children in college. This factor is both an economic pressure and family composition phenomenon. College is expensive and most of the expense is borne by the family of the college student. This expense is associated with the family composition phenomenon of having a child reach the age of 18 or so, and it can be anticipated several years in advance. We might expect that this expense or its prospect would raise the probability of work by mothers of high-school-age children as well as those of college students.

The income and welfare study provides a limited amount of information on this effect (Morgan *et al.*, 1962: 114). A composite variable, "Plan to help parents [in old age]" and "Plan to send children to college," produces net deviations from the grand mean as follows:

	N	Net deviation
Do not plan either	957	−.04
Plan to help parents	316	.03
Plan to send children to college	480	.02
Both	306	.06

The grand mean of the dependent variables, whether or not worked in 1959, is .38. Other variables in the analysis are age and education, race and age of children, husband's attitude toward wife working, family income less wife's earnings, and four other variables.

Employment Opportunities

We have already pointed out that the wage rate that a given woman with given characteristics can expect to receive would differ from place to place. Labor market characteristics also influence the probability of finding work at all, given the individual characteristics of the woman in question. Areas differ with regard to industrial composition of their employees. Thus areas differ in the number of employment opportunities for women (Belloc, 1950; also, Bowen and Finegan, 1965: 134–138). An economic base of textiles or electronics provides more employment opportunities for women than one of primary metals or industrial chemicals. Finally, areas differ with respect to unemployment levels. A number of economists have examined this effect on the labor force participation rates of women. It appears that the higher the unemployment rate, the lower the rate of labor force participation rate of women. This supports the "discouraged worker hypothesis" rather than the "additional worker hypothesis" (reviewed in Long, 1958: 181–201; Mincer, 1966: 73–112; and Cain, 1967). More women become discouraged and leave the labor force when jobs are scarce than are induced to enter the labor force because of the unemployment of primary workers.

One other set of areal influence has to do with areal variations in the acceptability of women working. This might suggest that women in small towns or rural areas or in more traditional parts of the country would have lower rates of employment (Hoffman, 1963: 36).

We will not consider any of these labor market characteristics in this study. Their interrelations with the individual characteristics is undoubtedly very complex. We will assume that they do not have effects that would modify the effects of the variables we will consider. There is no evidence that they do, nor is there any clear reason why they would. This is an important area of study which has not yet been dealt with at all.

Psychological Variables

There is a sizable literature relating psychological variables to work by wives. I will not review it here, but rather will refer to a summary of some of it prepared by Lois Hoffman (1963). She suggests that high need for achievement may lead to higher employment through two channels: a desire for upward social mobility and a "desire for a sense of competence." Furthermore, the association between educational attainment and employment may occur "not merely because education facilitates employment, but also because education is a manifestation of and a stimulation to the achievement motivation [p. 31]."

She also considers the "drive for actualization" as a potential influence on employment of wives. This is the drive to live up to one's own creative potential. This makes them "less satisfied with the housewife and mother roles, particularly with their less challenging and more mundane aspects." Work, presumably, would provide such self-fulfillment.

Hoffman also mentions the possible association between the need for power or dominance, the need for freedom and independence, the need for social contact, and the fear of aging and losing vitality as possible influences on the employment of wives.

An additional set of social psychological factors that may influence the work of wives operates through the husband's attitude toward wives working. Various American studies have found that a certain proportion of the husbands of working wives disapprove of wives working. A larger proportion of husbands of nonworking wives disapprove. The direction of causation here is unclear. It has been argued that work by the wife is threatening to some men because it symbolizes their own failure or inadequacy.

Other Variables

There are a number of other variables that have been found to be associated with differential levels of employment. Two of these which will be discussed here and used in the analysis are age and color.

Nonwhite wives have considerably higher rates of employment than white wives. Among the nonwhite women, blacks have the highest rates; women of other nonwhite racial groups have age-specific rates of employment which are more similar to the white than the black rates (see Table 1-9).

The employment pattern of black women has not yet been studied in any detail at all. The bulk of our knowledge comes from the census and Current Population Survey. In many cases the cross tabulations provided by color are quite inadequate for a detailed understanding of the employment patterns. Other sample surveys have too few nonwhites in the sample to permit separate analysis. In regard to the white–black differential, it has been asserted (for example, by Morgan *et al.*, 1966: 50) that, on the basis of such small samples, "Once one takes account of such factors as age, education, and husband's income, the differences become very small anyway." Published data from the 1960 census indicate that this is incorrect.

Several reasons for the higher rates of employment of black wives have been suggested by Cain (1966: 119–120):

1. For both white and black women, those who have been married more than once have higher rates of employment. Nonwhite wives are considerably more likely to fall in this category.

TABLE 1-9

Labor Force Participation Rates by Race, Nativity, and Parentage, by Age, for Females: United States, 1960[a]

	White					
Age	Native white	Native parentage	Foreign or mixed parentage	Foreign born	Black	Other races
14–17	14.7	14.5	16.7	16.9	9.4	9.8
18–19	48.0	47.4	55.7	52.6	34.5	36.7
20–24	44.7	43.9	51.1	49.1	45.7	45.3
25–29	33.1	32.9	34.5	38.2	47.8	36.5
30–34	33.4	33.6	32.6	36.8	51.6	38.5
35–39	38.3	38.6	37.6	40.3	55.0	44.3
40–44	43.9	43.8	44.0	45.9	57.6	51.6
45–49	46.3	45.8	47.5	47.7	57.0	48.7
50–54	45.2	44.7	46.8	44.7	52.9	44.1
55–59	39.4	38.7	41.5	37.5	45.2	40.8
60–64	29.5	28.9	31.0	26.1	34.4	30.0
65–69	16.9	16.4	18.3	13.5	19.5	17.7
70–74	9.9	9.6	10.9	7.7	11.4	12.2
75+	4.5	4.3	5.0	3.4	5.6	5.3
Total	34.1	33.7	35.9	28.3	42.1	36.8

[a]From U.S. Bureau of the Census (1964). *Employment status and work experience*, PC(2) 6A, Table 3.

2. Discrimination in housing forces blacks to live in less desirable dwellings which may necessitate or cause less desire for housework.
3. Discrimination in the male job market may cause substitution in market work from husband to wife.

The 1960 1/1000 census tape provides us with a unique resource for studying the determinants of the employment of black women. Cain has done some analysis of black employment from these data. This study will also.

The rate of employment of women has a distinctive pattern by age (see Table 1-9). There is a rise from ages 14–19 to ages 20–24; a decline from 20–24 to 30–34; a rise to a peak at 45–49; and a decline at each older age interval. In earlier years there was a peak at 20–24, followed by a gradual decline at all ages thereafter. The age pattern, at least at ages prior to 50 or so, is probably largely a result of differences in the various age groups in the distribution of women by child status variables. It also reflects intercohort change in employment. These matters will be considered in more detail in Chapters 2 and 3.

Fertility and Work

All of the studies that we have reviewed thus far are static and cross-sectional. There is another whole body of literature that views employment of wives in a more dynamic sense—in relation to marital history and, especially, fertility. The decision to work is made in the light of a family-building plan and preferences for work and children. Family aspirations and economic expectations and aspirations are closely intertwined. Empirical research from this perspective has thus far been inconclusive and unsatisfying. Cross-sectional data are of limited utility in examining questions of this sort.

Fertility and work are associated in a number of ways.

1. Children interfere with working in that they require care and make demands on the mother's time. Thus, at any given time, women who have more children or younger children are less likely to be able to work than women who have fewer or older children.
2. Fertility is subject to more or less rational control. If a woman wishes to work, she is likely to modify her fertility, both with regard to timing and total number of children. A woman who wishes to have children will probably have to resign herself to not working or to working less than she could in the absence of children.
3. Children are expensive and work is a source of income. A wife who feels strong economic pressures is likely to wish to work and/or to restrict her fertility. Thus both fertility and work may be expected to be influenced by family economic pressure (see, for example, Becker, 1960).
4. Related to this, both employment and restricted fertility by wives may be means of upward social mobility.
5. Work is a "modern" or nonfamilial activity, while childbearing is a "traditional" or "familial" activity. There are, presumably, women who are more familially oriented, independent of their current family status, and others who are oriented more toward extrafamilial activities (Ridley, 1959: 277–282).
6. For many women, one of the most substantial costs of having a child is the earnings she must give up when she drops out of the work force or reduces the number of hours that she works.

Since as early as 1941 in the Indianapolis fertility study, students of fertility have been interested in the relationship between fertility and work by wives. This interest has been pursued through the Growth of American Families studies, the Princeton fertility study, and the Detroit studies.

From the Indianapolis data, Lois Pratt selected a sample of fecund married women at the end of their childbearing period. She found work experience was negatively related to actual and desired family size, and positively related to the effective use of contraception (Pratt and Whelpton, 1958: 1245–1280).

Several analyses of work and fertility were undertaken using data from the 1955 Growth of American Families study (1957; partially summarized in Ridley, 1959). Jeanne Clare Ridley started with the hypothesis that women who wish to participate in activities outside the home will be more likely to accept some method of birth control in order to limit their fertility. Work and organizational participation were the two forms of activity outside the home. She sees the conflict between work and children as being primarily one of competition for the woman's time. She also argues that children compete in two ways with a higher standard of living: (1) they consume, and (2) they prevent the wife from working. The present-day emphasis of child-rearing literature on the quality of the mother–child relationship mitigates against the mother seeking work even if she could have time for both work and housework.

In order to avoid problems of confounding the effects of fecundity differentials with those of voluntary fertility, Ridley restricted her sample to women as fecund—couples for whom there was no evidence of impaired fecundity. (Fecundity classification is discussed in Freedman, Whelpton, and Campbell, 1959.) In order to avoid the *ex post facto* nature of the earlier Indianapolis analysis, and thus to draw more definite causal conclusions, she used expected completed family size and future expected births as two of the fertility variables. Her empirical conclusions are summarized as follows:

1. Women who have worked for long periods since marriage are more likely to be subfecund than women who have worked shorter periods or not at all.
2. Fecundity is not related to expectations of working in the future.
3. Working women expect slightly smaller completed families than non-working women. They have had fewer children to date, and they expect fewer in the future. This relationship persists after controls for socio-economic status are introduced.
4. Current labor force status better predicts whether any additional children at all are expected than it does the number expected.
5. Work experience is related to past use and expected future use of contraception. The crucial thing here is whether or not there is work experience, not the amount.
6. The longer the work experience since marriage, the more likely the woman was to have had completely planned fertility.
7. Expecting to work in the future is associated with current and expected use of contraception and with lower expected completed family size.

Clare points to the methodological dilemma when she notes:

> It is difficult to decide whether the high incidence of childlessness is due to a tendency for wives to work if they cannot bear children or to the deliberate avoidance of having children by wives who prefer to work. Nor, likewise, is it possible to decide whether families are smaller because wives desire to be employed or whether they are employed because their families are smaller [Ridley, 1959: 281].

She does conclude, however, from the GAF-I data that her original speculation, that the desire to work at a career or for contacts outside the family are important influences on fertility, is erroneous.

Using the same body of data, Namboodiri (1964: 65–77) investigated the association between work duration since marriage and the length of birth intervals. He reports that wife's work duration is directly related to the time taken after marriage to produce a given number of children. Namboodiri partialed out the effect of marriage duration, finding that the effect of years worked since marriage was reduced by a quarter for the length of the first birth interval and by 50–60% for the second. It retained a sizeable effect.

Using data from the longitudinal Detroit fertility study, Freedman and Coombs found (1966b: 197–222):

1. Family size *preferences* are inversely related to length of work since marriage, especially at earlier parities. The differences between preferences for women working less than 1 year and those working 5 or more years are from .5 to .9 children, and are not due to fecundity impairment.
2. Longer birth intervals and lower probability of having been premaritally pregnant are associated with longer work experience. These findings persist when duration of marriage is controlled.
3. Fertility in the 2-year interval between the interviews was *positively* related to work experience between marriage and the first interview. This last result may suggest that these women delayed fertility in order to work.

Perhaps more interesting and germane from the point of view of my own work is the more general conclusion of the two papers by Freedman and Coombs (1966a; 1966b: 631–648) that, for whatever reason, the shorter the first birth interval and the more rapidly the family is formed, the lower the level of current income and the lower the level of asset accumulation of the couple. Women who have children very shortly after marriage have much less chance to work and consequently make a lower contribution to asset accumulation. If the effect of early employment persists through time, the lack of early work experience might result in lower family income merely because of the lower contribution of the wife.

Using the Detroit data, Freedman, Coombs, and Friedman (1966: 327–344) have found that women who have been working have a higher fetal death rate than women who have not. They suggest several possible interpretations: (1) Working produces a greater fetal loss; (2) Women who are more prone to fetal deaths are more likely to work because they expect fewer children; and (3) Working women are more likely to have induced abortions. In connection with this latter point, they suggest that they may have greater access to information on the availability of abortions as a result of contacts made at work.

Westoff, Potter, Sagi, and Mishler (1961) see job and career as sources of personal satisfaction. This type of satisfaction is seen as an alternative to or an addition to traditional marital roles (e.g., bearing children). They point to two sources of conflict: (1) a conflict of values, and (2) a conflict of time. In order to test their original assertion, they use months worked since marriage as a measure of interest in job, and career and fertility performance (birth intervals) as a measure of interest in childbearing, admitting that these may not be highly valid. The following correlations with employment duration since marriage were obtained:

Number of children born	−.21
First birth interval	.70
Second birth interval	.32
Interval from marriage to second birth	.64

They abandon the interpretation of a conflict of values when they find that liking for children is correlated with neither months of employment nor future work plans. "There is neither evidence to support the hypothesis that job and career interests stand opposed to familial interests or, as hypothesized by Pratt and Whelpton, that there exists a direct relationship between extrafamilial participation and interest in and liking for children [Westoff *et al.*, 1961: 304]." The correlation between number of months since marriage spent not working and the number of children desired is −.17. They conclude that a "desire for a small family leads to long birth intervals, which in turn permit long duration of employment as well as nonemployment between marriage and second birth [Westoff *et al.*, 1961: 304]."

They suggest that, since the sample was composed of persons with two children, it selects out career women who would have fewer than two children or who would have two children later. This, they say, depresses the correlation between work duration and fertility. However, other studies of the reasons for working suggest that the career wife is very rare in the population.

The follow-up study of the same sample found that those women who had accidental pregnancies during the interval were those *most* likely to be working. Work in the interval had no association with number of children desired. The authors reach the conclusion that "rather than a conflict of interest hypothesis, data suggest socioeconomic class and the time available to the wife affect the choice of and intensity of extra-familial activity [Westoff, Potter, and Sagi, 1963: 190]."

Approaching the matter of fertility and work from a different perspective, Garfinkle, using 1960 census data, has done a multiple decrement life table analysis of the work life of married women. From that analysis he concluded that "the birth of a child reduces the average number of years a married woman can be expected to spend in the work force by about ten years. The birth of each additional child appears to further reduce the work life expectancy from two to three years for each child [U.S. Dept. of Labor, Manpower Administration, 1967]."

In summary, current work, work experience, and expectations regarding work are associated with various measures of past and expected fertility and with contraceptive practice. Each of the researchers we have cited concludes his analysis of these relationships with a statement that it is impossible to draw any causal conclusions regarding fertility and work. Freedman *et al.* (1959), for example, write:

> The association between the wife's working and the effectiveness of the couple's fertility planning has several explanations. One is simply negative selection: many of the couples not planning effectively have too many children to permit the wife to work easily. Unless forced to work by sheer economic necessity, these women tend to be excluded from the labor force by the lack of fertility planning or the ineffectiveness of the efforts made. More positively, if the wife wants to work and the husband wants her to do so, the couple has a strong motivation to plan family growth so as to make work possible. Moreover, it is likely that the wife's working contacts will put her in touch with other wives whose attitudes are favorable to contraception and who have information to communicate about effective practice [pp. 140–141].

Causally, there are four major possibilities, each of which undoubtedly occurs in the population in significant numbers.

1. The desire to work leads to restricted fertility.
2. Restricted fertility makes it possible to work.
3. The desire for increased fertility leads to restriction of work activity.
4. Work and fertility restriction both result from some third variable or combination of variables.

In connection with the first of these, there remains the question of the reason for wishing to work. It can be economic or simply a desire to work for the sake of working. In connection with the second, restricted fertility may be due to fecundity impairment, or purposeful for reasons other than the desire to work. Commenting on the historical changes in fertility and work by wives, Myrdal and Klein (1956) suggest a correlation between work and fertility which is due to the correlation of each with a third variable.

> When family limitation is spreading but is not a general pattern, the more alert type of woman who adopts voluntary control of her fertility will often be the type who is interested in retaining financial independence and intensely active life. Thus personality traits can act selectively in favor of both planned families and the gainful employment of women [p. 119].

Methodologically, the most important problem has to do with the inability to take history into accourt with currently available data. Retrospective data can do so to a limited extent, but as yet, the necessary data have not been collected. A decision to have a child at a particular time is influenced by a number of factors present at that time. Among them are the ages and number of children already present, the economic position of the family, the expected future economic position, and the desire of the wife to work. However, empirically:

1. Controls on the current socioeconomic status or need to work may not reflect very well the earlier state.
2. The number of children desired or expected now may not resemble the number desired or expected earlier. We are beginning to get some data on the temporal stability of this variable through panel studies.
3. Attempts to draw conclusions regarding causation from birth interval data encounter difficulty because a long birth interval may have occurred by choice, by chance, or because of a definite fecundity problem. A long interval by choice may be due to the desire to work for whatever reason (economic or noneconomic), or simply the desire not to have a child for any other reason. No study has every asked why particular intervals were long or short.
4. At any given point in time, the woman is not faced with a simple decision to have an additional child or to work. In deciding to work, she must, if she has already had children, contend with them in her decision-making process.
5. Finally, history also enters into the picture in that work experience in the past may modify both the probability of working in the present and also the fertility decisions.

2

Data and Methodology

In this chapter I will discuss the data I am using, describe the variables to be used in the analysis, present my interpretation of their significance in relation to predicting the probability of working, and finally describe the methods of analysis that will be utilized. Discussion of the data and methods used in the analysis of earnings will be deferred to Chapter 6.

The Data

Almost all of the data used are from the 1960 United States Census of Population. These data are in two forms: published tabulations and the .1% sample of households.

One-in-a-Thousand Sample

The 1/1000 sample tape contains almost all of the individual characteristic items collected in the census. The omitted information is primarily the precise geographic location of the person. In addition to individual characteristics, there are for each person in the sample some characteristics of the household, the family, and the subfamily of which he is a member; selected characteristics of an "associated person" in the household who, in the case of the married woman living with her husband, is the husband; and some characteristics of the housing unit in which the person lives.

In addition, since the unit that is sampled is the household, the records of all members of the household are together on the tape. Thus it is possible to obtain almost anything that is desired in the way of household composition data. I have utilized this last feature to construct several household composition and income variables from the records of all members of the household.

The specific sample that I have taken from the census tape consists of married women under the age of 60 who are living with their husbands, who do not live on farms nor in group quarters, and who are not members of secondary families. I have restricted the analysis to husband-present women, because to have included women of other marital statuses would have confounded the problem considerably. Certainly women of other marital statuses would have to be dealt with separately. I have excluded women living on farms because of the great inadequacy of applying the employment status concepts to them. An examination of the 1960 Current Population Survey-Census match leaves little doubt of this. I have discussed this matter further in Appendix A. Finally, secondary family members (that is, married women living in a household, the head of which is not related to her) were excluded because: (1) if they were domestic employees living in, their presence is not a family phenomenon, and (2) the application of the presence of other persons and family income concepts to these persons caused many complicated technical problems of programming. Husband-present women living as noninmates in group quarters were also excluded in order to simplify programming. Very likely, there were none of these in the 1/1000 sample anyway.

The upper age limit determines the extent to which it is possible to talk about the effects of the presence of children of older ages. A sample of women up to age 59 permits discussion of the effects of children up to the age of 17, since over 99% of the children under the age of 17, who are living with their mothers, have mothers who are under that age. I have estimated that more than 95% of the mothers of children aged 17 who are living with their mothers are covered with this age limit. The total sample size is about 32,500, of which 29,700 are white and 2800 are nonwhite. Of the 32,500, about 22,000 have one or more children under age 18. Much of the analysis will concern only these women, whom we will designate as "mothers."

Variables

It is convenient to classify the variables that we are using under the following headings: (1) labor force variables, (2) family composition variables, (3) family history variables, (4) economic variables, and (5) other variables. The analysis in the next three chapters will consider the association of family composition and family history variables with labor force variables. The "economic" and the "other" variables will be included in the analysis primarily to control their effects, thus avoiding the possibility of confounding the effects of the family composition variables. In addition, in Chapters 3 and 5 the effects of the family composition variables will be compared among various subpopulations defined on the basis of the "economic" and the "other" variables.

Labor Force Variables

Proportion Employed. I have chosen to use "percentage of the population group which is employed" rather than "percentage in the labor force" as my major dependent variable. Unemployment, which is a component of the labor force, is a very ambiguous concept when applied to women and other potential secondary workers (Wilcock, 1957). In the 1960 census the unemployed were identified as those persons who were not at work but were "looking for work." The census enumerators were given supplementary instructions regarding the meaning of "looking for work," which did not appear on the questionnaire. "Looking for work" includes making efforts to find work in the past 60 days if the person were still awaiting the results of such efforts. The unemployed did not include persons who would like to work but who have made no specific efforts to find it in the past 60 days, even if they believe that no appropriate work exists.

There is evidence that the employment status category "unemployed" is not very reliable, while the "employed" and the "not in the labor force" categories are classified fairly reliably. The Census Bureau has investigated the reliability of responses on various census items, including employment status. This has been done by matching the records of persons enumerated in the April 1960 Current Population Survey (CPS) with those from the 1960 census (U.S. Bureau of the Census, 1965). Census records were matched for about 93% of the CPS sample. There are reasons to believe that the CPS enumerators generally get better information. They are better trained, regular, hourly-paid employees. They generally find more persons in the less obvious, harder-to-identify categories such as "self-employed," "unemployed," and "with a job but not at work."

In Table 2-1 the comparisons of the classification of the female population on the basis of employment status in the 1960 census and the Current Population Survey match are shown. I have computed the percentages of the persons classified by the CPS within each employment status category who were classified in each category by the census. For each age group, about 90% of the "not in the labor force" and "employed" categories were classi-

TABLE 2-1

Comparison of Census and Current Population Survey Classifications of the Employment Status of Matched Women, by Age: United States, 1960[a]

Age and CPS classification	Percentage in each category in census classification				
	Employed	Un-employed	Not in labor force	Not reported	Total
20–24					
Employed	88.3	2.8	5.8	3.2	100.0
Unemployed	6.9	34.0	59.1	.0	100.0
Not in labor force	4.1	2.4	88.2	5.3	100.0
25–34					
Employed	87.8	.6	8.0	3.7	100.0
Unemployed	20.1	40.2	37.2	2.6	100.0
Not in labor force	5.0	1.1	91.5	2.4	100.0
35–44					
Employed	88.9	1.0	7.8	2.2	100.0
Unemployed	16.4	33.6	50.0	.0	100.0
Not in labor force	5.6	1.2	90.8	2.3	100.0
45–54					
Employed	85.6	1.2	9.7	3.5	100.0
Unemployed	13.3	48.6	38.1	.0	100.0
Not in labor force	6.8	1.1	90.3	1.7	100.0
Total–all ages					
Employed	84.6	1.3	10.5	3.2	100.0
Unemployed	15.6	30.8	52.5	1.0	100.0
Not in labor force	4.8	1.0	90.9	3.2	100.0
Nonwhite–all ages					
Employed	73.8	1.9	17.7	6.7	100.0
Unemployed	11.7	31.1	52.5	4.7	100.0
Not in labor force	8.4	3.2	81.6	6.9	100.0

[a] From U.S. Bureau of the Census (1965), *Evaluation and Research Program of the U.S. Censuses of Population and Housing: 1960*. Accuracy of data on population characteristics as measured by CPS-census match (ER 60, No. 5), Table 29.

fied in the same way by both the CPS and the census. Between 5 and 10% of the CPS "employed" category were classified as not in the labor force, and between 4 and 7% of the CPS "not in the labor force" category were classified as employed in the census. Fully half of the persons recorded as unemployed in the CPS were classified as not in the labor force, and an additional 10% or so were classified as employed in the census.

The last panel of Table 2-1 shows comparable data for nonwhite women. The reliability of employment status seems to be considerably lower for these women than for any of the age groups shown in the upper panels. Less than three-quarters of the women classified by the CPS as employed were in the same classification in the census; 18% of these women were classed as not in the labor force. The reliability of the "unemployed" and "not in the labor force" categories also appears somewhat lower for the nonwhite women. This is consistent with the fact that nonwhite women are more likely to be working part time and are more likely to be in rather marginal positions in the labor force and working sporadically.

Some of the deviation reflects actual movement from one employment status to another during the time between the Current Population Survey and the census enumerations. Most of the deviation is undoubtedly a result of the classification of the same situation in two different ways by the census and CPS enumerators.

The reliability of the category "unemployed" is clearly low. The greatest problem seems to be distinguishing the unemployed women from those who are not in the labor force. The reliability of classification of women between the "employed" and "not employed" categories is about as high as we find with other variables in the census. Of course, the real problem which arises when we begin to examine the association of one variable with another is whether the error in one variable is correlated with either the value of the other or its error (Bogue and Murphy, 1964). We have no information on this, nor is there any basis for speculation.

The use of the proportion employed during the week immediately preceding the census enumeration as the major labor force variable can be questioned on several grounds.

1. Women are very mobile into and out of the labor force; thus, the makeup of the labor force at any given time is quite unstable. Since we are not concerned with individual women, but with categories of women, this matter loses much of its relevance. We are assuming that the census week is a representative week for the period around 1960, and that if some other week had been chosen the levels would be about the same as they were at the time of the census, as would the differentials. (Actually, the census week is not a specific week, but the week immediately preceding the one in which the household was enumerated.)

2. The use of "employment" as a category weights women who work just a few hours per week equally with those who work full time. Clearly, employment is not a very adequate measure of the supply of labor effort, nor of productive contribution, nor of earnings, nor of the amount of time taken from housework and child care. We intend it to be none of these.

3. Labor force participation is a more adequate measure of labor force activity than employment, because it takes out the demand for labor component, leaving only the supply of labor. Or, in more motivational terms, it

measures the number of women who want to work, and not simply that subset of the women who want to work and are able to find acceptable jobs. Wanting to work, however, is a very ambiguous thing. There are numerous levels of wanting to work—wanting to work if the wage made it worthwhile; wanting to work if you could find someone to take care of the baby, or if you did not have the baby; wanting to work if you could get suitable work. In any case, the unemployment concept as it is now defined has nothing to do with wanting to work. The criterion is a behavioral one: seeking work. There is evidence that women who want to work and have been unsuccessful in finding it in the past tend to leave the labor force. Others, who want to work but believe that they would be unable to find a job, never enter the labor force. The concept is ambiguous at best; but not only is it ambiguous—the current operationalization of it is difficult for census enumerators to apply consistently to particular cases.

In the September 1966 Current Population Survey, an attempt was made to classify persons who were not in the labor force by reason for their nonparticipation (Stein, 1967). While this was only a test of a series of questions used on only about one-fourth of the CPS sample, the minimal published data may clarify somewhat the extent to which various factors constrain women from working and the extent to which nonemployed women desire work. The questions asked were:

"Does (this person) want a regular full-time or part-time job now?"
If yes or maybe:
"What are the reasons (this person) is now looking for work?"

Of the women who were not in the labor force, 9% expressed a desire for a regular job. Table 2-2 shows a distribution of reasons given by these 9%. Family factors, including inability to arrange child care, may be preventing 42% of the 9% (or perhaps 4% of all women who are not working) from seeking work. This figure would be slightly higher for married women, and perhaps considerably higher for mothers of young children.

The meaning of these data on reasons for not seeking work is quite uncertain. For example, does "family responsibility" as a reason for not seeking work include "would seek work if there were no children"? Does "inability to arrange child care" imply that an attempt has been made to do so? The published report on this preliminary study does not indicate whether there were more definite criteria for inclusion in one category or another.

Despite these ambiguities, it may be fruitful, if data of this kind become regularly available, to attempt to predict an employment variable which includes not only the employed and unemployed, but also those other persons who express a desire to work. Whether this proves useful or not, we

TABLE 2-2
Reasons for Not Seeking Work Given by Women Who Were Not in the Labor Force, but Who Wanted Regular Jobs, September 1966 (Percentage Distribution)[a]

Ill health or disability	16.4
In school	14.7
Family responsibilities	29.6
Inability to arrange child care	11.9
Miscellaneous personal reasons	7.9
Expects to be working or seeking work shortly	6.2
Believes it would be impossible to find work	13.4
Total	100.1
N (in thousands)	3651

[a]From Robert L. Stein (1967), Reasons for nonparticipation in the labor force, *Special Labor Force Report* No. 86, July 1967.

may still look forward to more detailed tabulations of reasons for not seeking work by, for example, color, husband's income, education, and child status. At the present time, there does not seem to be any satisfactory way to identify those women who "want" to work and are not working. The unemployment data collected in the census do not accomplish this, for it appears that there are more women who want to work and are not working who are classified "not in the labor force" than are classified "unemployed."

In defense of using employment status as a dichotomy as the major labor force variable, I would argue that whether or not to work is the major decision made by a woman and her family, within the context of the economic pressure under which the family is living, the employability of the wife, and the constraints imposed by the presence of children. How long to work is a secondary consideration. The presence of children, our major independent variable, probably constrains the decision to work or not to work much more than it constrains the decision of how long to work. Quite probably in most cases, after the decision to work is made, the decision as to how long to work is made on the basis of the work that is available. If a woman is interested in working part time and finds that no such work is available, she will have to choose whether to work full time or not to work at all. In any case, the outcome has its impact on the rate of employment. In Chapter 3 we will point out that the proportion of the employed population working full time has very little variation among population subgroups defined on the basis of child status variables—variables which ought to be correlated with preferences for part-time work.

Hours Worked per Week. There are other dimensions of work by wives which are of interest. Some of these can be examined with available census data. We can look at the number of hours worked per week during the census week. I have used this mainly as a dichotomy—part time and full time—following the convention of calling 1–34 hours part time, and 35 or more hours full time. (In the case of unpaid family work, 1–14 hours per week does not qualify as being employed.)

Data from the 1965 Current Population Surveys help to clarify the part-time–full-time distinction (U.S. Dept. of Labor, Bureau of Labor Statistics, 1966, Table D-7). In 1965, 31.8% of the working husband-present female population were working part time; 3.6% were working part time for economic reasons, and the remaining 28.2% were doing so for "other reasons." "Economic" reasons include slack work, material shortages, repairs to plant and equipment, start or termination of job during the week, and inability to find full-time work. "Other" reasons include industrial dispute, bad weather, illness, vacation, demands of home, housework, or school, no desire for full-time work, full-time worker only during peak season, and other such reasons. In the "part time for other reasons" category, 22.8% usually work part time and 5.4% usually work full time. These 22.8% can be considered as approximating the voluntary part-time workers—women who usually work part time and want to work part time. Of all the employed husband-present women, 51.3% were working 35–40 hours per week. The remaining 16.9% were working more than 40 hours per week. The mean

TABLE 2-3

Percentage of the Female Population Employed Part Time, by Reason for Part-Time Work and Whether Usually Work Part or Full Time, by Color: United States, 1965[a]

	Part time for economic reasons[b]			Part time for other reasons[b]			Total part time		
	Usually full time	Usually part time	Total	Usually full time	Usually part time	Total	Usually full time	Usually part time	Total
	Percentage of working population								
White	1.5	1.7	3.2	5.2	22.0	27.2	6.7	23.7	30.4
Nonwhite	2.2	7.9	10.1	5.0	19.4	24.4	7.2	27.3	34.5
Total	1.6	2.5	4.1	5.2	21.6	26.8	6.8	25.1	31.9
	Percentage of part-time workers								
White	4.9	5.6	10.5	16.9	72.5	89.4	21.8	78.1	100.0
Nonwhite	6.4	22.9	29.3	14.5	56.3	70.8	20.9	79.2	100.0
Total	5.2	8.1	13.3	16.8	69.9	86.7	22.0	78.0	100.0

[a]From U.S. Bureau of Labor Statistics, Labor force and employment in 1965, *Special Labor Force Report* No. 69, 1966, Table D-7.

[b]"Economic reasons" include: slack work, material shortages, repairs to plant or equipment, start or termination of job during the week, and inability to find full-time work. "Other reasons" include industrial dispute; bad weather; illness; vacation; demands of home, housework, or school; no desire for full-time work; full-time worker only during peak season; and other such reasons.

number of hours worked per week by husband-present women workers was 35.3. This compares to 32.8 for single women (many of whom were in school), and 37.5 for women of other marital statuses.

The percentage of the working nonwhite female population that worked less than 35 hours per week was 34.5. This compares with 30.4% of the white population. Nonwhite women work an average of 34.5 hours per week, and white women average 35.3 hours. Nonwhite women are much more likely to be part time for economic reasons and, within that category, to be usually working part time (see Table 2-3). They are less likely to be in the "part time for other reasons, usually part time" category—the category which we called voluntarily part time. Evidently, nonwhite women in considerable numbers would be willing to work more hours.

The more education a working woman has, the less likely she is to be working part time (U.S. Dept. of Labor, Bureau of Labor Statistics, 1965, Table C) (see Table 2-4). Among the part-time workers, the percentage

TABLE 2-4

Reason for Part-Time Work, by Education and Usual Hours Worked, for the Part-Time, Nonagricultural Female Labor Force: United States, March 1964[a]

Years of school completed	Usually work full time — Part time for: Economic reasons	Usually work full time — Part time for: Other reasons	Usually work part time — Part time for: Economic reasons	Usually work part time — Part time for: Other reasons	Total
	Percentage of total females at work				
1–4	2.8	3.2	4.4	18.3	28.7
5–7	2.7	3.0	5.2	19.3	30.2
8	2.9	2.8	3.5	16.7	25.9
9–11	2.0	3.5	3.7	18.1	27.3
12	1.3	3.0	1.5	16.3	22.1
13–15	.3	2.7	1.5	22.1	26.6
16	.4	1.6	.4	17.4	19.8
17+	.3	2.0	1.3	14.5	18.1
	Percentage of females working part time				
1–4	9.8	11.1	15.3	63.8	100.0
5–7	8.9	9.9	17.2	63.9	100.0
8	11.2	10.8	13.5	64.5	100.0
9–11	7.3	12.8	13.6	66.3	100.0
12	5.9	13.6	6.8	73.7	100.0
13–15	1.1	10.2	5.6	83.1	100.0
16	2.0	8.0	2.0	87.9	100.0
17+	1.7	11.0	7.2	80.1	100.0

[a]Computed from data in U.S. Bureau of Labor Statistics *Educational attainment of workers, Special Labor Force Report* No. 53, Table C.

working part time for economic reasons declines sharply with education (25% of the part-time workers with 8 years of education or less, and 4% of the college graduates). The proportion normally part time for "other" reasons increases with education from 64% for women with 8 years of education or less to 88% for women with a college education.

Thus, to summarize, about a third of the employed husband-present female population are working part time. Two-thirds are working full time. The majority of the women working part time are doing so for noneconomic reasons and are normally part-time workers. The proportion part time is greater for nonwhite women and for women with low education. Such women are more likely than white or well-educated women to be part time for economic reasons. With data from the 1960 census, we are unable to distinguish the voluntarily part-time workers from those whose part-time employment is involuntary.

Proportion Working in 1959. An additional labor force variable that is available is the proportion of women who worked at all in 1959. This category of women is normally larger than the number employed at the time of the census, for any given group of women, in that it includes women who work all year, women who seek employment sporadically during the course of a year, and women who terminated or began regular employment during the year. A comparison of the number of women who worked at all in 1959 and the number employed at the time of the census can give us an idea of the categories of women who are most mobile in their employment status.

Proportion Working 50–52 Weeks in 1959 and Proportion Never Worked. The final two labor force variables will facilitate identifying the extremes of labor force activity. On the one hand we can look at the proportion who worked full year in 1959, and on the other hand we can look at the proportion never having worked.

The category "never worked" was obtained from answers to a question regarding the year last worked. Respondents who were not currently at work were asked to check the time interval during which they had last worked. If they had never worked they were to check a box to that effect. I have followed the convention (adopted in most of the published tabulations of this variable by the Bureau of the Census) of combining persons reporting never having worked with unemployed persons who did not respond to this question. There is good reason to believe that the nonresponses were really persons who had never worked, since the question is labeled "When did he *last* work at all, even just for a few days?" Many persons who had never worked, thinking the question inappropriate, may have just skipped on to the next question.

The interpretation of the proportion never having worked is very complex. It is related to age in that there is an intracohort age pattern and an intercohort trend in labor force participation. Older women have had more time to work, but they were young at a time when fewer women were working.

Family Composition Variables

The sample being used consists of married women who are living with their husbands; thus, all the families have at least these two members. Most of my analysis will be confined to women with at least one child under the age of 18, although in Chapter 5 a separate analysis of the employment of wives with no children will be presented. The two classes of wives are analyzed separately because (1) the effects of various variables on employment are expected to differ between mothers and wives with no children, and (2) there are several variables which are important influences on employment which can be defined only for mothers (e.g., age of youngest child).

Women are classified with regard to the presence of children on two criteria: the number of own children in the family and the age of the youngest child. In the 1/1000 data, the number of own children under age 18 was obtained directly from the woman's record on the tape and is coded from zero to seven or more. The age of the youngest own child was constructed from information on the records of each woman's children. Own children were identified, their ages compared, and the age of the youngest own child was recorded in single years from 0 to 17. However, because of the relatively small number of cases for various subpopulations studied (blacks, for example), the ages from 10 to 17 were collapsed into 2-year intervals. This produces 14 categories of mother plus the category nonmother. In the published data used in Chapter 3, the classification of the two child-status variables is much less detailed than this.

The cross-classification of women in terms of number of children and age of youngest child has several aspects. In one sense, it is a classification of the amount and nature of their child-care responsibility and of the constraints placed on the possibility of working by the presence of children in the family. There are at least two dimensions to this: (1) the amount of household work varies with the size of the family and with its age composition, and (2) normally some arrangement must be made so that someone is responsible for the children during the time the mother is at work. It is more difficult to work with a preschool child than with one who is in school (if work and school hours coincide), since responsibility is provided by the school. Similarly, it is probably easier to find someone outside the family to care for one preschool-age child than for several; it is also probably easier to find someone to care for a child of 3 or 4 than for one under a year old. In addition, the larger the number of children, the greater the volume of household tasks. The number of household members available to do them is dependent on the age structure of the family, among other things.

Another interpretation of the classification of women by age, age of youngest child, and number of own children under the age of 18 has to do with the life cycle and the need for income. Children are themselves a direct cost; they consume food, clothing, medical services, and other things. In addition, there are other durable goods, the purchase of which is closely associated with marriage and the birth of children. These too are costs to the family which, if not caused by the children, are at least correlated with their presence. These include such things as the purchase of a washing machine, dryer, television, freezer, as well as the purchase of housing and the purchase of durables associated with that. (For a discussion of consumption patterns through the family life cycle, see David, 1962.) Still another use of income associated with the life cycle is the support of children in college.

A third more subtle facet of this classification is fertility. The classification categorizes women on the basis of their fertility to date (the number of children under 18) and the period of time since the last child was born. (The age of the youngest child is usually the same as the "open interval.") The longer the interval since the birth of the last child, regardless of the age of the woman, the lower the probability of her bearing another child. This is true both for reasons of fecundity and for reasons of volition. Thus a woman of age 30–34 with one, two, or even three children under 18, the youngest of whom is age 6 to 11, is likely to have deliberately limited her family size. She is probably still capable of having another child. She may have chosen to have fewer children than she might have for many reasons, including the desire to work. To the extent that women do limit their fertility in order to work, and to the extent that these women continue to work, we would expect to find an association between completed fertility to date and current labor force participation.

The interpretation of the effects of the presence of children and their number and ages is made more complex by the fact that the socioeconomic variables—education and income—are associated both with fertility patterns (number of children born, spacing, and age at marriage) and with employment patterns.

The interpretation of the effect of income on employment is confounded with the effect of children in an additional way. If income is to be used to measure economic pressure under which the family is operating and the degree to which economic pressure is inducing the wife to enter the labor force, it should be used as a ratio to the needs of the family. One basic set of needs is the direct cost of children and other household members. The more members consuming from a given dollar income, the more economic pressure the family is facing. The use of income adequacy rather than dollar income ought to be an improvement in this regard. (This measure will be discussed in detail later in this chapter.)

Presence of Related Adults. The inclusion of this variable is an attempt to analyze the effect of the presence in the household of potential baby-sitters. The nonemployed female adult under the age of 65 is the most likely to be a baby-sitter. The reasons for expecting the presence of such an adult to influence the employment of the mother have already been discussed. Its effect economically is to raise the real net earnings available to the family over those available if a baby-sitter had to be paid. Over and above that, in the absence of the relative, the mother might not be able to find a satisfactory paid baby-sitter. Finally, since there is emotion involved in the mother–child relationship, a relative living in the family is more likely to be entrusted with the care of young children than an outsider.

The variable that has been constructed to examine this effect can assume five values.

1. There is at least one not-employed female relative of the head or the wife aged 18–64 in the family. (For convenience in programming, subfamily heads or wives thereof were included even if they were under age 18. This undoubtedly makes very little difference.)
2. There is at least one female relative aged 18–64, and all such relatives in the family are employed.
3. There is a male, but no female, relative aged 18–64 in the family.
4. There is a relative over the age of 64 in the household, but no relatives under the age of 65.
5. There are no other adult relatives living in the household.

Family History Variables. In addition to the family history implied by the classification of women by age of youngest child, number of children, and age, I have constructed measures of two aspects of family history from the 1/1000 census data. These are age at marriage and length of the interval between marriage and the birth of the first child.

I am arguing that a woman who has work experience early in her marriage will be more likely to be at work at a later point in her marriage when all other factors related to her current situation and background are considered. There are several reasons for expecting this.

1. Early in the marriage, the family adjusts its consumption level to the income of both the husband and the wife. Later in the marriage it is difficult to accept the decline in the consumption level associated with the wife not working. Even if the woman is forced to leave the labor force for a while because of the birth of a child, she is more likely to return to work, and more likely to return sooner, than the woman who has no early work experience. Even in cases where there is no actual drop in income associated with the wife leaving the work force because the husband's income is increasing, the

wife's potential earnings and the increase in consumption that they permit tend to keep her in the labor force. The woman who has not worked earlier in marriage is content to consume at a level determined by her husband's income because she is not so clearly aware of her own earning potential.

2. The literature on attitudes toward work indicates that women who are not currently at work and their husbands have much stronger and more frequent negative attitudes toward working wives and mothers. These attitudes may be effective in reducing the likelihood of a woman seeking work.[1] Such attitudes are presumably less likely to be present if the woman has previous work experience.

3. Women with work experience early in marriage are selected for favorable dispositions toward work. The same factors that operated to dispose them to seek work early in marriage, at least to the extent that those factors were independent of the situation which they were in at the time, continue to operate later. I do not know of any adequate way to measure this propensity. Any measurable effect that early work experience may have on current work activity is confounded with the effect of the propensity to work.

4. To the extent that women find such intangible things as self-expression, independence, social contact, self-fulfillment, and escape from boredom by working, it would seem more likely that a woman who has worked in the past, and found these things by working, would be influenced by them to seek work later. Women who had not worked would be less likely to realize that such intangible benefits were available through work.

5. A woman who has worked early in her marriage has demonstrated to herself and to potential employers that she is employable and potentially productive. She has experience and perhaps some work skills.

6. Women with early work experience are likely to have modified their fertility as a result of it. Thus, with respect to responsibility for children, they are likely to be in a situation different from that of women with no work experience. The prevailing fertility pattern in the United States is to have two, three, or four children in quite rapid succession after marriage. This pattern, combined with an early age at marriage, enables a woman to complete childbearing and rearing of preschool children at a rather young age. From the point of view of working, this "strategy" of family formation produces a period early in the marriage in which work is difficult because of child-care responsibilities. This is a period in which the need for income for life-cycle-associated purchases is greatest. Later in the marriage—10–15 years after marriage—when the woman is 30–35 years of age, there

[1]James Morgan, Martin David, Wilbur Cohen, and Harvey Brazer, *Income and Welfare in the United States* (New York: McGraw-Hill, 1962), Chap. 9, found that of all predictors of employment of wives used in the analysis, husband's attitude toward work by wives was the best. Obviously, the direction of the association is unclear.

are no longer any preschool children in the family and the wife is relatively free to work. This may again be a time of economic pressure associated with supporting children in college.

An alternative strategy would be to intend to have the same number of children, but to space them at longer intervals of, say, 4 or 5 years. Such a pattern makes working between the births of the children considerably easier, as it is easier to work and find substitute care for a child of 2 to 4 than for a child of less than a year. Either of the two patterns might be combined with a late or an early marriage.

The second strategy or pattern has further implications for fertility. Since fecundity declines with age, fecundity impairment is more likely to occur before all of the intended children are born when early birth intervals are long. In addition, longer spacing of the first and second births means that the woman has more time to reduce her desired family size. This seems particularly likely if the woman enjoys working and/or enjoys the consumption level which her work permits.

Completed fertility, child-spacing, age at marriage, and work are very intricately associated. Cross-sectional data of the sort that we have at the present time cannot go very far in clarifying the relationships.

From the data on the census tape I have constructed the length of the interval between marriage and the birth of the first child for all women for whom the number of own children present in the family is equal to the number of children ever born, who have been married only once, and whose husbands have been married only once. This was done by subtracting the quarter and year of first marriage from the quarter and year of birth of the oldest child. It was possible to do this because the unit sampled on the 1/1000 sample tape is the household and the records of all the members of the household are together on the tape. Own children are identified and their ages are compared to identify the oldest. By performing this operation only for couples, both of whom were married only once and for whom the number of children ever born equals the number of children present, we avoid most of the problems associated with the absence of the oldest child from the family for reasons such as death, college, service in the armed forces, institutionalization, or marriage. We have not entirely avoided these problems because "own child" is defined as "a person under the age of 18 who is a never-married son, daughter, stepchild, or adopted child of the family head or subfamily head." It is thus possible for an own child by adoption to substitute for a missing child born to the woman in question. This is probably quite rare.

I use this variable to represent probable exposure to employment early in marriage. The longer the interval between marriage and the birth of the first child, the more likely the wife is to have been employed during the interval, and the longer she is likely to have worked. The very limited available data support this assumption. The 1960 Growth of American Families study asked the sample women how long they had been employed and whether part or full time during the interval between each birth. Table 2-5 is derived from these data. A very sharp gradient occurs, with 29% of the women having worked at some time during a first interval of less than ten months to 73% with an interval of 50 or more months. There is very little difference in the proportions working full time, of those who worked, by the length of the first birth interval.

Marital Stability. One additional family history variable, which I call marital stability, will be introduced in the analysis. Cain (1966, Chap. 3) has shown that wives who have been married more than once are more likely to be working than those who have been married only once. I have expanded this variable to include the previous martial history of the husband. The variable can assume four values.

1. Both spouses married only once;
2. Husband married once, wife married more than once;
3. Wife married once, husband married more than once;
4. Both spouses married more than once.

Further discussion of the interpretation of the effects of this variable will be deferred to Chapter 4 where the results are reported.

Income Adequacy. I am arguing that the economic pressure under which the family is living is an important determinant of the wife's labor force

TABLE 2-5

Work during Interval between Marriage and First Birth, by length of Interval for Husband-Present Women Aged 18–44, with at Least One Live Birth[a]

Length of interval (months)	Number of cases	Number worked	Percentage worked	Percentage of workers who worked full time
Less than 10	537	156	29.0	86.5
11–19	1151	503	43.7	88.5
20–29	448	256	57.1	87.5
30–49	388	263	67.8	92.0
50 or more	325	236	72.6	87.3

[a]Tabulated from 1960 Growth of American Families data (excludes 18 cases with inconsistent codes).

status. It would be incorrect to use family income to represent this economic pressure, because the wife's contribution to family income is included; and her income, to the extent that it consists of earnings, is a consequence, not a cause, of her employment. Thus the dollar income which is most relevant is either the family income minus the wife's earnings, or the husband's income. The former would be the most relevant if the entire family income was, in fact, pooled. The latter would be superior if there were other earning family members who did not pool their income. The two would, of course, be the same if there were no other earners than the husband and wife, and there were no nonearnings income. (Earnings are defined as wage and salary and self-employment income. Total income can also include various forms of income from assets and transfer income.) I have chosen to use family income minus wife's earnings since the family members with income who do not pool it with that of the head and wife cannot be identified, and their income and need for income will be included in the numerator and denominator of the variable described in the next paragraphs.

There are a number of reasons why dollar income does not adequately measure economic pressure. Most of them cannot be handled with the available data. It does not include any consideration of assets, either in terms of the need to accumulate them (especially housing and consumer durables) if you do not have them, or the possibility of living off of them (if they are in liquid form) when income is temporarily low. It ignores debt. Of two families with equal current income, the one with a large debt is under greater economic pressure than the one with little or no debt. Money income measures ignore various sorts of nonmoney income, as well as various forms of voluntary transfers of resources into or out of the family spending unit.

From our viewpoint, however, the most important deficiency is that money income measures ignore family composition. The economic pressure implied by a given family income is a function of the number of persons to be supported by it. The primary focus of this study, the effect of family composition on the employment of wives, makes it essential that we carefully separate the economic pressure and the family composition variables.

To this end, I have constructed a variable that I call income adequacy. The numerator of this fraction is family income minus the wife's earnings; the denominator is a measure of the minimum income needs of the family based on its composition. Table 2-6 shows the schedule of income needs that has been used. It is based on a 1959 budget study done in New York City for use by private agencies in determining eligibility for assistance. This is the same measure used by Morgan *et al.* in their study, *Income and Welfare in the United States* (1962: 188–196), except that the numerator used by them was family income rather than family income minus wife's earnings, and their family income measure was more refined than simply money in-

TABLE 2-6

Schedule of Estimated Annual Costs of Goods and Services Used in Constructing Income Adequacy Measure[a]

I. Food, clothing and other personal costs		
Head	— Employed or unemployed	$1144
	Other	676
Wife of head		1092
Other adults	— Employed, aged 18–40	1196
	Employed, aged 41 and over	988
	Not employed	546
Children	— Under 6	312
	6–11	416
	12–15	572
	16–17	676
II. Rent, utilities and other costs		
1 Person in spending unit		$1040
2		1248
3		1404
4		1508
5		1664
6		1924
7		2080
8 or more		2184

[a]From Morgan *et al.*, *Income and Welfare in the United States*, p. 189. Adapted from The Community Council of Greater New York, Budget Standard Service, *Annual Price Survey and Family Budget Costs*, 1959.

come. These differences reflect a difference in the focus of the two studies, and in the available data, rather than any disagreement.

The measure used in the denominator (i.e., the weights) are arbitrary in one sense. One might make somewhat different judgments of the various needs for income of the various categories of family members. The minimum acceptable standard is open to question, but this is not a problem since we are using the measure in a ratio and are not attributing any particular normative significance to a value of unity for the ratio.

I have used the measure rather uncritically for several reasons. It is clearly superior to any simple money income measure as an index of economic pressure. The weights seem reasonable to me when one is compared to another. The measure can be readily adapted to use with the data on the 1/1000 census sample tape. Finally, the measure was used by a group of highly competent economists who judged it to be adequate.[2]

[2]This problem is essentially the same as that of specifying whether a particular family is "poor." See Orshansky (1965); Froeder (1960); and Watts (1967, n.d.).

TABLE 2-7

Comparison of Distribution of Sample by Family Income Minus Wife's Earning and by Income Adequacy

Family income minus wife's earning	Income adequacy							Total
	.0–.3	.4–.7	.8–1.1	1.2–1.5	1.6–1.9	2.0–2.8	2.9+	
Nonblack families								
Less than $2000	93.7	14.4	—	—	—	—	—	5.3
$2000–3999	6.3	74.4	32.8	.1	—	—	—	15.0
$4000–5999	—	10.7	57.0	57.5	10.1	—	—	30.6
$6000–7999	—	.3	9.4	34.9	59.7	18.8	—	24.0
$8000–9999	—	.0	.7	6.1	23.1	41.6	.6	11.2
$10,000+	—	—	.1	1.6	7.1	39.6	99.3	13.9
Total	100.0	99.8	100.0	100.2	100.0	100.0	99.9	100.0
N	835	2064	4486	5429	3462	2699	1448	20,423
Percentage distribution	4.1	10.1	22.0	26.6	17.0	13.2	7.1	100.0
Black families								
Less than $2000	85.9	11.0	—	—	—	—	—	21.3
$2000–3999	14.0	70.4	34.1	—	—	—	—	36.8
$4000–5999	—	17.4	51.1	74.5	15.1	—	—	29.3
$6000–7999	—	1.1	11.4	14.9	58.5	13.8	—	7.5
$8000–9999	—	—	3.2	5.8	17.0	58.6	—	3.2
$10,000+	—	—	.2	4.8	9.4	27.6	100.0	1.9
Total	99.9	99.9	100.0	100.0	100.0	1000.0	100.0	100.0
N	313	545	411	188	53	29	6	1545
Percentage distribution	20.2	35.3	26.6	12.2	3.4	1.9	.4	100.0
All families								
Percentage distribution	5.2	11.9	22.3	25.6	16.0	12.4	6.6	100.0

Since this measure is unfamiliar, Table 2-7, showing the distribution of family income minus wife's earnings within income adequacy categories, is included. The lowest adequacy category, less than .3, includes 5% of the total population of families. Over 90% of these families have dollar income levels (family income minus wife's earnings) of less than $2000. Those families in the next higher income adequacy category (.4 to .7) comprise about 12% of the population and have money incomes that are heavily concentrated in the $2000–$3999 range. These two income adequacy categories constitute the lowest quintile of the income adequacy distribution, and roughly approximate the portion of the population that would be classified as "in poverty." The higher income adequacy categories exhibit a wider spread among family income categories. For example, the distribution of income adequacy 2.0–2.8 is composed of $6000–$7999 (19%), $8000–$8999 (42%), and $10,000 and over (40%). Over 99% of the families with an income adequacy of 2.9 and over have family income minus wife's earnings of $10,000 or more. There is a relatively high correlation between the two measures, but there appears to be sufficient departure from perfect correlation to justify the use of income adequacy as a more adequate measure of family economic pressure.

Education

I regard educational attainment as primarily an economic variable as it influences the employment of wives. I think of it as a measure of employability and earning potential. There are undoubtedly other factors associated with education which are also germane to the employment of wives. Some of these are a positive correlation with an inherent satisfaction derived from work; ability to find escape from boredom, satisfying social contacts, and self-fulfillment from work; a career orientation; and access to jobs that are clean, nonmanual, and nontedious (Bowen and Finegan, 1966: 568).

Other Variables

Age. Age, too, is relevant to the labor force activity of women in several ways.

1. Age is correlated with physical capacity to work. The older a woman, the higher the probability that she is physically unable to work.
2. Age has a life cycle aspect having to do with the need for income. A young woman who is married but has no children is likely to wish to work in order to accumulate assets in the form of a house or durable goods. An older woman can, to a certain extent, merely live on accumulated assets and durables without the need to work. Women between 40 and 60 who have no

children in the household may well be supporting a child who is living outside the household (e.g., a child in college).

3. Age locates a woman in a cohort, the members of which have lived through comparable periods of their lives in the same historical environment. There has been a trend in the employment of women in the United States such that the younger a woman is, the more likely she is to have been exposed to employment at any given earlier stage of her life. In addition, World War II was a historical event that had a marked accelerating effect on the previously slow trend in the increase in labor force participation. Women who completed their education immediately before the rapid increase in employment opportunities should probably show the influence of this event on their current labor force activity, at least if the idea of persistence has any validity.

4. In considering the question of whether or not a woman ever worked, age is relevant (in determining the period of exposure) to the possibility of ever having worked.

Color. Nonwhite wives have repeatedly been observed to have higher rates of employment than white wives. These differences appear to persist when other relevant characteristics are controlled. Color is included as a control variable in this analysis. In the published census data the color variable distinguishes between white and nonwhite wives, whereas in the analysis of the 1/1000 data, the distinction is between black and nonblack wives.[3] As we have already indicated, nonblack, nonwhite women have employment rates which are closer to the white rates than to the rates of blacks.

Methods of Analysis

The great bulk of our knowledge of the labor force participation of women is derived from an examination of differential rates of participation for various subgroups in the population. In the United States, there is a considerable amount of data from the last three decennial censuses, from the Current Population Survey reports, and from surveys conducted by university research workers. Much of the analysis of these data has been in the form of comparing rates of labor force participation.

There are at least three disadvantages to this approach:

1. The sample size is often too small to permit the reliable calculation of rates for subpopulations of interest to the investigator.

[3]O. D. Duncan (1967), suggests the distinction between black and nonblack rather than white and nonwhite, in order to maximize the homogeneity of the two categories. We have already shown that "other nonwhite races" have labor force paticipation rates that more closely approximate the white than the black rates.

2. The data are not sufficiently reduced to permit ready interpretation.
3. Desired controls are not introduced, either for lack of the necessary tabulations or because the sample size does not permit it. In such cases, the effects of the other variables may be confounded with those of the variable of interest.

I will utilize this approach in my analysis of the published census data. These data are from a 5% sample of the United States population, thus escaping disadvantage 1. My intent in using these tabulations is to analyze details which might be missed in the multivariate analysis and to test the adequacy of the model underlying it to the relationships I am examining. Thus disadvantage 2 is irrelevant. Disadvantage 3 is present to some extent, although, as we will point out later, the effects of the child status variables in particular are relatively uninfluenced by the introduction of socioeconomic variables into the analysis.

Various economists have utilized multiple regression in the analysis of female labor force participation. Dummy variables have been introduced to take account of categorical variables, and various transformations have been used to take account of nonlinear relationships. Only in Morgan's studies has there been an explicit attempt to take interactions into account.

The method of analysis which I will use most extensively is multiple classification analysis (discussed in Morgan *et al.*, 1962, Appendix E; and Andrews, Morgan, and Sonquist, 1967; discussed and illustrated in O.D. Duncan, 1964: 82–89; and B. Duncan, 1965: 78ff). This is a dummy variable regression technique which estimates a coefficient for each category of each independent variable. It is applicable when the dependent variable is on an interval scale or when it is a dichotomy. In our analyses, the major dependent variables are dichotomies—employed or not employed and, if employed, whether full or part time. In this case, the results are expressed in terms of the probability of being in one or the other category.

The results are presented in the form of net deviations from the grand mean of the dependent variable for the entire sample or, in our case, from the total sample proportion in the employed category. These net effects are then compared among the various categories of each variable. They can also be compared with the "gross effects" or the category mean minus the grand mean. This comparison indicates the extent to which the other included variables modify the effect on the dependent variable of the variable in question.

The underlying model assumes that the effects on the dependent variable of the various independent variables are additive. Chapter 3 and 5 will be devoted, in part, to examining the nature of the interactions that are present. These interactions can then be taken into account in the analysis in two ways: (1) a composite variable can be constructed by cross-classifying the two or three interacting variables, or (2) separate multiple classification analyses can be performed within categories of an "independent" variable.

For the purpose of this study, the particular advantage that this technique has over the more conventional multiple regression analysis is its ability to isolate and describe nonlinear relationships in a way which is both unambiguous and easy to comprehend. Some of the relationships that we are most interested in are expected to be nonlinear. For example, the literature cited earlier leads us to expect a discontinuity in the rate of employment by age of youngest child as school age is reached. In addition, this study is intended to be a detailed description. We have a very large number of sample cases and we wish to take the fullest advantage of this large sample size. One of the things that is important to our detailed description is the ability to locate any substantively significant nonlinearity that occurs in the relationship between child status variables and employment variables. Does the employment rate of mothers increase faster in the high school ages than in the grade school ages? Are there major discontinuities in this relationship? Exactly where do they occur; in particular, do they occur at the time of entry of the youngest child into grade school, into junior high school, or into high school? What is the precise shape of the number of children–employment relationship? One of the great merits of the usual regression procedure is the ability to use small samples efficiently to describe relationships when, for example, there are not enough cases for a sufficiently detailed cross tabulation. Here we are able to obtain the advantage of the regression procedure of not needing a large enough number of cases to obtain multiple-dimensional cross-tabulations (by the assumption of the additivity of the effects of the independent variables) without imposing linearity on the relationships.

Another major advantage of the usual multiple regression analysis is the ability to make very succinct summary statements about the nature of a relationship—i.e., specify a single slope. This is lost with the multiple classification procedure, where a coefficient is estimated for each category of each independent variable. However, when the pattern of multiple classification effects for the various categories of a given variable are plotted, slopes can be estimated for those relationships which appear to be reasonably linear (B. Duncan, 1965: 78–83).

A final advantage of this procedure is its ability to handle variables in a regression context that are not scored on an interval scale. Dummy variables, especially dichotomies like color or sex, are now commonly introduced into regression analyses. The multiple classification procedure is no more than a large scale dummy variable regression analysis with all variables treated as dummy variables. Variables such as region, size of place, or husband's occupation can be simply introduced into the analysis.

Labor Force Activity of Wives in Relation to Family Composition: A First Description

In this chapter we present a detailed description of the relationship of age of youngest child, number of children in the family, and age of the mother to various employment variables for all husband-present wives in the United States. This chapter will utilize published census data, primarily. The following two chapters will examine the results of the multivariate analyses of data from the 1/1000 census sample. This chapter will be almost entirely devoted to description; it will include only a minimum of interpretation.

A Note on the Child Status Classification and Its Use in Reaching Conclusions about Cohort Behavior

We will classify women by child status both by the cross-classification of age of youngest child and number of children under age 18, and by age of youngest child alone. Before going on to report on the differentials in employment among child status categories, some discussion of the appropriateness of this cross-sectional analysis for describing the behavior of real cohorts is necessary. In this study we want, among other things, to answer questions like, "To what extent is there a jump in the rate of employment of mothers at the age when the youngest child enters school?" or "To what extent does the life-cycle pattern of employment differ from one educational or economic class to another?" These are questions which can most adequately be dealt with by comparing the employment patterns of actual cohorts. Here

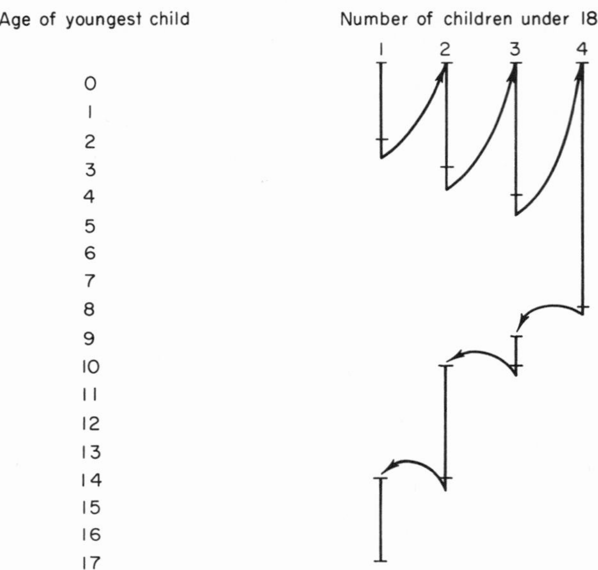

Figure 3-1. *Illustration of the path through the child status classification taken by a hypothetical mother through time.*

we want to discuss two problems: (1) The independent variable we are most interested in, child status, does not have a perfect one-to-one relationship with cohort time; and (2) We have cross-sectional data and we want to make inferences about cohort behavior.

If one is concerned with labor force activity through a family life cycle, the two-way classification of women by age of youngest child and number of children might be somewhat misleading. A woman does not move along the rows or down columns of this classification. Consider a detailed table showing single years of age of youngest child in the rows and number of children under 18 in the columns (see Fig. 3-1). Through time a mother moves down each column, starting with column 1, for a period equivalent to each birth interval until she has had her last child, say her fourth. Then she moves down the fourth column until her first child reaches 18 or leaves home. This continues until all children have reached 18 or have left home. Then the woman leaves the classification completely—she is a woman with no children under 18.

Another implication is that certain of the cells in this classificatory scheme can be occupied only under very special conditions. For example, one-child women, the youngest aged 6–11, are probably either women who will have completed their families with one child, or who have had other children, or will have more children with unusually long birth intervals. Similarly, a woman with four or more children under the age of 18, with the youngest 13 or more, has probably either had a multiple birth or has had children at relatively close intervals.

A final point with regard to this classification of women is that, if we ignore the "number of children" dimension and consider only the "age of youngest child" dimension, women proceed through it in something like the following pattern:

none, 0, 1, 2, 0, 1, 2, 3, 0, 1, 0, 1, 2, 3, 4, 5, 6, 7, 8, 9, 10, 11, 12, 13, 14, 15, 16, 17, none

marriage — first birth — second birth — third birth — fourth birth

Only a proportion of the women in the 0-, 1-, 2-, or 3-year old age of youngest child categories have completed their families, but almost all of the women with youngest child over the age of 4 have. Thus, if we plot proportions employed by single year of age of youngest child beyond age 4, we are plotting the sort of path that actual women might take if there were no intercohort change in employment occurring. The only problem we have then in interpreting these data is that there is intercohort change. For the women with younger children, however, we have the additional problem that women do not move through the age of youngest child categories year by year, but instead keep jumping back to the zero category as each additional child is born.

From the point of view of explaining or predicting employment, it may be quite a significant distinction whether a youngest child of age 0, 1, 2, 3, or 4 is regarded by the woman in question as her last child, or just one along the way to a completed family. With data from the 1965 National Fertility

TABLE 3-1

Employment Rates by Age of Youngest Own Child and Whether or Not Another Child Is Wanted, for All Mothers and for Mothers of Two or More Children: United States, 1965

Age of youngest own child	All mothers				Mothers of two or more children			
	Has all wants		Wants more		Has all wants		Wants more	
	N	Percentage employed	*N*	Percentage employed	*N*	Percentage employed	*N*	Percentage employed
0	638	12.9	545	14.1	243	12.4	122	8.2
1	600	17.8	494	22.3	224	13.8	122	18.0
2	515	23.9	328	23.5	204	24.4	88	19.3
3	443	24.4	201	24.9	182	26.4	57	22.8
4	419	25.3	159	27.0	161	23.0	46	21.7
5	301	33.6	115	26.1	126	30.2	41	22.0
6	354	33.9	94	56.4	131	30.5	28	60.7

Study it was possible to compute employment rates for women classified simultaneously by age of youngest child (in single years) and whether or not the couple has had all of the children that they *want*. Table 3-1 presents a summary of these data. When number of children in the family is not taken into account, there seems to be very little difference in the age-of-youngest-child–specific employment rates by whether or not the couple has all the children they want. If anything, the wives who want more children are more likely to be working. However, as we will note later, the wives who have only one child are much more likely to be working than those who have more children, while beyond two children, the differences in employment rates are not large. These women with only one child are also more likely to want additional children.

TABLE 3-2

Labor Force Participation Rates of Women in the United States, 1890–1965[a]

Year	Rate
1890	18.2
1900	20.0
1920	22.7
1930	23.6
1940	25.7
1950	29.3
1955	30.7
1960	34.5
1965	37.9

[a]Data for 1890–1955 from Gertrude Bancroft, *The American Labor Force: Its Growth and Changing Composition*, Table D–1a. These data have been adjusted by Durand and by Bancroft to improve comparability. Data for 1960 from 1960 Census of Population, U.S. Summary, Population Characteristics, Table 195. Data for 1965 from U.S. Bureau of Labor Statistics, *Special Labor Force Report* No. 69, Labor force and employment in 1965, Table B-2. Data for 1965 are the annual average of the monthly labor force. Because they are Current Population Survey figures, they are probably biased slightly in the direction of being too high in comparison with census figures. This bias would probably be especially pronounced for the youngest ages who are enrolled in school in large proportions.

The right side of Table 3-1 shows the employment rates of those women with two or more children by whether more children are desired. Among these mothers there is a tendency for those who report having already had all of the children that they want to be working in greater proportions at most age of youngest child categories. If this relationship is being confounded by the number of children, it is in a direction opposite to that necessary to confirm our hypothesis. That is to say, the women who have had all the children they want are likely, on average, to have had more children, and for that reason less likely to be working. Any further subdivision of the sample, however, into number of children categories would leave very small cell frequencies. A multivariate analysis might permit a more definite conclusion. From these data, there is some weak evidence that women are more likely to be working, whatever the age of their (preschool) youngest child if they do not desire to have additional children.[1]

The crude rate of labor force participation of women has been rising continuously in the United States over the 75 years for which data are available. These rates are shown in Table 3-2. Table 3-3 arranges the data on age-specific labor force participation of all women in the United States from the 1920 through the 1960 censuses, as well as from 1955 and 1965 Current Population Surveys, into rates for actual birth cohorts. Since the lower age limit for eligibility as a member of the labor force was 14, the data are presented for ages 14–19, and then for conventional 5-year age groups. The first observation for each cohort is, then, not exactly the same cohort as succeeding observations. Since change has occurred rather slowly, this makes very little difference.

For all cohorts for which we have observations, the rate rose sharply between ages 14–19 and 20–24, and fell again rather sharply in ages 25–29. This reflects the changes in educational, marital, and fertility statuses which typically occur in this age range. Many women 14–19 are enrolled in school. By ages 20–24, many are out of school and not yet married or, if married, not yet mothers. By ages 25–29, many women are mothers of one or more small children. The earlier cohorts of 1886–1890 and 1891–1895 have a rather flat curve beyond age 30. The more recent cohorts show successively steeper rises beginning at ages 30–34. Thus, the intracohort pattern of rising rates after age 30 becomes more and more pronounced with successive cohorts. The intercohort pattern is remarkably regular: At all ages above 30–34, the curves of later cohorts lie entirely above those of earlier cohorts.

[1]These data were made available to me by Professor Norman Ryder and Professor Larry Bumpass. Further thought on the matter suggests that the fertility variable of most relevance is not whether additional children are desired, but rather whether further children are expected. Some couples expect to have additional unwanted pregnancies, while others would like to have additional children, but realize that they are subfecund.

TABLE 3-3

Labor Force Participation Rates by Age for Birth Cohorts of American Women[a]

Birth cohort	14–19	20–24	25–29	30–34	35–39	40–44	45–49	50–54	55–59	60–64
1856–1860										13.0
1861–1865									15.4	
1866–1870								17.5		13.9
1871–1875							18.8		16.5	
1876–1880						18.3		19.0		14.7
1881–1885					19.6		20.3		18.2	
1886–1890				19.8		21.1		21.0		20.8
1891–1895			27.0		22.3		23.5		26.1	24.5
1896–1900		37.5		23.6		26.0		31.0	31.0	29.5
1901–1905	28.4		30.2		28.4		35.0	35.0	39.7	34.0
1906–1910		41.8		30.8		36.6	41.2	45.8	47.1	
1911–1915	22.8		35.6		34.0	40.5	47.4	50.1		
1916–1920		45.6		31.2	35.4	45.3	51.7			
1921–1925	19.0		32.8	32.9	40.3	48.5				
1926–1930		43.6	32.4	35.5	43.6					
1931–1935	23.0	43.0	35.1	38.2						
1936–1940	21.1	44.8	38.9							
1941–1945	23.8	49.9								
1946–1950	29.2									

[a]See Table 3-2 for sources.

The observations which we have in the 1960 census on labor force activity of mothers are for the birth cohorts of 1901–1905 to 1941–1945. It is clear that a sizable amount of change in the age-specific employment levels has occurred and is occurring among these cohorts—change both in levels of employment and in the age pattern of employment. Each successive cohort has higher age-specific rates of employment than its predecessors, and each successive cohort has a steeper positive slope of employment on age beyond the age of 30. It is clear, then, that we are not describing very closely the labor force activity of any real cohort with our 1960 cross-sectional data.

Child Status and Employment

The proportions of wives employed by detailed age of youngest child category are plotted in Fig. 3-2. These data are taken from 1/1000 census sample. There is a continuous increase in the proportion employed from age of youngest child 0 to age of youngest child 12–13. After age 13, the proportion is constant at about 43%. After a sharp jump from 10 to 17% between age 0 and age 1, the slope is quite constant to age 12–13. The proportion increases at a rate of slightly more than two percentage points per year. There

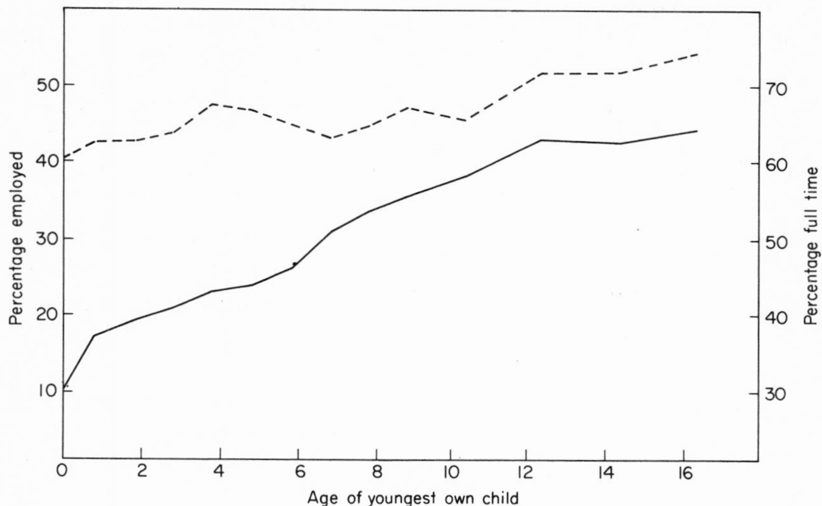

Figure 3-2. *Percentage of married women employed (—) and percentage of employed women working full time (– – –) by age of youngest child: United States, 1960.*

is a slight increase in the slope between ages 6 and 7, but not nearly as sharp a jump as might be expected either from the sudden decline in child responsibility as the youngest child enters school or from the social psychological argument presented earlier.

The proportions of the employed mothers working full time by age of youngest child are also shown in Fig. 3-2. Three-fifths of the mothers of children under the age of 1 are working full time. Between age 1 and ages 10–11, the proportion fluctuates around 65%, never deviating from that figure by more than three percentage points. After the age of 11, the proportion of employed mothers working full time climbs to over 70%.

The probability of working is closely related to child responsibility, but it is clear that considerable numbers of mothers of preschool-age children do not combine child responsibility and work by working part time. This may be a result of the shortage of part-time work rather than of preferences. We cannot conclude from this observation that there would be no response of mothers of young children to an increase in the availability of part-time jobs.

Figure 3-3 plots the proportion employed by number of own children under the age of 18. This proportion drops quite sharply from 43% for wives with no children to 33% for mothers of one child, and to 20% for mothers of three children. After three children, the proportion drops slowly to 17% for mothers of six children. For mothers of seven or more children, the proportion working is only slightly more than one-tenth.

In Fig. 3-3 we also see that the proportion of the employed wives who are

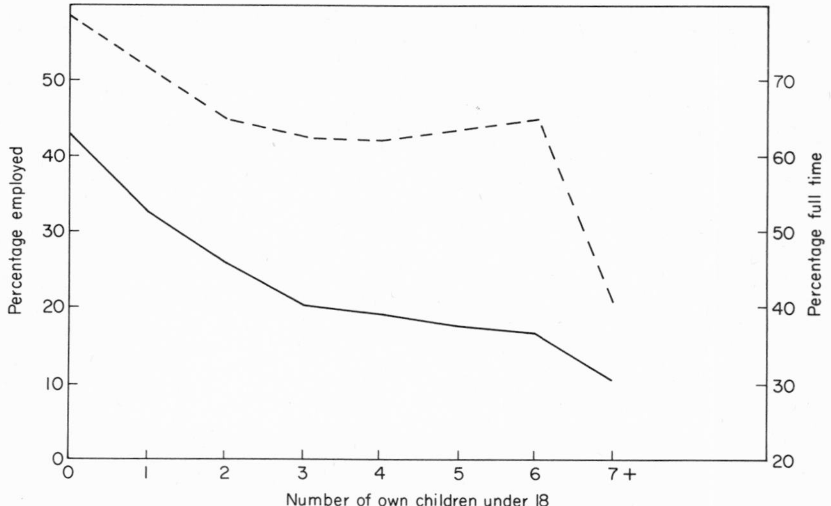

Figure 3-3. *Percentage of married women employed (—) and percentage of employed women working full time (---) by number of children under 18: United States, 1960.*

working full time is, again, considerably less influenced by the number of children than is the proportion employed. The proportion declines from 77% for wives with no children to 64% for mothers of two children. Beyond two children, the proportion is constant at about 62–64% until five children. After five children it again declines sharply.

We can consider simultaneously the effects of age of youngest child and number of children on the employment of mothers with data from the 1960 census in Table 8 of the Subject Report on "Employment Status and Work Experience." The labor force activity rates which have been derived from the data in this table are:

1. Percentage of women employed.
2. Percentage of women employed full time.
3. Percentage of employed women working full time.
4. Percentage of women working at all in 1959.
5. Percentage of women working in 1959 who worked 50–52 weeks.

In addition, the *Subject Report* on the "Labor Reserve" (PC(2)6C) provides information on the number of women who have never worked at all for the same categories of women. Consequently we were able to compute:

6. Percentage of women who have never worked.

I will begin by outlining the relationship of age of youngest child and number of own children under 18 to the various labor force variables, without taking account of the age of the woman.

TABLE 3-4

Percentage of Husband-Present Women Age 14–59 Who Are Employed, by Age of Youngest Own Child, Number of Own Children Under 18, and Color: United States, 1960 [a]

Age of youngest child	Number of own children under 18				
	1	2	3	4 or more	none
White women					
0–2	18.8	14.1	12.2	11.0	—
3–4	28.3	20.5	18.7	18.2	—
5	30.5	23.5	22.9	23.0	—
6–11, without children 12–17	34.6	30.1	28.4	27.0	—
6–11, with children 12–17	—	34.7	32.8	30.1	—
12–17	40.9	42.1	39.6	37.0	—
None	—	—	—	—	42.6
Nonwhite women					
0–2	28.6	25.3	23.6	21.0	—
3–4	42.0	37.8	36.2	33.0	—
5	44.9	43.8	38.4	36.7	—
6–11, without children 12–17	47.5	48.6	43.5	41.4	—
6–11, with children 12–17	—	48.4	44.9	41.4	—
12–17	49.5	49.8	45.1	38.9	—
None	—	—	—	—	48.6

[a] From U.S. Bureau of the Census (1963). *Employment status and work experience*, PC(2) 6A, Table 8.

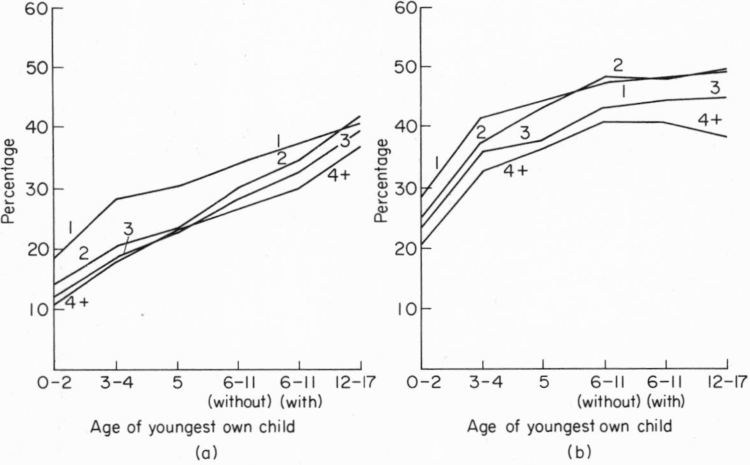

Figure 3-4. *Percentage of husband-present women, aged 14–58 who are employed, by age of youngest child, number of own children under 18, and color. (a) White population; (b) nonwhite population. Numbers on curves refer to number of own children under 18.*

Percentage Employed

For the white population, about one-fifth of the mothers with only one child work if the child is under 3 (see Table 3-4 and Fig. 3-4). The proportion increases to about one-third for mothers of a child aged 6–17. For mothers of more than one child, one-eighth work if the youngest child is under 3; one-quarter work if the youngest child is age 5. This proportion rises further to two-fifths for mothers of children the youngest of whom is 12–17.

For nonwhite women, the proportions are considerably higher. Approximately one-quarter of the mothers of children under 3 are working; this proportion increases to about two-fifths of the mothers of children, the youngest of which is 3–5 and up to half of the mothers of older children.

Figure 3-4 plots the relationships between employment and age of youngest child and number of own children under 18 for white and nonwhite women. For the white women, there is a clear positive effect of the age of the youngest child. Within each "number of children" category, there is a pronounced upward slope. Only for the women with only one child over the age of 11 is the positive slope absent. This is a group of women who are older than any other. Their child responsibility is nearly over; most have had other children who have left home.

The number of own children under 18 exerts a significant influence on the proportion employed independent of the effect of age of youngest child. Women with more children are less likely to work than women with fewer children. In particular, among the white women, mothers of two children under 18 are at least five percentage points less likely to work than mothers of one child, at every age of youngest child, with the single exception of 12–17. The differences between having two, three, or four or more children are much smaller–in the 1–4% range.

For the white women, the curves are approximately parallel. This suggests that the effects of age and number of children under 18 on employment may be adequately depicted with an additive statistical model. The two variables will be used additively in the multivariate analysis in the following chapters.

For white women with more than one child, the youngest of which is 6–11 years, the effect of having another child age 12–17 is as great as the difference between the other age of youngest child categories. Thus if a woman with children 6–11 has an older child in the household, she is more likely to be employed than if she has none. This leads to the inference that the older children are left with the responsibility of caring for the younger ones, although it may be due to the uncontrolled effects of socioeconomic variables. We do know from the 1965 Children's Bureau and Women's Bureau study of child care arrangements of working mothers that 6% of the children ages 6–11 receiving care while their mothers work are cared for in the home by relatives under the age of 16 (U.S. Dept. of Health, Education, and Welfare, 1965, Table 6).

One other possible explanation for this differential is that the youngest child aged 6–11 with siblings in the 12–17 age range are on the average closer to the upper limit of the 6–11 age range, whereas those who have no older siblings are nearer the younger limit. We have already shown that the rate of employment of mothers increases more or less linearly in this range. For all women, white and nonwhite combined, the mean age of youngest child aged 6–11 without an older sibling aged 12–17 is 8.08 years, while for those with one or more older siblings 12–17, the mean age is 8.55 years. A difference of age of youngest child of about a half year would result in a differential in employment of somewhat more than one percentage point. The overall difference in the employment of the two categories of mothers of children ages

TABLE 3-5

Percentage Distribution of Husband-Present Women Age 14–59, by Age of Youngest Own Child and Number of Own Children Under 18, for White and Nonwhite Women: United States, 1960[a]

Age of youngest child	Number of children: 1	2	3	4 or more	None	Total
White women						
0–2	6.2	7.1	5.6	6.1	—	25.0
3–4	1.6	3.0	2.4	2.0	—	9.0
5	.6	1.4	1.0	.7	—	3.7
6–11, without children 12–17	9.1	2.7	.6	.1	—	12.5
6–11, with children 12–17	—	4.6	3.1	1.7	—	9.4
12–17	4.2	3.5	.6	.1	—	8.4
None	—	—	—	—	32.0	32.0
Total	21.7	22.3	13.3	10.7	32.0	100.0
Nonwhite women						
0–2	5.6	6.0	5.3	13.2	—	30.1
3–4	1.8	1.9	1.6	3.3	—	8.6
5	.8	.8	.6	1.1	—	3.3
6–11, without children 12–17	5.1	1.7	.6	.2	—	7.6
6–11, with children 12–17	—	2.0	2.1	3.0	—	7.1
12–17	3.8	2.2	.7	.1	—	6.8
None	—	—	—	—	36.8	36.8
Total	17.1	14.6	10.9	20.9	36.8	100.0

[a]From U.S. Bureau of the Census (1963), *Employment status and work experience*, PC(2)6A, Table 8.

6–11 is 3–4%, depending on the number of children. We have, therefore, explained at best only a third of this differential by the differential in the age of the youngest own child within the range 6–11 years.

The effect of age of youngest child appears to be greater than that of the number of children in the sense that there is considerably greater spread among the rates of the various categories.

The rates of nonwhite women have the same general pattern as those of the white women. The probability of being employed is greater, the older the youngest child. Within age of youngest child categories, the probability decreases as the number of own children increases. The slopes by age of youngest child are much less steep for the nonwhite than for the white women, at

TABLE 3-6

Percentage Distribution of Employed, Husband-Present Women Age 14–59, by Age of Youngest Own Child and Number of Own Children Under 18, for White and Nonwhite Women: United States, 1960[a]

	Number of children					
Age of youngest child	1	2	3	4 or more	None	Total
White women						
0–2	3.8	3.2	2.2	2.2	—	11.4
3–4	1.5	2.0	1.5	1.2	—	6.2
5	.6	1.0	.7	.5	—	2.8
6–11, without children 12–17	4.7	2.6	.6	.1	—	8.0
6–11, with children 12–17	—	5.2	3.3	1.6	—	10.1
12–17	12.0	4.7	.7	.1	—	17.5
None	—	—	—	—	44.0	44.0
Total	22.6	18.7	9.0	5.7	44.0	100.0
Nonwhite women						
0–2	4.1	3.9	3.1	7.0	—	18.1
3–4	1.9	1.8	1.4	2.7	—	7.8
5	.9	.8	.6	1.1	—	3.4
6–11, without children 12–17	4.6	2.1	.6	.2	—	7.5
6–11, with children 12–17	—	2.5	2.4	3.1	—	8.0
12–17	6.3	2.7	.8	.1	—	9.9
None	—	—	—	—	45.3	45.3
Total	17.8	13.8	8.9	14.2	45.3	100.0

[a] From U.S. Bureau of the Census (1963). *Employment status and work experience*, PC(2) 6A Table 8.

least after age of youngest child of three to four. For the nonwhite women, the difference between two, three, and four children is relatively greater than for white women. For mothers of children 6–11, it makes little difference whether or not there is an older child.

Distribution of the Employed Population among Child Status Categories

The contribution of various subpopulations to the labor force depends on both the relative rates of participation and the percentage distribution of the total population among the categories into which it is divided. To indicate the numerical importance of married women in the labor force and the relative weights of the various child-status subpopulations, the percentage distribution of the total husband-present population by child status is presented in Table 3-5.

Table 3-6 gives a similar percentage distribution of employed husband-present women. Since husband-present women comprised 55.4% of the total employed females and 18.1% of all employed persons, the figures in Table 3-6 can be converted to either of these bases by multiplying by these proportions.

Eleven percent of the white employed women have children under the age of 3. The corresponding figure for nonwhite women is 18%. An additional 9% and 11% have children age 3–5. Thus, 20% of the white and 29% of the nonwhite working wives have preschool-age children. Thirty-six percent of the white and 25% of nonwhite working wives have school-age children, and 44% and 45%, respectively, have no children.

Another way of looking at these data that may be of some interest, particularly with regard to the differentials between blacks and nonblacks, is the proportion of all children of particular ages with working mothers. Table 3-7 presents data from the 1/1000 sample on the proportions of all *children* in each of four age intervals who have working mothers. Data are also shown on proportions of children of working mothers whose mothers work full time. From the standpoint of the effects of working mothers on the social and psychological development of children, these figures are more germane than the figures using mothers as units.

The chances are about one in four that a black child under the age of 3 will have a working mother, while those for a white child are closer to one in eight. A similar differential exists for children between the ages of 3 and 5. Overall, it is about 72% more likely that a preschool black child living in an intact family will have a working mother than it is for a white child. Of course, the probability that a black child will be living in an intact family is considerably lower than for a white child. The lower panel of the table indicates that these observed differentials are only slightly mitigated, in terms of the poten-

TABLE 3-7

Percentage of the Children of Husband-Present Mothers Whose Mothers Are Employed and Who Are Working Full Time, by Color and Age of Child: United States, 1960[a]

Age of child	Black (1)	Nonblack (2)	Difference: (1) − (2)	Relative difference (%): (1) − (2) / 2
0–2	22.4	12.5	9.9	79
3–5	26.5	15.8	10.7	68
6–9	34.4	21.3	13.1	61
10–17	35.2	30.7	4.5	15
0–6	24.3	14.1	10.2	72
0–9	27.4	16.6	10.8	65
0–17	30.4	22.1	8.3	37
Percentage of employed working full time				
0–2	61.9	61.0		
3–5	58.6	62.2		
6–9	58.9	61.4		
10–17	57.2	67.8		
0–6	60.2	61.6		
0–9	59.7	61.5		
0–17	58.6	64.9		

[a]From 1/1000 sample.

tial effects on the child, by the greater probability that the working black mother will be working part time. In fact, the working mother of a black child under the age of 3 is slightly more likely to be working full time.

Even where the family is intact, the black child may be relatively deprived of the social and psychological advantages of having a mother present in the home throughout the day. The effects of working mothers on the social and psychological development of the child are not yet known, however. Much undoubtedly depends on the sort of substitute care (see Nye and Hoffman, 1963; see also Herzog, 1967; and Lewis, 1967).

Proportion Who Worked at All in 1959

The 1960 census contained the question, "Last year (1959) did this person work at all, even for a few days?" We turn now to a discussion of the proportion of each child-status subgroup for whom the answer to this question was yes. For the white women (see Table 3-8), over a quarter of the women with children under 3, almost a third of the mothers whose youngest child was 3

TABLE 3-8

Percentage of Husband-Present Women Age 14–59 Who Worked in 1959, by Age of Youngest Own Child, Number of Own Children Under 18, and Color: United States, 1960[a]

Age of youngest child	Number of own children under 18				
	1	2	3	4 or more	None
White women					
0–2	46.0	25.6	20.8	17.9	—
3–4	41.3	29.2	25.9	25.4	—
5	41.5	31.6	30.3	31.0	—
6–11, without children 12–17	43.2	38.3	37.4	36.2	—
6–11, with children 12–17	—	42.3	40.9	38.2	—
12–17	48.6	49.8	47.2	43.6	—
None	—	—	—	—	53.0
Nonwhite women					
0–2	48.0	40.2	36.6	36.5	—
3–4	55.5	49.7	47.1	36.2	—
5	58.6	52.9	50.5	53.9	—
6–11, without children 12–17	59.1	57.8	52.0	49.6	—
6–11, with children 12–17	—	57.6	55.8	47.6	—
12–17	59.2	59.6	58.2	50.9	—
None	—	—	—	—	59.5

[a]From U.S. Bureau of the Census (1963). *Employment status and work experience*, PC(2) 6A, Table 8.

to 5, and nearly half of the mothers whose youngest child was 12–17 worked during 1959. For the nonwhite population, fully two-fifths of the mothers of the youngest children, over half of the mothers whose youngest child was age 5, and nearly three-fifths of the mothers of youngest children 12–17 worked at some time during the year.

Among mothers of one child, the proportion is higher for women with children 0 to 2 than for mothers of older children. This reflects the fact that many of the women in this category did not have children during part or all of 1959 and, therefore, were more likely to have worked. Virtually all of the other women would have had youngest child during 1959 who would have been only about a year younger than they were at the time of the census. The only exceptions would be mothers of two children, youngest 0 to 2, who had twins in the last year; women who adopted older children within the last year or so; and women who married a man with older children.

The same basic pattern appears for the proportion working in 1959 as for the percentage employed. There is an increase in the proportion with increases in age of youngest child, and a decrease with increases in the number of children under 18. Again, the nonwhite women show about the same pattern as the white women. The proportion who worked at all in 1959 increases with age of youngest child and is negatively related to the number of children under 18. The nonwhite levels are higher, and the slope on age of youngest child is less steep in comparison with the whites.

In Table 3-9, the ratio of the number of women working some in 1959 to those employed during the census week is shown for women by age of youngest child and number of children. (For a discussion of the regularity of work by wives, see Bancroft, 1958: 100–106, 113–114.) For both the white and the nonwhite women, this ratio increases as age of youngest child decreases. Within each age of youngest child group there is little difference by number of children except for white women with children under age 3.

One might argue that this pattern further shows the effect of the difficulties of working while there are young children in the family. Quite likely there is a sizable number included in the "worked in 1959" category who, feeling economic pressure, gave work a try and gave up because it was too difficult to combine work with family responsibilities. Probably of greater signifi-

TABLE 3-9

Ratio of Number of Husband-Present Women Age 14–59 Who Worked in 1959 to Those Working at the Time of the 1960 Census, by Age of Youngest Own Child, Number of Children Under 18 and Color: United States, 1960[a]

	Number of own children under 18				
Age of youngest child	1	2	3	4 or more	None
White population					
0–2	2.447	1.816	1.705	1.627	—
3–4	1.459	1.424	1.385	1.396	—
5	1.361	1.345	1.323	1.348	—
6–11, without children 12–17	1.249	1.272	1.317	1.341	—
6–11, with children 12–17	—	1.219	1.247	1.269	—
12–17	1.188	1.183	1.192	1.178	—
None	—	—	—	—	1.242
Nonwhite population					
0–2	1.678	1.589	1.551	1.738	—
3–4	1.321	1.315	1.301	1.400	—
5	1.305	1.208	1.315	1.351	—
6–11, without children 12–17	1.244	1.189	1.195	1.150	—
6–11, with children 12–17	—	1.190	1.243	1.302	—
12–17	1.196	1.197	1.290	1.308	—
None	—	—	—	—	1.224

[a]From U.S. Bureau of the Census (1963). *Employment status and work experience*, PC(2) 6A, Table 8.

cance, however, is the fact that young wives report that the major reason for quitting work is pregnancy (Rosenfeld and Perrella, 1965: 1081). The mothers who are most likely to be pregnant are those who already have a child 0 to 2, particularly if they have only one or two children already. In addition, a sizable fraction of women with children under age 3 had their most recent baby in late 1959 or early 1960 and, thus, could have been working in 1959 prior to the birth. Whether, therefore, these women provide labor force flexibility, in the sense of being ready to enter the labor force in fairly sizable numbers in response to a change in the demand for labor, is doubtful. The differentials in this ratio probably reflect to a large degree the differential incidence of pregnancy.

Proportion Employed Full Time

Both from the viewpoint of labor supply in a labor market and from the viewpoint of the individual's time budget and the constraints placed on work

TABLE 3-10

Percentage of Employed, Husband-Present Women Who Are Working Full Time, by Age of Youngest Own Child, Number of Children Under 18, and Color: United States, 1960[a]

	Number of own children under 18				
Age of youngest child	1	2	3	4 or more	None
White women					
0–2	71.8	64.1	60.0	59.5	—
3–4	74.8	64.4	60.5	61.3	—
5	73.4	63.2	61.0	62.1	—
6–11, without children 12–17	69.8	62.7	60.2	63.8	—
6–11, with children 12–17	—	65.0	64.0	66.2	—
12–17	72.1	70.2	71.3	70.4	—
None	—	—	—	—	79.9
Nonwhite women					
0–2	70.4	70.1	63.6	56.5	—
3–4	70.7	68.6	62.8	56.7	—
5	68.7	66.7	57.4	57.7	—
6–11, without children 12–17	69.1	68.7	65.8	67.4	—
6–11, with children 12–17	—	64.6	62.4	59.4	—
12–17	64.5	64.2	60.6	63.4	—
None	—	—	—	—	65.6

[a]From U.S. Bureau of the Census (1963). *Employment status and work experience*, PC(2) 6A, Table 8.

by the presence of children, the number of hours worked per week, as well as the percent employed, is of interest. In the 1960 census those persons who were reported as having worked in the last week were asked how many hours they had worked. A person is regarded as a full-time worker if he worked 35 or more hours during the week.

Table 3-10 shows the proportion of the employed population working full time by child status. The most striking impression that these figures convey is the relatively small differentials among the various child status groupings. There is, to be sure, a decline in the proportion working full time as the number of children increases, and an increase with increasing age of youngest child. The figures range from a high of 80% for wives with no children to a low of 59% for mothers of four or more children under the age of 18, the youngest of whom is 0–2. Among mothers, the highest rate is 75% for mothers of one child age 3–4. The argument presented in the literature and earlier in this study, that the child status variable has its effect on employment primarily because it is correlated with the demands on the mother's time, would suggest that working mothers with heavy child care demands would prefer to work only part time. There are at least two countervailing forces:

1. Most available jobs are full-time jobs. This includes most office and factory positions as well as professional activities. Regular part-time employment opportunities are relatively concentrated in retail trade and service activities (see Table 3-11). Thus, the choice confronting many women who are considering working is whether to work full time or not at all.
2. In addition, the wives with high child-care responsibility who do work are selected in two ways:
   (a) They are women who have high family economic pressure and thus need to earn as much as possible;
   (b) They are disproportionately women with a strong preference for work either by virtue of their training and education or by personal preference.

Klein (1965a) concludes from a survey of representatives from Organization for Economic Cooperation and Development member nations that, in areas of severe labor shortage, one way to increase the supply of labor has been to provide part-time jobs at convenient hours for married women. She points out several disadvantages to part-time work, both to the worker and to the employer. For the worker, the full costs of transportation to and from work and other costs of working are present even though the hours worked and earnings are less. For the employer, there are additional administrative and social insurance costs and problems of utilizing productive capacity to its fullest (Klein, 1965a: 47ff).

TABLE 3-11

Occupational Distribution of the Female Labor Force by Number of Hours Worked per Week: United States, 1960[a]

Occupation	Total labor force	1–14 hours	15–29 hours	30–34 hours	1–34 hours
Professional, technical and kindred	*13.1*	*12.3*	*13.8*	*16.9*	*13.2*
Nurses	2.7	1.5	3.1	1.7	2.1
Teachers	5.7	3.5	5.7	11.6	6.0
Managers, officials and proprietors	*3.7*	*1.7*	*2.1*	*2.3*	*1.9*
Clerical	*30.0*	*17.6*	*25.3*	*18.5*	*19.6*
Sales	*7.8*	*12.7*	*14.1*	*8.2*	*11.4*
Retail trade	6.6	9.8	11.8	6.9	9.3
Craftsmen and foremen	*1.2*	*.6*	*.9*	*1.0*	*.8*
Operatives	*15.3*	*6.8*	*13.3*	*19.4*	*11.7*
Service (except private household workers)	*13.5*	*16.2*	*21.1*	*15.9*	*17.0*
Private household workers	*7.9*	*23.7*	*14.8*	*9.8*	*16.0*
Farm	*1.6*	*2.6*	*4.0*	*2.5*	*2.9*
Laborers	*.5*	*.5*	*.5*	*.6*	*.5*
N. A.	5.3	5.3	5.6	4.9	5.0
Total	100.0	100.0	100.0	100.0	100.0
N (in thousands)	20,454	2009	2321	1324	5658

[a]From U.S. Bureau of the Census (1963). *Occupational characteristics*, PC(2) 7A, Table 13.

Klein's survey indicates that in many countries employers have been successful in recruiting married women by offering part-time work and more flexible schedules. One example is a biscuit factory in London which found it necessary to reorganize its production to fit the part-time employment needs of married women when other labor in the area became quite scarce. A detailed study (Jephcott, Seear, and Smith, 1962) of this factory and its apparently successful experiment has been made by a group of social scientists from the London School of Economics.

Klein (1965a) concludes her discussion:

> Speaking generally, part-time employment is, in present conditions, the adjustment *par excellence* of working hours to the domestic needs of working women with family responsibilities. For this reason it is very much sought after by married women, whether trained or untrained, who wish to work outside their homes. Part-time jobs may therefore fulfill an urgent social need, as well as providing employers with an expedient for increasing their labor force at a time of full employment, or enlisting the services of particular kinds of trained personnel in short supply [p. 51].

If such work were generally available in the United States, we might expect the differential of working full time by child status to be quite wide. To my knowledge, no American survey has ever asked women who were not employed whether they would be interested in taking a part-time job if one were available. A study of Swedish women asked women working full time whether they would prefer part-time work. A quarter of the women responded that they would. About a tenth of both the part-time and the full-time working wives indicated that they would prefer not working at all (Gendell, 1963, Table VI-3).

We do have American data on unemployed women (of all ages and marital statuses) as to whether they are seeking part- or full-time work. In recent years some 80% of the unemployed women were seeking full-time work and only a fifth part-time work (U.S. Dept. of Labor, Bureau of Labor Statistics, 1966, Table F-8). Data are not available by child status. The difficulty with these data is that the meaning of umemployment is rather ambiguous when applied to secondary workers. The women who might be drawn into the part-time labor force may be more likely to be in the "not in the labor force" category, rather than unemployed. The measured unemployed are more likely to be women who need to work by virtue of family economic pressure and who are unable to find jobs. Very little is known about the unemployment of married women.

Extremes of Labor Force Involvement

If we wanted to locate women with maximum labor force involvement, we would select those who worked full time, full year. Unfortunately, the census did not ask a question on usual hours worked while working last year, so we cannot do this. The closest we can come with census data is to examine differentials in the proportion working full year (i.e., 50–52 weeks). A note of caution should be introduced here—some occupations, such as that of school teacher (6% of all employed females) are generally not performed full year. This fact should, however, not influence the differentials by child status since there is no strong reason for positing a high correlation between employment in these occupations and child status.

About 4% of the white women with youngest child aged 0–2, and one or more other children, worked full year in 1959 (see columns 1 and 4 of Table 3-12). This proportion rises to 10% of the mothers with youngest child age 5, and to 18% of mothers with youngest child aged 12–17. For nonwhite women, about 8% of the mothers of very young children were at work 50–52 weeks in 1959; 18% of the mothers of youngest children age 5; and a quarter of the mothers of youngest child age 12–17. We again find an increase with

TABLE 3-12

Decomposition of the Percentage of Women Working 50–52 Weeks in 1959 into Percentage Working in 1959 and the Percentage of the Working Women Who Worked 50–52 Weeks, by Age of Youngest Own Child, Number of Own Children Under 18, and Color: United States, 1960[a]

	White women				
Child status	Percentage worked in 1959	×	Percentage of workers working 50–52 weeks	=	Percentage of women working 50–52 weeks
No child under 18	53.0		50.1		26.6
One child under 18					
0–2	46.0		14.8		6.8
3–4	41.3		37.0		15.3
5	41.5		38.9		16.2
6–11	43.2		41.2		17.8
12–17	48.6		45.2		22.0
Two children under 18					
Youngest 0–2	25.6		16.0		4.1
3–4	29.2		30.3		8.8
5	31.6		33.2		10.5
6–11, with children 12–17	42.3		37.4		15.8
6–11, without children 12–17	38.3		33.3		12.8
12–17	49.8		42.7		21.2
Three children under 18					
Youngest 0–2	20.8		16.8		3.5
3–4	25.9		28.6		7.4
5	30.3		31.3		9.5
6–11, with children 12–17	40.9		34.6		14.2
6–11, without children 12–17	37.4		28.3		10.6
12–17	47.2		41.8		19.7
Four children under 18					
Youngest 0–2	17.9		18.9		3.4
3–4	25.4		28.2		7.2
5	31.0		31.0		9.6
6–11, with children 12–17	38.2		33.4		12.9
6–11, without children 12–17	36.2		27.0		9.8
12–17	43.6		39.3		17.1

age of youngest child and a decrease with number of children under 18 for white women. Working women with only one child are much more likely to be full-year workers than women with two children, while the difference between two and four children is smaller. The nonwhite pattern is generally similar to the white, but more irregular.

We can decompose the proportion of each subpopulation working full

TABLE 3-12—(*Continued*)

	Nonwhite women		
Child status	Percentage worked in 1959 ×	Percentage of workers working 50–52 weeks =	Percentage of women working 50–52 weeks
No child under 18	59.5	41.6	24.7
One child under 18			
0–2	48.0	19.9	9.6
3–4	55.5	37.0	20.5
5	58.6	38.9	22.8
6–11	59.1	40.6	24.0
12–17	59.2	42.2	25.0
Two children under 18			
Youngest 0–2	40.2	19.8	7.9
3–4	49.7	37.6	18.7
5	52.9	35.0	18.5
6–11, with children 12–17	57.6	42.1	24.4
6–11, without children 12–17	57.8	40.8	23.6
12–17	59.6	43.4	25.9
Three children under 18			
Youngest 0–2	36.6	18.7	6.9
3–4	47.1	35.6	16.7
5	50.5	35.4	17.9
6–11, with children 12–17	55.8	36.2	20.2
6–11, without children 12–17	52.0	39.2	20.4
12–17	58.2	42.2	24.6
Four children under 18			
Youngest 0–2	36.5	17.4	6.4
3–4	46.2	30.2	13.9
5	49.6	30.2	15.0
6–11, with children 12–17	53.9	34.2	18.6
6–11, without children 12–17	47.6	40.8	19.4
12–17	50.9	27.8	14.2

[a]From U.S. Bureau of the Census (1963). *Employment status and work experience*, PC(2) 6A. Table 8.

year into two components: the proportion working in 1959, and the proportion of those working in 1959 who worked full year (see Table 3-12). For both the white and nonwhite populations, both of the components increase with age of youngest child to produce the increase in the proportion of all women working full year as age of youngest child increases. The slopes of each of the components and the total are less steep for nonwhite than for white women.

At the other extreme of minimum labor force involvement are persons who have never worked. The 1960 census asked, "When did he last work at all, even for just a few days?" There was a category "never worked." In addition, all persons for whom the question was appropriate (those not currently at work) and for whom the question was not answered were included in the tabulations as never having worked. These proportions are shown in Table 3-13. For white women, the proportion never having worked rises with both age of youngest child and number of children under 18. The pattern is not very regular. The major difference occurs between three and four or more children. The curves for one and two children are very close together, while the curve for three children lies closer to them than to the curve for four or more children.

The proportion of nonwhite women who have never worked also increases with number of children. In the case of nonwhites, three children is as far away from one and two as four or more is from three. Nonwhite women differ from white women in that the proportion who have never worked decreases with increasing age of youngest child.

TABLE 3-13

Percentage of Husband-Present Women, Age 14–59. Who Have Never Worked, by Age of Youngest Own Child. Number of Own Children Under 18, and Color: United States, 1960[a]

	Number of own children under 18				
Age of youngest child	1	2	3	4 or more	None
White women					
0–2	14.8	13.9	15.5	27.1	—
3–4	12.1	12.5	14.7	22.0	—
5	11.9	12.7	15.5	22.1	—
6–11, without children 12–17	14.3	15.0	17.6	24.5	—
6–11, with children 12–17	—	11.5	13.4	17.8	—
12–17	17.7	17.0	21.4	27.3	—
None	—	—	—	—	17.4
Nonwhite women					
0–2	26.5	26.9	26.9	29.6	—
3–4	17.8	19.1	20.3	24.1	—
5	16.7	16.3	19.8	23.4	—
6–11, without children 12–17	14.9	15.4	18.3	21.9	—
6–11, with children 12–17	—	15.2	20.3	22.6	—
12–17	16.4	17.6	19.5	22.6	—
None	—	—	—	—	15.4

[a]From U.S. Bureau of the Census (1963). *Employment status and work experience*, PC(2) 6A, Table 8 and *Labor Reserve*, PC(2) 6C, Table 6.

It is very difficult to interpret these differentials in the proportions never having worked. Age is correlated with both number of children and age of youngest child. Furthermore, age is associated with work experience in two ways. Younger women with children have had fewer years of "exposure" to the possibility of having worked. However, the exposure of older women to the possibility of working, particularly prior to the birth of their first child, occurred at a time when fewer women were working.

Added to this is a further factor in the comparison of the white and black proportions never having worked. There has been a long-term increase in the proportion of white women in the work force, while the proportion of black women in the work force has been higher, but approximately constant, since prior to 1900. Given these considerations, no attempt will be made to interpret these differentials. These data are available for 5-year age groups and could be analyzed cohort by cohort.

Effects of Age of Women on Labor Force Activity

In Tables 3-14 through 3-16, the population of husband-present females is divided by age and child status groups. The employment rates of women in the detailed child status classification by age of women will be examined later. Table 3-14 shows that, at all ages of wife between 20–24 and 40–44,

TABLE 3-14

Percentage of Husband-Present Women Age 14–59 Who Are Employed, by Age, and Presence and Age of Children: United States, 1960[a]

Age	All women	Women with children under 6	Women with children 6–17	Women with no children under 18
14–19	21.9	11.3	—	32.7
20–24	27.6	16.9	35.5	59.0
25–29	24.1	16.8	36.9	61.8
30–34	26.3	16.6	37.4	57.9
35–39	31.2	17.2	38.0	53.4
40–44	36.3	18.3	37.4	48.6
45–49	37.7	20.6	34.6	43.1
50–54	34.9	24.0	31.1	36.6
55–59	27.5	—	24.7	27.8
Total 14–59	30.6	16.9	36.0	41.8

[a]From U.S. Bureau of the Census (1963). *Employment status and work experience*, PC(2) 4A, Table 12.

TABLE 3-15

Percentage of Employed Husband-Present Women Who Are Working Full Time, by Age, and Presence and Age of Children: United States, 1960[a]

Age	All women	Women with children under 6	Women with children 6–17	Women with no children under 18
14–19	76.0	65.6	—	80.1
20–24	78.7	69.5	74.5	86.6
25–29	72.1	64.4	73.1	84.8
30–34	68.4	60.0	69.0	83.0
35–39	68.6	58.7	68.0	80.6
40–44	69.9	60.1	66.7	78.4
45–49	70.9	61.4	65.7	75.8
50–54	71.3	60.9	64.7	73.7
55–59	69.4	—	64.4	70.1
Total 14–59	70.9	63.0	67.2	77.6

[a]From U.S. Bureau of the Census (1963). *Employment status and work experience*, PC(2) 4A, Table 12.

TABLE 3-16

Mean Number of Hours Worked per Week,[a] *by Working Husband-Present Women, by Age, and by Presence and Age of Children: United States, 1960*[b]

Age	All women	Women with children under 6	Women with children 6–17	Women with no children under 18
14–19	35.8	33.3	—	36.7
20–24	36.2	34.2	35.8	37.9
25–29	35.0	33.2	35.8	37.8
30–34	34.6	32.4	35.0	37.8
35–39	34.9	32.4	34.9	37.5
40–44	35.5	33.1	34.7	37.4
45–49	35.9	33.5	34.7	37.0
50–54	36.1	32.6	34.7	36.6
55–59	35.7	—	34.4	35.8
Total 14–59	35.4	33.1	34.8	37.0

[a]Means were computed by assigning midpoints of intervals to persons in the intervals. The intervals are 1–14, 15–29, 30–34, 35–39, 40, 41–48, 49–59, and 60 or more. A value of 65 was assigned to the 60 and over category.

[b]From U.S. Bureau of the Census (1963). *Employment status and work experience*, PC(2) 4A, Table 12.

about a sixth of the women with children under 6 are at work. Between 34 and 38% of the women under 50 with children 6–17 and with no children under 6 are working. Thus, if a woman with children is under 50, it is the ages of her children and not her own age which influences her labor market participation. For women with no children under 18, age makes a great difference. A third of the women ages 14–19 who have no own children under 18, about 60% of women ages 20–34, and a steadily decreasing proportion through the older ages are at work.

Table 3-15 presents the percentage of working women in each "age-presence of children" group who were at work full time during the census week. For women with no children (with the exception of the youngest age group) the older the woman, the less likely she is to be working full time. Older childless women have both lower participation rates and work shorter hours. Younger women with children 6–17 and none under 6 are more likely to be working full time than older women. Full-time work seems to be more common among younger working wives.

Table 3-16 presents the mean number of hours worked by employed women in each age group. Women with children under 6 work an average of 33 hours per week; those with children 6–17 work 35 hours; and those with no children work an average of 37.5 hours. Age of woman makes little difference in these means when there are children present, and makes a difference for childless women only after age 45.

This is not an adequate description of the effect of age of woman, for within the broad "age of child" categories there is room for a great deal of variation as a result of differences between age groups in the distribution of age of youngest child and number of children. Women of ages 20–24 have a distribution of children under 6 that is weighted more heavily in the 0 to 2 range, whereas women 35–39 would be more likely to have a child age 5. We have already described the differences in the proportion employed within these broad "age of youngest child" categories. In addition, a younger woman would be less likely to have several children than an older woman.

Figure 3-5 plots the percentage employed by age for women with two children under 18. There is a separate curve for each age of youngest child category. For both the white and nonwhite populations, this figure shows that, as the age of the youngest child increases, the slope of age goes from moderately positive for youngest child 0–2 to rather strongly negative by age of youngest child 6–11 and 12–17. This figure for mothers of two children under 18 shows this pattern most perfectly, but it is also present for other numbers of children. The older a mother of a child 0–2 is, the more likely she is to work. Twenty percent of the mothers of youngest child 3 to 4 work, regardless of their age. Mothers of older children show even steeper declines

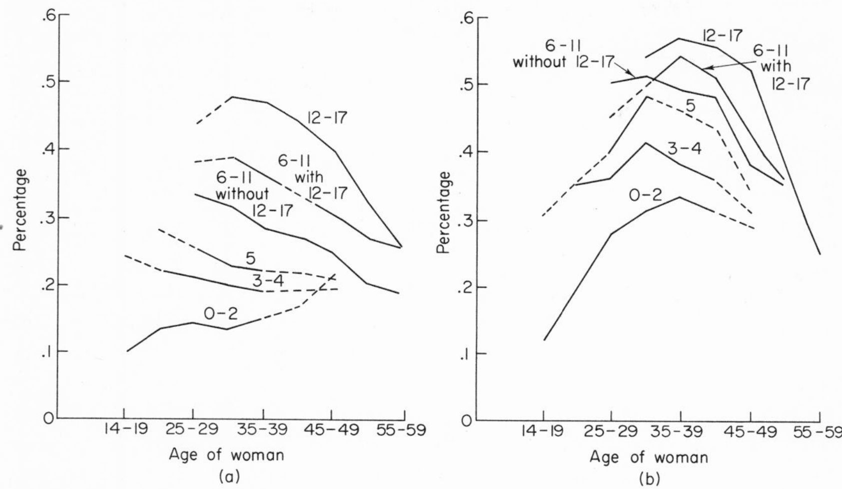

Figure 3-5. *Percentage of husband-present women with two children under 18 who are employed, by age of youngest own child and color: United States, 1960. (a) White women; (b) nonwhite women. Numbers on curves refer to age of youngest own child.*

with age in rate of employment. The pattern is considerably more pronounced for nonwhite than for white women.

The rise in employment rates with age for mothers of very young children may be a result of the older women's later age at marriage or a longer first birth interval, following the argument presented in Chapter 2.

At least part of the basis for this phenomenon of changing slope is the fact that it is only at the older ages of women, say over 40, that age has any real influence on labor force participation. The influence is both physiological and a cohort phenomenon. A woman of 35–39 is probably as able to work as a woman of 20–24. Both had completed high school after the start of World War II when rates of employment of women increased markedly. The slopes we are looking at and comparing are formed at progressively older ages of women. The positive slope of mothers of children 0 to 2 is a curve drawn primarily between ages 20–24 and 35–39. The curve for mothers of youngest child 12–17 is drawn only for women who are over age 35.

In addition, within an age group where there are sizable numbers of women both with older children and with very young children (e.g., age 35–39 or 40–44), the women in the different age of youngest child categories are selected in quite different ways. For example, a woman of age 40 with a child under three is likely to have married late in life, or to have borne many children, or to have spaced her children at long intervals. Women in the same age group with youngest child 12–17 have either married at a very young age or have had very few children. Age at marriage and child spacing and associated socioeconomic factors are probably exerting the influence here, and age is relatively unimportant, at least until after age 40, when physical ability to work may begin to be important.

White–Nonwhite Differentials in Labor Force Activity

We have compared the pattern of variation of employment for black and white wives in relation to family status. Let us briefly turn our attention to a more explicit comparison of black and white employment. The measure which I have used to make comparisons between the white and nonwhite labor force rates is the difference between the two rates expressed as a proportion of the rate for the white population. I have used this proportion in addition to simply the absolute difference in order to make comparisons between groups of women with quite different levels more meaningful.

TABLE 3-17

White-Nonwhite Differentials in the Percentage of Husband-Present Women Aged 14–59 Who Are Employed, by Age of Youngest Child and Number of Own Children Under 18: United States, 1960[a]

	Number of own children under 18				
Age of youngest child	1	2	3	4 or more	None
Absolute differentials					
0–2	9.8	11.2	11.4	10.0	—
3–4	13.7	17.3	17.5	14.8	—
5	14.4	20.3	15.5	13.7	—
6–11, without children 12–17	14.9	18.5	15.1	14.4	—
6–11, with children 12–17	—	13.7	12.1	11.3	—
12–17	6.6	7.7	5.5	1.9	—
None	—	—	—	—	6.0
Relative differentials					
0–2	52.1	79.4	93.4	90.9	—
3–4	48.4	84.4	93.6	81.3	—
5	47.2	86.4	67.7	59.6	—
6–11, without children 12–17	43.1	61.5	53.2	53.3	—
6–11, with children 12–17	—	39.5	36.9	37.5	—
12–17	16.1	18.3	13.9	5.1	—
None	—	—	—	—	14.1

[a]From U.S. Bureau of the Census (1963). *Employment status and work experience*. PC(2) 6A. Table 8.

I will consider separately the differences within child status categories between the white and nonwhite population for each of the labor force activity variables.

Percentage Employed

For mothers of one child under age 12, the nonwhite rate is almost half again as large as the white (see Table 3-17). For mothers of more than one child, the youngest of which is under 5, the nonwhite rates are 80–95% higher than the white rates. For mothers of older children the relative differentials are smaller. Only when there are children 12–17 is the differential as small as 40%.

Clearly, the nonwhite rates specific for age of youngest child and number of children are uniformly higher than those for white mothers. How does the composition of the two populations, with respect to family size and age of youngest child, affect the crude employment rates? Table 3-5 showed a relative surplus of nonwhite women in the younger age of youngest child and the larger family size categories, reflecting their higher fertility. How do

TABLE 3-18

White–Nonwhite Differentials in the Percentage of Husband-Present Women, Working in 1959, by Age of Youngest Child and Number of Own Children Under 18: United States, 1960[a]

	Number of own children under 18				
Age of youngest child	1	2	3	4 or more	None
Absolute differentials					
0–2	2.0	14.6	15.8	18.6	—
3–4	14.2	20.5	21.2	20.8	—
5	17.1	21.3	20.2	18.6	—
6–11, without children 12–17	15.9	19.5	14.6	11.4	—
6–11, with children 12–17	—	15.3	14.9	15.7	—
12–17	10.6	9.8	11.0	7.3	—
None	—	—	—	—	6.5
Relative differentials					
0–2	4.3	57.0	76.0	103.9	—
3–4	34.4	70.2	81.8	81.9	—
5	41.2	67.4	66.7	60.0	—
6–11, without children 12–17	36.8	50.9	39.0	31.5	—
6–11, with children 12–17	—	36.2	36.4	41.1	—
12–17	21.8	19.7	23.3	16.7	—
None	—	—	—	—	12.2

[a]From U.S. Bureau of the Census (1963). *Employment status and work experience*, PC(2) 6A. Table 8.

these countervailing influences affect the crude rate of employment? The overall difference in the rate of employment of white and nonwhite mothers is 8.7 percentage points (34.2 – 25.5). The nonwhite rate is thus slightly more than a third higher than the white. If the nonwhite mothers had their own child-status specific (i.e., age of youngest child by number of children specific) employment rates and the white child status composition, their crude rate of employment would be 37.4. Thus the white–nonwhite differential increases, rather than diminishes, when the rates are standardized on child status. The nonwhite family status composition is relatively unfavorable to employment, given the nonwhite specific rates.

Percentage Who Worked in 1959

Again we find wide differentials, which are widest for mothers of more than one child, the youngest of which is under 5 years of age (see Table 3-18). There is not a single differential of less than 30% for any category of women with more than one child, the youngest of whom is under 12. For the mothers

TABLE 3-19

White–Nonwhite Differentials in the Percentage of Employed Husband-Present Women, Aged 14–59, Who Are Working Full Time, by Age of Youngest Child and Number of Own Children Under 18: United States, 1960[a]

Age of youngest child	Number of own children under 18: 1	2	3	4 or more	None
Absolute differentials					
0–2	–1.4	6.0	3.6	–3.0	—
3–4	–4.1	4.2	2.3	–4.6	—
5	–4.7	3.5	–3.6	–4.4	—
6–11, without children 12–17	–0.7	6.0	5.6	3.6	—
6–11, with children 12–17	—	–0.4	–1.6	–6.8	—
12–17	–7.6	–6.0	–10.7	–7.0	—
None	—	—	—	—	–14.3
Relative Differentials					
0–2	–1.9	9.4	6.0	–5.0	—
3–4	–5.5	6.5	3.8	–7.5	—
5	–6.4	5.5	–5.9	–7.1	—
6–11, without children 12–17	–1.0	9.6	9.3	5.6	—
6–11, with children 12–17	—	–0.6	–2.5	–10.3	—
12–17	–10.5	–8.5	–15.0	–9.9	—
None	—	—	—	—	–17.9

[a]From U.S. Bureau of the Census (1963). *Employment status and work experience*, PC(2) 6A, Table 8.

of more than one child, the differential is as high as 104%. Mothers of more than one child, the youngest of whom is 12–17, show a differential of 17–23%.

Mothers of one child age 0 to 2 show only a 4% differential. This group is composed of women, many of whom spent all or part of the year with no children. Many were unmarried during 1959. This smaller differential might therefore be expected, since nonwhite single women participate in the labor force with lower frequency than white single women.

Proportion Working Full Time

Table 3-19 shows that the differentials in percentage of employed working full time are rather small in absolute magnitude and extremely small as proportions of the white percentages in comparison with the figures we have been examining. The range of the proportional differences is from 1 to 15%, with almost all between 5 and 10%. In most cases the signs are negative, which means that the nonwhite women are less likely to be working full time than the white employed women. Five of the eight exceptions occur in categories of mothers with two or three children, the youngest of whom is

TABLE 3-20

White–Nonwhite Differentials in the Percentage of Husband-Present Women Aged 14–59 Who Worked 50–52 Weeks in 1959, by Age of Youngest Child and Number of Own[a]

	Number of own children under 18				
Age of youngest child	1	2	3	4 or more	None
Absolute Differentials					
0–2	2.8	3.8	3.4	3.0	—
3–4	5.2	9.9	9.3	6.7	—
5	6.6	8.0	8.4	5.4	—
6–11, without children 12–17	6.2	10.6	9.8	9.6	—
6–11, with children 12–17	—	8.6	6.0	5.7	—
12–17	3.0	4.7	4.9	−2.9	—
None	—	—	—	—	−1.9
Relative differentials					
0–2	41.2	92.7	17.1	88.2	—
3–4	34.0	112.5	125.7	93.0	—
5	40.7	76.2	88.4	56.2	—
6–11, without children 12–17	34.8	84.4	92.4	98.0	—
6–11, with children 12–17	—	54.4	42.2	44.2	—
12–17	13.5	22.2	24.9	−17.0	—
None	—	—	—	—	−7.1

[a]From U.S. Bureau of the Census (1963). *Employment status and work experience*, PC(2) 6A, Table 8.

under 6. Here nonwhite women are 3–6% more likely to be working full time than white mothers.

Percentage Worked 50–52 Weeks in 1959

Despite the nature of the employment opportunities open to nonwhite women and their marginal position in many jobs, a much higher proportion of the nonwhite population worked full year (see Table 3-20). The differential is again smaller for mothers whose youngest child is 12–17 (−17–+25), and for mothers with only one child under 18 (35–41%) than for other categories of mothers. Apart from mothers with children 12–17, the range of the differentials is 56–126%, with most of the differentials over 80%. The differential tends to be greater, the younger the child.

Percentage Who Never Worked

We have already shown that nonwhite women are more likely to be employed. They are also considerably more likely to have never worked (see Table 3-21). Again, the exceptions and smallest differentials occur for

TABLE 3-21

White–Nonwhite Differentials in the Percentage of Husband-Present Women Who Have Never Worked, by Age of Youngest Child and Number of Own Children under 18: United States, 1960[a]

	Number of own children under 18				
Age of youngest child	1	2	3	4 or more	None
Absolute differentials					
0–2	11.7	13.0	11.4	7.5	—
3–4	5.7	6.6	5.6	2.1	—
5	4.8	3.6	4.3	1.3	—
6–11, without children 12–17	.6	3.7	6.9	4.8	—
6–11, with children 12–17	—	.4	.7	−2.6	—
12–17	−1.3	.6	−1.9	−4.7	—
None	—	—	—	—	−2.0
Relative differentials					
0–2	79.0	93.5	73.5	33.9	—
3–4	47.1	52.8	38.1	9.5	—
5	40.3	28.3	27.7	5.9	—
6–11, without children 12–17	4.2	32.2	51.5	27.0	—
6–11, with children 12–17	—	2.7	4.0	−10.6	—
12–17	−7.3	3.5	−8.9	−17.2	—
None	—	—	—	—	−11.5

[a]From U.S. Bureau of the Census (1963). *Employment status and work experience*, PC(2) 6A, Table 8.

mothers whose youngest child is 12–17. There is a tendency for the differentials to be greater, the younger the youngest child. The differential is smallest for women with four or more children. This makes sense in that women who have spent a large share of their lives with very young children, regardless of their color, particularly if they married young, have been very limited in their opportunity for employment. We have previously pointed out how difficult it is to interpret these proportions never worked, particularly white–nonwhite comparisons.

In some of our multivariate analyses in the following chapters, color will be used as an independent variable additively with the child status variables. This means that we are forcing the asbolute differentials to some constant across all child status categories. In the case of differentials in the rate of employment, this is not too unreasonable since the differentials lie largely within a range of 10–15%. The exceptions are mostly in the 12–17 years of age of youngest child category.

Completed Fertility and Labor Force Participation

In the first chapter we discussed the relationship between fertility and labor force participation. This discussion concluded that it was very difficult

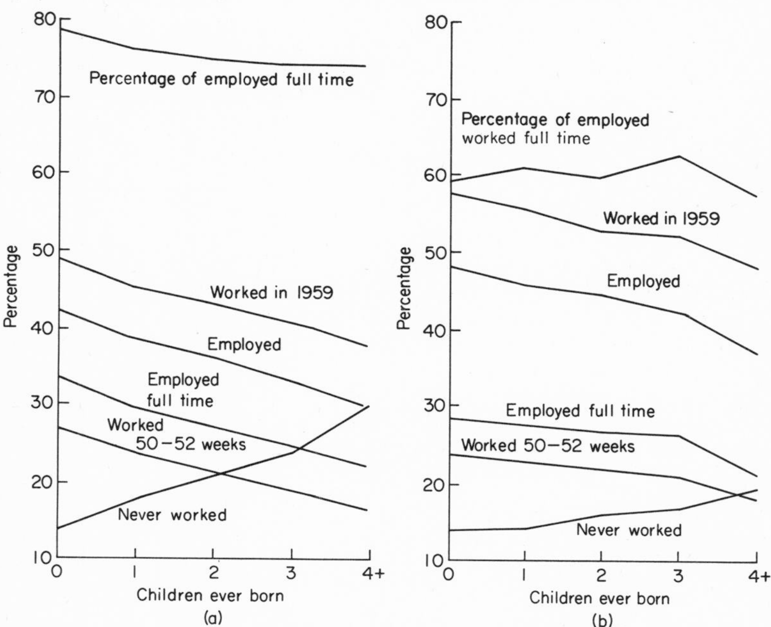

Figure 3-6. *Labor force activity rates for women 50–54 with no own children under 25, by number of children ever born: United States. 1960. (a) White women; (b) nonwhite women.*

to deal causally with this question using cross-sectional data. One problem with causal analysis was that present child care responsibility was confounding the relationship. One way to examine the relationship between fertility and employment, independent of present child care responsbilities, is to examine the labor force activity of women who have completed their fertility and have no children present in the household by the number of children ever born. Figure 3-6 plots six labor force proportions by number of children ever born for women ages 50–54 with no own children under 25 in the household. In all cases the five measures of current labor force activity decrease as children ever born increases. The proportions employed, employed full time, worked in 1959, and worked full year in 1959 all decline at approximately the same rate for the white population. There is about a 10% difference between women with no children ever born and women with four or more children ever born, and a 7% differential between one and four children ever born. For the nonwhite population the slopes are less steep and the curves are less regularly shaped. Similar results are found when the same rates are plotted for women 55–59.

The proportion never having worked increases quite rapidly with children ever born, from 14% for white women with no children ever born to 30% for those with four or more children ever born. While the effect of fertility on work experience may be confounded by education and economic pressure and thus be overstated in these comparisons, I would argue that these observed differentials are probably largely independent effects of fertility.

Labor Force Activity of Married Women in Relation to Child Status and Family History–Multivariate Analysis

This chapter reports the results of a multivariate analysis of the employment of mothers with one or more children under 18 in the household. The primary concern will be to describe the effects of the child status variables on employment. We will also examine the effects of the family history variables. The chapter concludes with an analysis of the conditional probabilities of full-time work, given that the mother is working. Throughout this chapter particular attention is focused on black–white differences in employment.

Despite the probable existence of interactions in the effects of our major independent variables on the employment of mothers, we will, as a first approximation, consider their additive effects in this chapter. The one exception to this is that we will consider separately the black and the nonblack mothers. In Chapter 5 the presence and substantive importance of other interactions will be considered.

In all analyses of the employment of mothers, I have used five independent variables: (1) age of youngest own child, (2) number of own children under the age of 18, (3) educational attainment, (4) income adequacy, and (5) age. The categories into which these variables were divided and the distribution of sample cases among the categories are shown in Table 4-1. I will refer to this set of five independent variables as the "basic variables." To this set of variables I will add, one at a time, a number of other family history and family composition variables in order to assess their effects on employment, independent of their correlations with the basic variables.

TABLE 4-1

Multiple Classification Analysis of Employment of Mothers in Relation to Age, Child Status Variables, and Socioeconomic Variables, by Color: United States, 1960

	Nonblack mothers				Black mothers			
			Deviations				Deviations	
	N	Distri-bution	Gross	Net	*N*	Distri-bution	Gross	Net
Age of youngest child								
0	3205	15.7	−.17	−.20	355	23.0	.13	.12
1	2566	12.6	−.09	−.12	229	14.8	−.04	−.04
2	1858	9.1	−.07	−.08	142	9.2	−.07	−.07
3	1498	7.3	−.05	−.06	107	6.9	−.05	−.05
4	1214	5.9	−.03	−.03	81	5.2	−.00	−.01
5	1117	5.5	−.03	−.03	89	5.8	−.04	−.03
6	987	4.8	.00	.00	58	3.8	−.03	−.04
7	953	4.7	.04	.06	62	4.0	.13	.12
8	778	3.8	.08	.09	54	3.5	.05	.05
9	777	3.8	.08	.10	59	3.8	.27	.26
10–11	1555	7.6	.12	.14	89	5.8	.18	.19
12–13	1623	7.9	.18	.20	104	6.7	.10	.11
14–15	1276	6.2	.17	.21	61	3.9	.09	.09
16–17	1014	5.0	.19	.23	55	3.6	.17	.16
Income adequacy								
.0–.3	835	4.1	.03	.08	315	20.4	−.00	.03
.4 .7	2064	10.0	.02	.09	545	35.3	.01	.03
.8–1.1	4486	22.0	.03	.07	411	26.6	−.04	−.05
1.2–1.5	5428	26.6	.02	.02	188	12.2	.04	−.02
1.6–1.9	3462	17.0	−.02	−.04	53	3.4	.08	.01
2.0–2.8	2699	13.2	−.04	−.09	29	1.9	—	—
2.9+	1447	7.1	−.10	−.20	6	0.4	—	—
Age								
14–19	378	1.9	−.14	−.02	62	4.0	−.13	−.05
20–24	2321	11.4	−.08	.02	231	15.0	−.08	−.02
25–29	3293	16.1	−.07	.02	279	18.1	−.05	−.00
30–34	3999	19.6	−.03	.02	320	20.7	.03	.04
35–39	4196	20.5	.03	.02	251	16.2	.04	.02
40–44	3092	15.1	.07	−.02	182	11.8	.08	.03
45–49	1998	9.8	.08	−.06	117	7.6	.07	−.03
50–54	876	4.3	.08	−.10	77	5.0	.00	−.13
55–59	268	1.3	.06	−.13	26	1.7	—	—
Education								
No H.S.	3768	18.5	−.01	−.07	582	37.7	.00	−.01
H.S. 9–11	4821	23.6	−.01	−.03	496	32.1	−.02	−.02
H.S. 12	8336	40.8	.00	.01	343	22.2	−.00	.00
Col. 1–3	2187	10.7	.01	.05	76	4.9	−.02	−.02
Col. 4+	1309	6.4	.05	.13	48	3.1	.29	.28

TABLE 4-1—(*continued*)

	Nonblack mothers				Black mothers			
			Deviations				Deviations	
	N	Distribution	Gross	Net	*N*	Distribution	Gross	Net
Number of children								
1	6553	32.1	.08	.04	436	28.2	.05	.03
2	6823	33.4	.00	−.01	368	23.8	.05	.04
3	3951	19.3	−.05	−.03	264	17.1	−.04	−.04
4	1823	8.9	−.07	−.03	178	11.5	−.04	−.03
5	706	3.5	−.10	−.05	123	8.0	−.00	.02
6	314	1.5	−.11	−.05	80	5.2	−.05	−.02
7+	251	1.2	−.17	−.08	96	6.2	−.17	−.13
Grand mean		.25				.34		

Table 4-1 presents the results of the multiple classification analysis of the probability of being employed in relation to the five basic variables for the two color groups. The first column contains the distribution of sample cases among categories of each variable. The second column presents the same information in the form of a percentage distribution. The third column, called gross deviations from the grand mean, is simply the category-specific proportion employed minus the proportion of the entire sample which is employed. Finally, the fourth column shows net deviations from the grand mean, or the deviation of the category proportion employed when the effects of the remaining four variables are statistically controlled. The difference between the net and the gross deviations from the grand mean, then, represents the effect of controlling the effects of the other included variables on the effect attributed to the variable in question.

I will begin by describing the effects of education, income adequacy, and age, even though they are not our primary concern.

Education

For nonblack mothers, education (short of having completed college) has an extremely weak zero-order effect on employment. Having completed college raises the probability of working by about five percentage points. When the effects of the other variables, particularly income adequacy, are taken into account, the effect of education becomes quite pronounced. The employment rate is depressed by seven percentage points below the grand mean of .25 for women with no high school. The net deviations increase by four percentage points over each of the next three education categories, and by eight percentage points between the "some college" and the "college graduate" categories.

For black mothers, education in the range less than college graduate has no appreciable gross or net effect on employment. Having graduated from college raises the probability of working by almost 30% above the black grand mean of 34%.

If the interpretation of the effect of education suggested earlier is correct, it would appear that increments in education, short of completing college, make little difference in the earning capacity and/or employability of black women. Bowen and Finegan (1969), however, correctly point out that there is a similar upward gradient in earnings by education for both black and white women. They suggest as an alternative hypothesis that the differential shape of the education effect (i.e., the lack of a rise in employment with additional education) may be due to the fact that the occupational options available to black women do not improve as much with increases in education as they do for white women.

One might also argue that occupational segregation by race, and resultant differential norms regarding the "appropriate" jobs for women in general and for black and white women in particular, may serve to raise the employment rates of poorly educated black women. White women may be unwilling to compete with black women for jobs as domestic servants, hospital aides, and operatives in such undesirable industries as laundries because these jobs have become defined as "black jobs," beneath the "dignity" of white women.

There is also the possibility that black women may be more heavily concentrated in those urban areas, and in those neighborhoods of urban areas, where unskilled employment opportunities are concentrated. Neither we nor Bowen and Finegan have attempted to introduce any region or size and type of place of residence in our analyses. We know virtually nothing about the geographic location of various types of employment opportunities within urban areas. Some social scientists, such as John Kain (1964: 260–269), have argued that occupational opportunities are increasingly sparse in central cities, particularly in ghetto areas. This is undoubtedly true for the more "desirable" opportunities, but may be relatively less true for the most undesirable unskilled jobs.

The very high proportion of black women with college degrees who are employed, both in relation to the white women with college degrees and to black women with less education, may reflect in part the very high demand for the relatively few college-educated women to teach in the segregated school system. Two-thirds of the employed nonwhite college-educated women are teachers.

Income Adequacy

Income adequacy is the measure of family economic pressure that we have adopted in order to more adequately discriminate the effects of family size and family composition from the effects of economic pressure. A more detailed discussion of the measure has been presented in Chapter 2.

For nonblack women, income adequacy has a strong negative net effect on the probability of employment. The range of the net deviations is from +9% deviation for an income adequacy of less than .8 to a −20% for the highest category of 2.9 and over. The pattern of net deviations is approximately linear in that range.

Income adequacy does not have a strong, nor even a monotonic effect on the employment of black mothers in the range less than 2.0. There are too few black families with income adequacy of more than 2.0 to compute reliable coefficients. This lack of strong negative effect may be explainable in several ways. There is probably more year-to-year variability in the income of black husbands than in that of white husbands. If this is the case, the black families with high income in any year include a larger proportion of families with a positive "transitory component" of income than white families at the same income level. Work by wives, then, may be related to the permanent component or the usual income of the husband. Recall, however, that the economists argue quite the opposite. They say that the wife works in order to maintain the family income when the transitory income is negative. In fact, the wives of men whose income is temporarily high may be working simply because the income of their husband is unstable. Even though his income is adequate now, it may not be next year. If jobs are difficult to find, the most satisfactory strategy may be to continue working even when the husband's income is high.

An alternative explanation for the lack of a strong negative effect of income adequacy may have to do with the possibility that the moderate-income black family may have more extrafamilial or extrahousehold claimants on their income. Clearly all of this is speculation that goes far beyond the available data.

Before leaving the matter of the effect of economic pressure on the probability of employment, there is one other issue to be considered. The conventional income measure that has been used in studies of labor force participation of married women has been family income minus wife's earnings. We now turn to a consideration of the difference that the use of this new measure, income adequacy, made in the analysis. Two types of differences are of interest. One income measure may have a greater or lesser effect on the employment of wives than the other. Here the major test is the ability of the variable to explain variance in the dependent variable. Second, the inclusion of one or the other variable may cause the net effects of the other included variables to differ.

In order to assess the extent of the difference between the use of income adequacy and family income minus wife's earnings, I have run two multiple classification problems which were identical except that in one economic pressure was measured with income adequacy and in the other it was measured with family income minus wife's earnings. For nonblack mothers, coefficient of determination was .106 when family income minus wife's earnings was included with the four other basic variables; when income adequacy was used instead, the coefficient was .111. This small difference may be, to some extent, due to the fact that income adequacy has seven categories and family income minus wife's earnings has only six. In any event, the increase in the R^2 is very small. The shape of the economic pressure–employment relationship is approximately the same for each measure.

In Table 4-2, the patterns of net effects of the four basic variables on the employment of nonblack women are compared when economic pressure is measured in the two alternative ways. There is virtually no difference in the effects of age of youngest child, age, or education. The number of children under 18 has almost no effect when family income minus wife's earnings is used, and a moderate negative effect when income adequacy is included.

The number of children in a family has two conceptually distinct effects on the probability of employment of a mother. On the one hand, the more children in a family, the greater, *ceteris paribus*, the economic pressure implicit in a given dollar income and thus the higher the probability of employment. Yet, the more children, the greater the child care responsibility and the lower the probability of employment. When economic pressure is measured by the family income minus wife's earnings variable, both effects are operating entirely through the number of children variable, and it has little net effect on employment. By taking the economic pressure aspect of the number of children into account in the construction of the economic pressure variable, we are attempting to get a purer measure of the effect of the presence of children as a constraint of work, independent of its economic incentive effect.

Age

For the nonblack woman, the gross deviations show a sharp monotonic increase in employment from ages 14–19 to ages 45–49, followed by a small decline to ages 55–59. The net effects exhibit quite a different pattern.

TABLE 4-2

Comparison of Multiple Classification Results Using Two Alternative Measures of Economic Pressure: Income Adequacy and Family Income Minus Wife's Earnings (Nonblacks Only)

	Using income adequacy			Using family income minus wife's earnings		
		Deviations			Deviations	
	N	Gross	Net	*N*	Gross	Net
Income adequacy						
.0– .3	835	.033	.082			
.4– .7	2064	.023	.087			
.8–1.1	4486	.033	.067			
1.2–1.5	5429	.018	.022			
1.6–1.9	3562	–.017	–.039			
2.0–2.8	2699	–.042	–.093			
2.9+	1447	–.104	–.197			
Family income minus wife's earnings						
Less than $2000				1080	.035	.068
$2000–3999				3067	.037	.086
$4000–5999				6252	.027	.043
$6000–7999				4900	–.010	–.019
$8000–9999				2297	–.019	–.053
$10,000+				2826	–.081	–.140
Education		*Net deviation*			*Net deviation*	
Less than 9 years		–.068			–.062	
9–11 years		–.029			–.025	
12 years		.014			.013	
13–15 years		.049			.040	
16+ years		.130			.115	
Age of youngest child						
0		–.199			–.203	
1		–.119			–.124	
2		–.083			–.088	
3		–.058			–.061	
4		–.034			–.038	
5		–.026			–.028	
6		.004			.006	
7		.055			.055	
8		.090			.092	
9		.099			.101	
10–11		.143			.146	
12–13		.203			.212	
14–15		.213			.221	
16–17		.228			.238	

Table 4-2—(*continued*)

	Using income adequacy			Using family income minus wife's earnings		
		Deviations			Deviations	
	N	Gross	Net	*N*	Gross	Net
Age						
14–19		−.022			−.012	
20–24		.020			.020	
25–29		.018			.013	
30–34		.020			.015	
35–39		.025			.024	
40–44		−.015			−.011	
45–49		−.056			−.049	
50–54		−.099			−.094	
55–59		−.126			−.118	
Number of children						
1		.044			.021	
2		−.006			−.010	
3		−.030			−.014	
4		−.032			−.000	
5		−.052			−.009	
6		−.046			−.002	
7+		−.083			−.036	

After a slight increase from ages 14–19 to ages 20–24, there are almost constant positive net deviations of about two percentage points through ages 35–39. This is followed by an almost linear decline to −12% by ages 55–59. This reinforces what we observed earlier—up to age 40, age has very little effect on the employment of mothers, independent of child status. After age 40, the rates of employment drop quite quickly given the child status.

For black mothers, the effect of age takes the shape of an inverted U with a peak at ages 30–34, and a very rapid decline beginning at age 50. The very young wives in each color group are evidently less employable than the older wives. They have also had less time to seek work and to have gained work experience. For black women, this handicap of youth evidently persists beyond the age of 20. More will be said regarding the employment of young black women when we discuss employment rates of nonmothers.

Age of Youngest Own Child

We have already described the pattern of gross deviations of employment in relation to the child status variables. All that remains to consider here is the extent to which the inclusion of the socioeconomic variables modifies these effects. A comparison of the net and gross deviation columns in Table 4-1 shows that the effects of the age of youngest child on the employment of nonblack mothers are somewhat strengthened by including education, age, number of children under 18, and income adequacy in the analysis. This change in slope is not great, suggesting that the detailed comparisons in Chapter 3 of the employment rates by child status are valid. We were not reaching conclusions as a result of uncontrolled effects of socioeconomic variables. For black women, the pattern of gross deviations is very little different from that of net deviations. This is not surprising since, of the other included variables, only age is very closely associated with employment.

The net effects of age of youngest child are compared for black and nonblack mothers in Fig. 4-1. Because of the smaller sample size, the black rates are less stable than the nonblack rates. Thus, very detailed year-by-year comparisons would be misleading.

Over the entire age range 0–17, the slope for nonblacks is .027, and for blacks it is .019. These are regression coefficients computed from the net

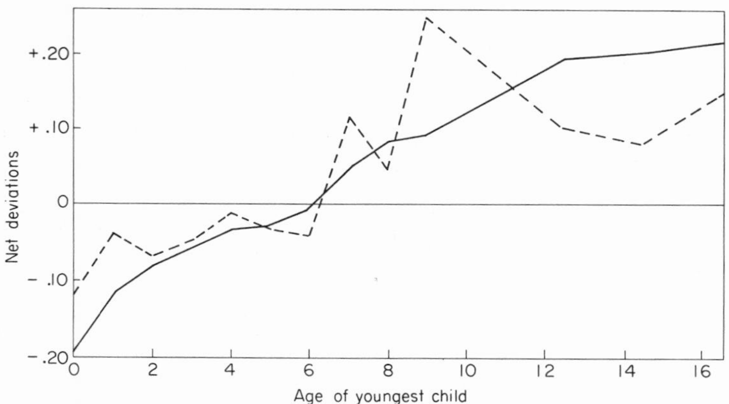

Figure 4-1. *Comparison of the net effects of age of youngest child for black (– – –) and nonblack (—) women. (Other variables included are age, education, income adequacy, and number of children under 18.)*

Slopes	*Black*	*Nonblack*
0–5	.026	.036
6–11	.047	.028
12–17	.009	.009
Total	.019	.027
Mean	.25	.34

deviations where each age of youngest child category is weighted by its number of observations. Thus, for each additional year of age of youngest child, nonblack employment increases by 2.7% while for blacks the increment is 1.9% (procedure used in B. Duncan, 1965: 80). Dividing the "age of youngest child" range into three intervals corresponding roughly to preschool-age, grade-school-age, and high-school-age children, the slopes within each of these age ranges were computed. These are shown in Fig. 4-1. The instability of the black pattern of effects makes the computed slopes sensitive to the age interval selected. Consequently, the difference or similarity in slopes between the color groups, particularly in the 6–11 range, may be deceiving. It is fairly clear that the slope for black mothers is less steep than that for nonblack mothers in the "age of youngest child" range 0 to 5 or 6.

Black mothers of preschool children may have a greater "propensity" to work in some psychological sense. That is a matter about which we have no information and thus cannot discuss. In order to work, however, a mother must arrange for child care. There are several possible reasons that black families may be in a better position than nonblack families to find suitable baby-sitters while mothers work.

1. The black family is more likely to contain extra adult relatives than the nonblack family. Our data from the 1/1000 sample indicates that 19% of the black families with one or more children under the age of three contain a related adult other than the wife and husband. This contrasts with 9% of the nonblack families. For families with youngest child aged three to five, these percentages are 23 and 12%, and for families with youngest child 6–11 they are 29 and 21% respectively. The effect of these extra adults in the family on the employment of mothers will be examined in Chapter 5. Unfortunately, we cannot compare the effects for the two color groups.

2. Blacks are segregated residentially from the white population. If there is a relative living in the same community who might act as a baby-sitter, it is more likely that she is living close to the family than in the case of nonblack families.

3. It may be also that a black family is more likely than a white family to have a relative in the same community. Black families are more likely to be migrants than white families. However, migration of black families may be more focused to a specific area than that of white families. In other words, black migrants may choose their destination with greater frequency in terms of the presence of relatives or move in larger familial units than white families. I know of no data on the extent to which persons have relatives in the same neighborhood.

4. Access to paid baby-sitters may be greater in the black community. Lacking a related person living in the household or nearby, it is probably more likely that a black family would live in the vicinity of someone who would be willing to care for a child for pay than in the white community. The black population is of lower socioeconomic status than the white population. Black mothers who are at home caring for their own children might be likely to want to earn additional income. The black population includes a larger proportion of mothers who are in the marital statuses married, spouse-absent; divorced; widowed; and never married. Data on the labor force participation rates, unemployment rates, and hours worked indicate that young black women—ages 25 and under—have particular difficulty in finding acceptable employment. They may be potential baby-sitters for their relatives and neighbors.

5. If the black family is, in fact, more likely to be wife-dominated than the nonblack family, it is possible that the black woman who wishes to work is less likely to meet resistance from her husband. She may also be more likely to be able to get her husband to care for the children during her absence. This may involve his changing shifts or jobs, or at least constrain him in his choice of a job. One additional matter of some potential importance here is the fact that it is also possible that black men are more likely to be working night shifts anyhow. If they have low seniority in factory work, or are service workers, this is quite probable.

6. Finally, the employment of black women is more likely to be part time and more likely to be evening work than that of white women. Black female employment is concentrated in private household service, largely a part-time employment opportunity. There are also many black women engaged in such service occupations as nurses' aides, cleaning of offices and stores, and other jobs which are often performed during the evening hours. Again, these facts might make it easier for the husband and wife to share the baby-sitting responsibilities.

A 1965 study of child care arrangements of working mothers permits us to indirectly check the validity of some of these hypotheses. Table 4-3 shows the distributions of child care arrangements of full- and part-time working mothers, by color.

(*a*) Nonwhite fathers are somewhat less likely to be caring for the children than are white fathers (10.0 versus 15.9%). The differential is much greater for children of part-time rather than for those of full-time working wives.

(*b*) Nonwhite children are more likely to be cared for in their own homes by a relative other than the father than are white children (28 versus 19%). The color differential is greater for care by relatives over the age of 15

TABLE 4-3

Percentage Distribution of Child Care Arrangements for Children under 14 of Working Mothers by Color and Full-Time, Part-Time Status: United States, 1965[a]

	White			Nonwhite		
	Total	Full time	Part time	Total	Full time	Part time
Care in own home by	**45.7**	**50.8**	**35.3**	**43.5**	**41.8**	**47.7**
Father	15.9	14.5	18.9	10.0	10.8	8.2
Other relatives	19.4	23.6	10.7	28.4	25.4	35.7
Under 16	(4.2)	(4.8)	(2.9)	(6.6)	(4.6)	(11.5)
16 and over	(15.2)	(18.8)	(7.8)	(21.8)	(20.8)	(24.2)
Nonrelative	10.4	12.7	5.6	5.1	5.7	3.9
Only child care	(4.8)	(5.3)	(3.9)	(4.4)	(4.7)	(3.9)
Also other chores	(5.6)	(7.4)	(1.7)	(.7)	(1.0)	(—)
Care in other's home	**14.6**	**18.9**	**5.6**	**22.0**	**24.0**	**17.1**
Relative	7.0	9.2	2.5	11.7	12.0	11.2
Nonrelative	7.6	9.7	3.1	10.3	12.0	6.0
Other care	**39.8**	**30.5**	**59.1**	**34.6**	**34.3**	**35.1**
Group care center	2.1	2.9	.5	2.2	2.7	.9
Child looked after self	7.7	9.3	4.3	10.4	11.3	8.3
Mother, while working	14.1	7.0	28.9	7.7	7.0	9.3
Mother worked only during school	15.5	10.8	25.1	13.3	12.0	16.3
Other	.4	.5	.3	1.0	1.3	.3
Total	100.0	100.0	100.0	100.0	100.0	100.0

[a] Reproduced from S. Low and P. Spindler, *Child care arrangements of working mothers in the United States*, U.S. Department of Health, Education, and Labor Children's Bureau and U.S. Department of Labor, Women's Bureau, 1968, Table A-10.

than for younger relatives, although relatives under 15 account for a substantial share (11.5%) of the child care of nonwhite part-time working mothers. (Relatives include other older children.)

(*c*) Nonwhite children are disproportionately cared for by relatives (and also by nonrelatives) outside the home.

(*d*) Nonwhite children are less than proportionately cared for by the mother while working.

(*e*) Differences in the proportions receiving group care are small, while part-time working white mothers are more likely to be working only while the child is in school.

With the exception of our hypotheses suggesting that nonwhite fathers may be more likely to be available to care for children, our speculation on the sources of the color differentials in employment of mothers of young children seems to be consistent with these data. This is not, of course, an assertion that these hypotheses have been verified.

Within the preschool age of youngest child range, the slope of age of youngest child on employment is steeper for nonblack than for black women. This may reflect the fact that the living arrangements and access to baby-sitters inside and outside of the family are such that black women with infants can work or not work in accord with their own "propensities." The presence of the very young child is not such a constraint. The nonblack woman with a very young child is constrained from working by the lack of a baby-sitter. Gradually, as the child grows up, the constraint becomes less and less because of the greater ease of finding someone (including group care) to care for an older child. There is a great deal of potential child care service in the black community. In the white community there is a shortage of such services. One way that this shortage may be equilibrated is by the potential paid baby-sitters rationing their services to older children who are easier to care for.

An alternative explanation would be in terms of difference in the feelings about the child's need for the mother or the role of the mother. The belief that the wife's place is in the home is certainly present in the American population.[1] Census data from the late nineteenth century to the present indicate that black women have worked in very high proportions, primarily out of economic necessity (Table 4-4). The idea that the wife's, and particularly the mother's, place is in the home has probably not become established to the extent that it has in the society at large. Child-rearing literature in recent years has stressed the importance of the early mother–child relationship to the child's personality development. It is likely, also, that the white population has greater access to and pays greater heed to this literature (see Blau, 1964: 595–608).

To the extent that the black wife has relatively more power within the family, feelings of the husband that the wife should be at home are more irrelevant to the wife's employment. In other words, the husband's negative attitudes toward the wife working may not influence the wife's decision to work as much. Black husbands may, on average, be less likely to have such negative attitudes (see Morgan *et al.* 1966: 326–333) and, to the extent that they do have them, be less influential.

There is evidence that black husbands are less likely than white husbands to oppose work by mothers. Morgan *et al.* (1966) report a multivariate analysis of the attitude of American husbands toward mothers working. A sample

[1]Robert Smuts (1959) discusses the historical origins of contemporary American attitudes toward women working, while Morgan *et al.* (1966: 326–333), show empirically the distribution of attitudes of American men toward working mothers.

TABLE 4-4

Female Labor Force Participation Rates, by Color: United States, 1890–1965[a]

	White	Nonwhite
All women		
1890	15.8	37.7
1900	17.2	41.2
1920	20.7	40.6
1930	21.8	40.4
1940	24.5	37.3
1950	28.4	37.1
1955	30.0	37.3
1960	33.6	41.8
1965	36.9	46.0
Women aged 25–34		
1890	14.5	36.2
1900	16.8	39.9
1920	21.5	42.7
1930	24.9	44.6
1940	31.8	45.8
1950	30.5	44.4
1955	31.0	45.6
1960	33.5	48.6
1965	36.3	54.0

[a]Data for 1890–1955, from Gertrude Bancroft, *The American Labor Force: Its Growth and Changing Composition*, Table D-la. Data for 1960 from U.S. Census of Population, *Characteristics of the population*, U.S. Summary, Table 194. Data for 1965 from U.S. Bureau of Labor Statistics. Labor force and employment in 1965, *Special Labor Force Report*, No. 69, Table B-5.

of American married men was asked, "Suppose a family has children, but they are all in school—would you say it is a good thing for the wife to take a job, or a bad thing, or what?" The 2214 cases were distributed:

Favorable	15%
Favorable with qualifications	17
Pro–con or depends	17
Unfavorable with qualifications	14
Unfavorable	35
NA, Don't know	2
	100%

They note that younger husbands are somewhat more likely to be favorable toward working mothers, and that less educated husbands are less favorably disposed. The largest differential in the proportion approving (in the two favorable categories) is found by color. For husbands under the age of 55, 54% of the nonwhite and 35% of the white husbands approved of mothers working. The authors warn:

> There is always a question whether we are explaining an attitude, or relating it to a behavior which it rationalizes. The racial relation, in particular, may reflect merely the acceptance of a necessity. [p. 326ff]

The white woman may tend to change her mind about her role as the child grows up—within the preschool age. The family's need for additional income, her boredom, or other factors may convince her that the value of being with the child is less important than she had previously thought. In addition, the crucial time for the mother to be with the child may be believed to be in the first couple of years. It is possible that they feel that the experience of being with other children, either in a nursery school context or in another household, may be more important than being in the constant presence of the mother.

Number of Children under 18

The effect of the number of children on employment is attenuated when other variables, particularly the income adequacy measure, are taken into account. For nonblacks, the effect is a monotonic decline from a positive net deviation of .04 for mothers of one child to a negative net deviation of .08 for mothers of seven or more children. For blacks, the pattern is not so regular. There is no reduction in employment between one and two children; a sharp reduction from three to four children; a slight increase to five children; and a sharp reduction thereafter.

The Effects of Family History Variables on Employment of Wives

Age at Marriage

Table 4-5 shows the gross and net deviations for the various categories of age at marriage. The other variables included in the analysis are the basic variables. Age at marriage has no orderly association with employment for either the black or nonblack mothers.

TABLE 4-5

Effects of Wife's Age at First Marriage on the Probability of Employment of Mothers, by Color: United States, 1960

Age at Marriage	Nonblack			Black		
	N	Gross deviation	Net[a] deviation	*N*	Gross deviation	Net[a] deviation
Less than 18	3530	−.01	.01	461	−.01	.01
18–20	7191	.03	.01	482	−.02	−.01
21–24	6434	−.01	−.01	334	.01	−.01
25–29	2447	.02	.01	174	.06	.02
30 and over	820	.02	.00	94	.03	.01
Grand mean	.25			.34		

[a]Other variables included in this multivariate analysis are age of youngest own child, number of children under 18, age, education, and income adequacy.

Length of the First Birth Interval

Table 4-6 shows that the length of the first birth interval also has no effect on the employment of mothers. In view of our rather elaborate argument in support of our expectation that both of these variables would be related to employment later in marriage, further discussion is necessary. Freedman and Coombs (1966b) report that early marriage and short first birth intervals both tend to depress family income and asset accumulation. These effects of early marriage and rapid births appear to persist for some time. In particular, we might expect that the couple with a long first birth interval during which the wife works will be able to accumulate a down payment on a home before the first child is born. At least such a couple ought to be able to remain relatively free of debt. On the other hand, the couple who have a child very early in marriage may be unable to accumulate these assets in a sufficiently short time unless the wife works after all the children are born or between them. When asked why they are working, wives respond primarily in terms of the economic welfare of their family. I know of no study in which responses were coded in terms of specific plans for use of wife's income. We do not know the extent to which women are working to save for a house.

If, in fact, saving for a down payment on a house is an important reason for wives working, young wives in families who are renters ought to have, *ceteris paribus*, a higher rate of employment than wives in home-owning families. In addition, we might expect that longer first birth intervals would be related to homeownership. When tenure is included in a multiple classification analysis along with the basic variables, its effect on the employment of mothers is very small. The net deviation for home owners is

TABLE 4-6

Effects of Length of First Birth Interval on the Probability of Employment of Mothers, by Color: United States, 1960

First birth interval (in quarters)	Nonblack			Black		
	N	Gross deviation	Net[a] deviation	N	Gross deviation	Net[a] deviation
Less than 3	4831	−.043	−.003	453	−.041	.012
3–4	3309	−.038	−.017	118	−.031	−.018
5–9	1580	−.017	−.004	60	.163	.141
10–14	943	−.044	−.029	31	—[c]	—[c]
15–19	607	.007	.004	23	—[c]	—[c]
20 or more	1468	.009	−.003	66	.027	.147
Not ascertained[b]	7675	.050	.014	781	.013	−.017
Grand mean	.25			.34		

[a]Other variables included in this multivariate analysis are age of youngest own child, number of children under 18, age, education, and income adequacy.

[b]Women whose number of children ever born is not equal to the number of own children under 18, or who have been married more than once, or whose husbands have been married more than once.

[c]Less than 50 cases.

+.004 and for renters and others is −.009. These questions could be answered more fully with the data on the 1/1000 sample census tape. Unfortunately, I had not thought of them until after I had made my tabulations.

To summarize, the explanation proposed here for the lack of an effect of length of first birth interval on employment later in marriage is that a short first birth interval without an opportunity for the wife to work puts the family at an economic disadvantage in comparison to couples who have had a longer birth interval and more of an opportunity for the wife to work, given the level of the husband's income. This then raises the probability of work by wives with short first birth intervals. A long first birth interval, on the other hand, has a positive effect on employment for reasons of persistence operating mainly through the desire to maintain an accustomed standard of living. These two sorts of influences counteract one another. This discussion has by no means been conclusive. It does, however, begin to indicate the complexity of the interrelationships among family history variables, including fertility, family economic position, and work by wives.

Marital Stability

Another family history variable which has been found by Cain to be of some significance in influencing the employment of wives is whether or not the woman was married more than once (Cain, 1966: 105ff). Data from our

TABLE 4-7

Effects of Marital Stability on the Probability of Employment of Mothers, by Color: United States, 1960

	Nonblack			Black		
Marital stability category	*N*	Gross deviation	Net[a] deviation	*N*	Gross deviation	Net[a] deviation
Both spouses married only once	17,208	−.01	−.01	1,175	−.01	−.00
Wife married once, husband more than once	1,115	.04	.04	158	−.03	−.04
Husband married once, wife more than once	1,184	.05	.04	102	.10	.05
Both spouses married more than once	915	.08	.06	110	.04	.01
Grand mean		.25			.34	

[a]Other variables included in this multivariate analysis are age of youngest own child, number of children under 18, age, education, and income adequacy.

1/1000 sample of women with children show that if either spouse has been married more than once the probability of the wife working is increased. These data are presented in Table 4-7. In the case of nonblack women, if only one spouse has been married more than once, regardless of which one, the probability of the wife being employed is raised by four percentage points. If both spouses have been married more than once, the probability is raised by six percentage points. The pattern for blacks is different. It appears that the effect of marital instability is positive if the wife has been married more than once and negative if the husband has been married more than once. If both spouses have been married more than once, the husband and the wife effects cancel each other. The number of cases on which these rates are based are fairly small—102, 110, and 158—so the differences observed may well be due to sampling fluctuation.

Cain has suggested that marital instability has its effect as a result of the wife feeling that the present marriage is also likely to be temporary (Cain, 1966: 82–83). The woman is working for security. There is also likely to be simple persistence operating. The woman was likely to have been working in the interval between marriages. The Current Population Survey supplement which asked about reasons for starting and stopping work indicates that most young women who stop working do so because of pregnancy (Rosenfeld and Perrella, 1965). Unless a pregnancy has intervened, the remarried woman is likely to be still working.

Proportion Working Full Time

The results of a multiple classification analysis of the probability of working full time in relation to the five basic variables are shown in Table 4-8. The analysis is confined to mothers who worked during the census week. In this analysis the sample has not been subdivided into two color groups, since there were too few working black mothers in the sample. I shall briefly describe the effects of each of the five variables.

Income Adequacy

Income adequacy has a fairly strong negative effect on the probability of working full time. The net deviations range from +.05, in the income adequacy range of .4 to .7 to −.17 for income adequacy of 2.9 or more. The grand mean is .66. There is a considerable jump in the proportion working part time between an income adequacy level of 2.0–2.8 and 2.9 and above. This suggests that, if my reasoning about the difficulty of finding part-time jobs is correct, these women who are under minimal economic pressure may be able and willing to wait to enter the labor force until a part-time job is available. On the other hand, women who are living under extreme economic pressure (.4 or below) are no more likely to work full time than women in the next two higher income adequacy categories, although the probability of working does decline with increasing income adequacy within this range. Why this should be the case is not clear.

Education

Education appears to have a slight, but irregular, positive influence on full-time employment. For some reason, women who have gone to college, but for less than 4 years, are the least likely to be working full time among all education categories. Again the effect of both income adequacy and education are augmented by the inclusion of the other variables.

Age

Age has only a very small zero-order relationship with working full time, except that the 14–19-year-old mothers are seven percentage points less likely to be working full time than the average. When the child status and socioeconomic variables are taken into account, age has a fairly

TABLE 4-8

Multiple Classification Analysis of the Probability of Working Full Time in Relation to Age of Youngest Own Child, Number of Own Children Under 18, Age, Education, and Income Adequacy, for Employed Mothers Aged 14–59: United States, 1960

	N	Gross deviation	Net deviation
Age of Youngest Child			
0	350	–.066	–.109
1	476	–.040	–.082
2	382	–.041	–.073
3	332	–.028	–.040
4	296	.009	–.003
5	286	.001	–.003
6	270	–.019	–.012
7	310	.038	.030
8	279	–.022	–.010
9	294	.003	.018
10–11	623	–.015	.004
12–13	743	.047	.068
14–15	568	.048	.066
16–17	472	.072	.085
Income Adequacy			
Less than .4	344	–.001	.032
.4–.7	758	.025	.052
.8–1.1	1403	.026	.038
1.2–1.5	1541	.001	–.004
1.6–1.9	840	–.005	–.027
2.0–2.8	578	–.034	–.065
2.9 and above	217	–.152	–.171
Education			
Less than 9 years	1110	–.008	–.022
9–11 years	1323	.001	–.011
12 years	2224	.016	.018
13–15 years	592	–.045	–.026
16 or more years	432	–.004	.036
Age			
14–19	56	–.074	–.020
20–24	459	.020	.062
25–29	679	.005	.050
30–34	1000	–.021	.000
35–39	1301	.007	.012
40–44	1060	.018	–.007
45–49	716	–.009	–.050
50–54	317	–.023	–.085
55–59	93	–.018	–.080
Number of Children			
1	2301	.048	.042
2	1871	–.021	–.021
3	866	–.044	–.039
4	388	–.048	–.036
5	149	–.033	–.017
6 or more	106	–.107	–.084
Grand mean		.66	

strong negative effect on full-time employment at ages 20–24 and above. Given that the woman is working, the probability of working full time declines as age increases.

Age of Youngest Own Child

We have already looked at the pattern of gross deviations for the child status variables. The effect of age of youngest child is increased by the inclusion of the other variables. The general pattern is that the probability of working full time increases from 11% below the grand mean of 66% to a 0% deviation between age of youngest child of 0 and 4. Between ages 4 and 10 to 11, the net effects remain very close to zero. Then, at age 12–13, the effect jumps to seven percentage points above the grand mean, where it remains through ages 16–17.

Again, these results indicate that there is no great change in the distribution of working mothers by part- or full-time status at the time the youngest child reaches school age. It does appear that when the youngest child reaches junior high school age, the probability of working full time increases considerably. It also increases quite sharply during the early preschool ages.

Number of Children under 18

The pattern of net deviations is almost identical to that of the gross deviations. The proportion of one-child working mothers employed full time is six percentage points greater than that of two-child mothers. There is, then, very little change through five children. Working mothers with six or more children are considerably less likely to be working full time than those with fewer children.

White–Nonwhite Differentials in Employment

We showed in Chapter 2 that nonwhite mothers had considerably higher rates of employment than white mothers. The differential was particularly large in the case of mothers of preschool-age children. Our multivariate analyses of employment of black and white mothers have demonstrated that the effects of education and family economic pressure on employment are quite different for the two racial groups.

What can be said by way of a single summary statement about the differential between the employment levels of black and white wives? To what extent are black-white differentials in employment attributable to differences in composition with respect to education, family economic need, family status, and other factors?

TABLE 4-9

Nonwhite Rates of Employment Standardized on the Education by Family Income Minus Wife's Earnings Composition of the White Population, by Child Status: for Mothers in the Unites States, 1960[a]

Age of youngest child	White rate of employment	Nonwhite rate of employment		Differential	
	Crude	Crude	Standardized	Crude	Standardized
Under 6	16.7	27.9	28.6	11.2	11.9
6–17	36.4	46.5	48.2	10.1	11.8
Under 18[b]	25.5	34.4	37.4	8.9	11.9

[a]Derived from United States Bureau of the Census (1963). *Families*. PC(2) 4A, Table 42.
[b]Here the standardization is not only over income and education, but also over child status in two categories–youngest child under 6, and 6–17.

Bowen and Finegan (1969: 87ff) report that the black–white differential in labor force participation narrows from 12.3 to 6.8 percentage points when race is included in an additive regression model along with education, age, other family income, presence of children, and employment status of husband. Thus, about 45% of the differential is attributable to composition with respect to these characteristics.

Alternatively, one could compare the actual nonwhite employment rate with that which we would obtain if the education by husband's income by family status specific nonwhite rates were applied to the white population distribution. These results are shown in Table 4-9. Among mothers of children under age 6, the standardized rate is .7 points higher than the crude rate, suggesting a population composition with respect to education and husband's income that is, on balance, relatively unfavorable to employment. Similarly for mothers with youngest child age six to seventeen, the standardized rate is 1.7 points greater than the crude rate. When we standardize over education, husband's income, and age of youngest child, the standardized rate is fully three points greater than the crude rate. We conclude that, contrary to Bowen and Finegan, the black–white differential is not in any sense attributable to compositional differences. Quite the contrary, the nonwhite composition is *un*favorable to high levels of employment. If population composition were identical for the two races, the race differential would be 12 points, rather than only 9 points.

Our comparison is different from theirs in three respects. We include only mothers; they include women with no children. We have controlled fewer variables. The major difference is that Bowen and Finegan have adjusted for the confounding variables in an additive regression framework in which the average rate structure (dominated by the white) is the basis for control whereas we have applied the category-specific black rate pattern to the white composition. When race interacts with education, husband's income and family status (as we have shown it does), the standardization procedure used here is a better adjustment for purely compositional differences. We are answering the question, "If the black and white populations had identical compositions with respect to other factors associated with employment, and all that differed was the category-specific rate functions, what would be the differential in employment?"

Their procedure answers a question with one additional if—if the employment of black and white women responded in identical ways to differentials in education and family economic need. This is clearly an assumption that is not empirically tenable and seriously distorts the conclusions.

Family Status, Education, Economic Need, and Labor Force Activity: Some Interactions

In the analysis reported in Chapter 4, education, income adequacy, and the family status variables were assumed to be additive in their effects on employment. In this chapter we will examine a number of "interactions" that seem to be of particular substantive significance. We will look first at the interactions between the family status variables and the economic variables—education and income adequacy. Our substantive concern here is whether the family life cycle pattern of employment differs depending on the level of family economic need and/or the level of education. We will then turn to an analysis of the employment patterns of married women with no own children under 18. In this analysis we divide the sample by age in an attempt to separate out recently married women prior to childbearing, women whose children have left home, and those who have been and are likely to continue to be childless. How do the economic variables and family history variables differentially affect the employment of women in these three additional life cycle categories?

Our attention then turns to the interaction between education and family economic need. We raise the question, how does the responsiveness of employment to family economic need vary, depending on the education (i.e., the employability and earning capacity) of a married woman?

The Employment of Mothers

Does the effect of family income adequacy on the employment of wives vary depending on their family status? The alternative would be that income adequacy has the same effect on employment at all family status positions—i.e., that the two variables are additive in their effects on employment status. Our expectation is that the effects of family economic pressure will be greater, the older the youngest child, or at least that the employment of women with very young children will not be very responsive to differences in income. Women with very young children and low levels of income adequacy will be constrained from working in response to economic pressure for several reasons.

1. Young children are highly dependent on their mothers or other adults for a variety of needs. Mothers, presumably, feel some compulsion to remain with their own children and provide the necessary care.
2. This psychological compulsion to care for one's own young children is supported by, if not created by, the widespread belief in American society that the mother's place is in the home, especially if she has an infant or older preschool-age children.
3. For a mother of preschool-age children to work, it will in many, if not most, cases be necessary for the mother to spend some portion of her earnings on child care services. Thus the net gain derived from working will be lower, *ceteris paribus*, for the mother of young children than for mothers with older children.
4. Finally, in order to work, a mother of young children must make arrangements for child care. There is some evidence that the sheer inability to arrange child care is presently keeping a substantial segment of the very poor from responding to their economic pressure.

Similar reasoning would apply with respect to the effect of education on employment. We regard the effect of education on the employment of wives largely as a reflection of its association with earning potential and employability. Thus a woman with a high school education would be more likely to be successful in finding an acceptable job at an acceptable rate of remuneration than a woman with less education. In addition, education is probably positively correlated with a work or career orientation. We would expect that the effect of education on employment would be positive at all child statuses, but that, for the same reasons just enumerated, the effect should be smaller for mothers of young children than for mothers of older children. More generally, we expect that any characteristic of wives which either puts pressure on them to work or facilitates work would have a larger effect on

TABLE 5-1

Multiple Classification Analysis of Employment in Relation to Income Adequacy, Education, and Other Variables,[a] *for Four Child-Status Categories of Mothers*

	Age of youngest own child											
	0–2			3–5			6–11			12–17		
		Deviations			Deviations			Deviations			Deviations	
	N	Gross	Net	*N*	Gross	Net	*N*	Gross	Net	*N*	Gross	Net
Income adequacy												
.3 or less	499	.042	.068	184	.104	.125	246	.039	.089	219	.025	.090
.4–.7	1244	.048	.064	462	.057	.080	554	.086	.120	349	.027	.089
.8–1.1	2098	.020	.028	923	.040	.057	1110	.061	.085	766	.064	.077
1.2–1.5	2152	−.001	−.004	1081	.022	.020	1402	.025	.028	982	.047	.054
1.6–1.9	1223	−.032	−.045	692	−.040	−.053	873	−.040	−.054	727	.013	.000
2.0–2.8	818	−.064	−.089	503	−.085	−.109	735	−.076	−.106	672	−.050	−.076
2.9 and over	321	−.084	−.120	262	−.131	−.162	452	−.156	−.215	418	−.207	−.267
Education												
Less than 5 years	171	−.028	−.065	84	−.044	−.088	140	−.109	−.161	141	−.197	−.256
5–6 years	242	−.012	−.052	120	.019	−.032	210	.003	−.055	195	−.113	−.161
7 years	257	.007	−.030	123	.038	−.003	230	−.052	−.100	200	−.021	−.062
8 years	669	.008	−.014	351	−.003	−.033	592	−.043	−.077	625	−.028	−.056
9–10 years	1390	−.018	−.029	723	−.016	−.038	935	−.003	−.033	723	−.019	−.040
11 years	625	−.007	−.020	294	.019	−.005	342	.009	−.009	286	−.008	−.040
12 years	3558	.001	.008	1721	.001	.008	2041	.005	.014	1359	.038	.050
13–15 years	878	−.002	.019	445	.007	.052	554	.003	.058	386	.035	.139
16 years	472	.039	.074	209	−.002	.060	253	.060	.168	161	.078	.179
17 years and over	93	.102	.143	37	.021	.105	75	.349	.436	57	.183	.096
Grand mean		.145			.223			.331			.431	
R^2		.051			.042			.072			.064	

[a]In each regression age, race, and number of children under 18 are also included. They are also expressed as dummy variables.

TABLE 5-2

Regression[a] of Employment on Income Adequacy within Four Child-Status Categories

Age of youngest child	N	b	$\overline{X}$	$\overline{Y}$
0–2	8355	–.064	1.36	.145
3–5	4107	–.085	1.52	.223
6–11	5372	–.102	1.60	.331
12–17	4133	–.105	1.69	.431

[a]Computed on net deviations from grand mean from multiple classification analysis. For explanation, see text.

the employment of mothers with school-age children than on that of mothers with younger children.

Table 5-1 presents the results of multiple classification analyses of employment in relation to several variables previously shown to be related to employment, performed within four, age-of-youngest-child categories (0–2, 3–5, 6–11, and 12–17).

An examination of the pattern of net effects in Table 5-1 reveals that there is a clear tendency for the slope of employment on income adequacy to increase as the age of youngest child increases. The pattern in each case is approximately linear. In order to provide simple summary measures of this pattern among age of youngest child groups, regression coefficients are shown in Table 5-2. These regression coefficients have been computed on the net deviations shown in Table 5-1, weighting each point by the number of

TABLE 5-3

Regression[a] of Employment on Education within Four Child-Status Categories

Age of youngest child	N	b	$\overline{X}$	$\overline{Y}$
0–2	8355	.010	11.2	.145
3–5	4107	.012	11.1	.223
6–11	5372	.025	10.8	.331
12–17	4133	.030	10.5	.431

[a]Computed on net deviations from grand mean from multiple classification analysis. For explanation, see text. Education is coded in years of schooling completed.

observations in the category. These would be approximately the same coefficients that would have been obtained if income adequacy had been entered in the equation as a single variable.

Thus the probability of employment of women with no preschool-age children increases by a greater amount per unit increase in income adequacy than does that of mothers of younger children. There is a substantial difference in the slopes of the two categories of mothers of preschool-age children: the younger the youngest child, the less the slope. Comparing the two-school-age child categories, there is virtually no difference in slopes.

Table 5-3 shows the net effects of education on employment. The pattern is not nearly as neat as it was in the case of income adequacy. The relationships again appear to be roughly linear, particularly if we discount the first three points at the low end of the education scale and the last point at the upper end because they represent a rather small proportion of the total sample. Again, our general hypothesis is supported. The younger the youngest child, the less the response of employment to education. The regression coefficients for the two categories of mothers of preschool-age children are very similar. For each additional year of education, the probability of employment rises by about one percentage point. For the mothers of children aged 6–11 and 12–17, the probabilities increase by 2.5 and 3.0 percentage points per year of education, respectively.

Life Cycle Employment Patterns

There is here, as with any statistical interaction, an alternative way of looking at these data. We can ask the question, "What are the life cycle patterns of employment of the various socioeconomic categories of wives?" We will look first at the pattern among education categories, then among income adequacy categories.

To use Schnore's terminology, educational attainment can be thought of as an achieved, changeable, but irreversible status (Schnore, 1961: 407–423). For a woman, it is normally fixed by the time the first child is born. Thus we can conceive of our division of the population of mothers by educational attainment as four populations, the memberships of which remain fixed through time (subject, of course, to exit from the population by death, marital dissolution, or through change in status from "mother" to "non-mother" when the last child reaches 18 or leaves home before that age). Looked at in this way, we can think about the pattern of employment within educational categories among age of youngest child categories as approximating the pattern of employment through the "family life cycle." These are synthetic and not real cohorts. Employment levels and age patterns are changing year by year. In addition, women do not pass through the age of youngest child classification year by year, but rather return to the zero category each time they have an additional baby. However, as we have argued earlier, these limitations are not so great as to preclude useful comparisons within the age range 5–14 or so, since "secular" change is occurring at a slow, regular pace, and since, beyond age of youngest child of 4 or so, relatively few women have an additional child and revert back to the age of youngest child category zero.

The sample was divided into four parts, based on educational level: less than 9 years, 9–11 years, 12 years, and 13 and more years. Multiple classification analyses were performed within each educational level. The variables included in these analyses, in addition to the age of the youngest child, are income adequacy, color, age, and number of children. We expect that the greater the educational level, the greater the relationship between age of youngest child and employment. As the youngest child ages and child status constraints on employment are weakened, the better-educated woman is in a better position to enter the labor market, and the net return she can expect to receive is greater. More important than these slopes, however, is the comparison of employment patterns by age of the youngest child among education categories. In particular, are there any categories of women whose employment rates show a discontinuity at about the ages at which the youngest child first enters school? Even with the large sample that we are working with here, it is difficult to reach very firm conclusions of this sort since the numbers of cases within the child status-education categories are often small.

As a simple summary device, regression coefficients were computed, as they were earlier, on the pattern of net deviations and also on the gross deviations from the grand mean (see Table 5-4 and Fig. 5-1). The pattern

TABLE 5-4

Regression Analysis of Employment on Age of Youngest Own Child, within Four Education Levels

	Education level			
	0–8	9–11	12	13+
Regression coefficients computed on gross deviations from grand mean				
Entire age range	.016	.022	.025	.025
Regression coefficients computed on net deviations from grand mean				
Entire age range	.021	.026	.028	.026
Age range 0–5	.028	.035	.036	.037
Age range 6–11	.019	.030	.038	.024
Age range 12–17	.016	−.001	.014	−.008

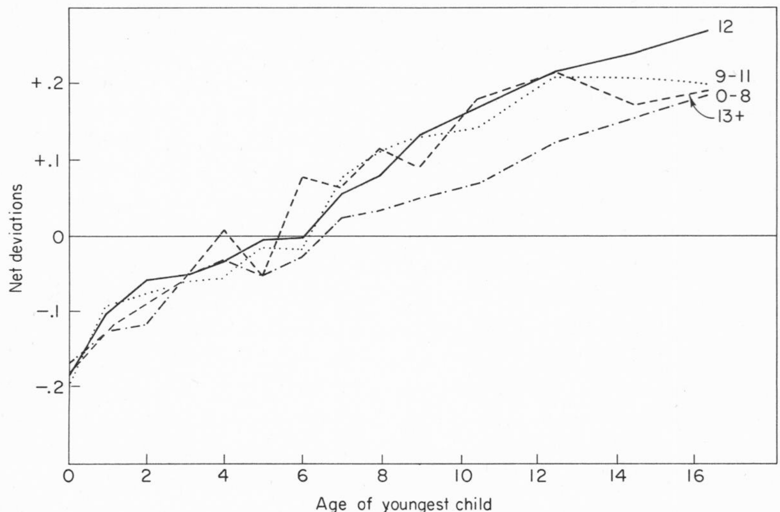

Figure 5-1. *Net effects of age of youngest own child on employment, within four education categories. (Net of the effects of color, income adequacy, and number of children.)*

of gross deviations is a more accurate description of what happens to the employment rates of these synthetic cohorts as they pass through the life cycle. Clearly other variables are also changing with age of the youngest child. In particular, the woman is aging, her husband's income and family income adequacy are increasing, and the number of children is changing. The pattern of net deviations indicates the change in employment uniquely associated with increasing age of youngest child, independently of the other correlated variables.

The slopes of employment on age of youngest child for each of the four education categories are presented in Table 5-4. In each educational category the slope on the net deviations is greater than that computed on the gross deviations. That is to say, the other variables correlated with age of youngest child (particularly increases in husband's income) tend to reduce age of youngest child specific employment rates. The expected pattern of increasing slopes with increasing education is found between the first three education categories, but the slope for college-educated women is smaller than that for high school graduates.

A closer examination of the age of youngest child patterns plotted in Fig. 5-1 reveals:

1. The increment in employment between age of youngest child 0 and age of youngest child 1 is greater, the greater the level of education. The employ-

ment rate of college-educated women with a child aged 1 is 11.4 points higher than that for women with child aged 0. The comparable figures for the other education groups are: 12, 9.0; 9–11, 5.6; and 0–8, 4.5. The increments between ages 1 and 5 or 6 are very similar from one education group to another. Overall, the employment of the better-educated women increases more in the preschool ages than does that of the less well educated. These data suggest that the college-educated women, and to a lesser degree the women who are high school graduates, probably return to work earlier after the birth of a child. They are, at least, considerably more likely to be at work when the child is in the age interval 1 to 2. This might possibly reflect differentials in birth-spacing patterns. That is, the women with lower levels of education may be more likely to be pregnant by the time their youngest child is in his second year, and thus are less likely to want to continue working if they have resumed working, or to return to the labor force if they have not. However, a recent Current Population Survey report showed rather small differences in birth spacing by education for second-, third-, and fourth-order births occurring between 1955 and 1959 (see Table 5-5). For example, 46% of second-order births to women with no high school occurred within 24 months of the first birth, while for women with a high school or college education the figure is 43%. For third births, the proportions occurring within 2 years of second births are 39% for women with no high school, 36% for women with a high school education, and 31% for those with a college education.

TABLE 5-5

Intervals between Births of Children of Second- to Fourth-Order to White Women during 1960 to 1964, by Education of Mother (Cumulative Percentage)[a]

Birth interval since preceding birth (months)	Second			Third			Fourth		
	No high school	High school	College	No high school	High school	College	No high school	High school	College
12	5.9	5.0	3.0	3.5	4.0	3.9	4.1	3.0	3.8
24	48.4	44.4	43.1	38.7	35.7	31.3	38.7	34.2	37.2
36	69.9	69.1	73.2	58.3	55.2	57.2	60.9	57.4	54.9
48	80.4	83.7	86.4	70.3	69.7	70.4	70.5	71.3	72.2
60	88.1	89.1	90.9	77.9	78.9	81.0	79.4	82.5	80.9
120	97.7	97.6	97.7	94.3	96.1	95.0	96.6	98.2	97.6
121 and over	100.0	100.0	100.0	100.0	100.0	100.0	100.0	100.0	100.0
Median interval	24.4	26.2	26.3	30.5	32.3	32.2	29.6	31.7	32.2

[a]From U.S. Bureau of the Census, *Current Population Reports, Population Characteristics* (Series P-20), No. 186, *Marriage, fertility and childspacing, June, 1965,* 1969, Table 24.

An alternative explanation would be that well-educated women have longer marriage to first birth intervals, and are more likely to have worked both during that interval as well as prior to marriage. Women with recent work experience may be more employable in some objective sense, have greater contacts with the labor market and knowledge of opportunities, and a greater subjective employability—i.e., they realize that employment is an available option. The persisting effect of past employment experience on current employment is also undoubtedly influenced by the fact that consumption standards are adapted to two incomes, rather than only one.

In addition, the poorly educated woman has greater difficulty finding a job when she wants one, and may still be searching long after the better-educated woman has found suitable employment.

2. In no education group is there clear evidence of a jump in the rate of employment when the youngest child reaches school age. The curves wobble randomly too much to make a firm statement in this regard, however. Over the age range from 2 or so to 8 or so, the patterns are on the whole quite linear for each education group.

3. An anomaly that can be observed in these data is that for the lowest education category and for the high school graduates there is a continuous increase in the employment rates through the high school ages. For the mothers in the 9–11 and 13 and over education categories, rate of employment does not continue to increase, but rather declines. Until further evidence is available, I would tend to regard this difference as random variation.

Income adequacy cannot be conceived of as a fixed status like education or color. Hence, it is not as useful to examine the implicit life cycle pattern of employment within education categories. Incomes change through time. For a substantial segment of the population, there are wide year-to-year fluctuations of income. This is particularly true of the men who, on average, have a relatively low earning capacity and are likely to experience unemployment. In addition, there is a career pattern of increasing income for most husbands. This career pattern would suggest that, on average, a father would be earning less, the younger his youngest child.

Income adequacy (IA) depends on both family income and family composition. A given family can move out of one IA category because its income changes from one year to the next, either temporarily or permanently, or because its family composition has changed. It seems likely that the family with all children in the 12–17 age range which is in the lowest IA category would be more likely to have spent more of its life in the lowest category than the family with a very young child. For these reasons, as well as for those cited earlier, the synthetic cohort interpretation of these results is suspect. However, since there is widespread concern with poverty and the behavior

TABLE 5-6

Composition of the Four Income Adequacy Categories

	Distribution of total sample	
Income adequacy range	*N*	Percentage
Less than .6	2,222	10.1
.6–1.1	7,885	35.9
1.2–1.9	7,678	35.0
2.0 and over	4,181	19.0
Total	21,966	100.0

Percentage distribution of family income minus wife's earnings within each income adequacy category

	Family income minus wife's earnings						
Income adequacy	Less than $2,000	$2,000–3,999	$4,000–5,999	$6,000–7,999	$8,000–9,999	$10,000–and over	Total
Less than .6	62.6	36.0	1.5	.0	.0	.0	100.0
.6–1.1	.2	36.0	52.3	10.1	1.2	.2	100.0
1.2–1.9	.0	.0	33.2	48.2	14.3	4.2	100.0
2.0 and over	.0	.0	.0	12.3	27.4	60.3	100.0

of the poor in comparison to the more affluent, I will present a synthetic cohort analysis of the employment rates of four income adequacy levels.

Since the income adequacy scale is arbitrary and unfamiliar, it is informative to indicate the percentage distribution of the entire sample among the four income adequacy levels, and the dollar income distributions among the IA categories (see Table 5-6). The lowest category represents the lowest income decile. Fully three-fifths of this category are in the family income minus wife's earnings category of less than $2000. These families would be included in the poverty population by most anyone's definition. At the other extreme, the income adequacy level of 2.0 and above includes the upper fifth of the income distribution. Three-fifths of this category have an income level of more than $10,000. The two intermediate IA categories have modal money incomes of $4000–5999 and $6000–7999, respectively. Table 5-7 indicates that the overall slopes of employment on age of youngest child are very similar for the first three income adequacy levels (.027 – .029), while the slope for the most affluent group is somewhat less (.021) (see also Fig. 5-2). Within the preschool ages the slopes of employment on age of youngest child are steeper, the lower the level of income adequacy (.043, .037, .039, and .019). The two extreme categories appear different from the intermediate catego-

TABLE 5-7

Regression Analysis of Employment on Age of Youngest Own Child, Within Four Income Adequacy Levels

Regression coefficients	Income adequacy .6	.6–1.1	1.2–1.9	2.0+
Computed on gross deviations from grand mean				
Entire age range	.020	.025	.025	.019
Computed on net deviations from grand mean				
Entire age range	.029	.027	.028	.021
Age range 0–5	.043	.037	.039	.019
Age range 6–11	.042	.034	.022	.034
Age range 12–17	.009	.006	.006	.006

ries, but the two intermediate categories are indistinguishable from one another.

A detailed examination of the age of youngest child pattern of employment of the lowest IA category shows that the employment rate increases very rapidly from age 0 to 3, followed by stability from 3 to 6, and a further rapid rise from 6 to 8. Beyond age 8, the employment rate increases only very slowly. The employment pattern of the women in the next higher income adequacy category shows a similar pattern, but with less sharp discontinu-

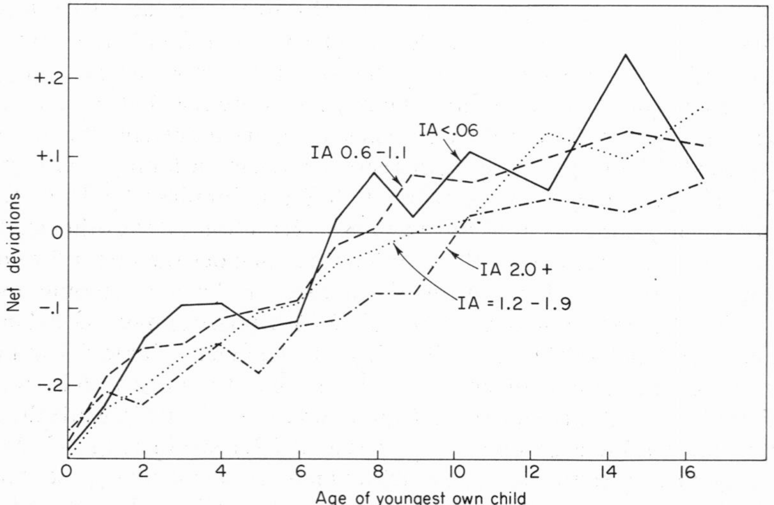

Figure 5-2. *Net effects of age of youngest own child on employment, within four income adequacy categories. (Net of the effects of education, color, age, and number of children.)*

ities. After a slow steady increase in employment year by year between ages 1 and 6, there is a more rapid, steady increase to age 9. After the age of 9, the increase in employment is considerably slower. The upper two income adequacy categories exhibit a slower, smoother progression of employment rates through the preschool and early school ages. In no case does there appear to be much of an increase in the rates of employment after the age of 12.

The Employment of Wives with No Children under the Age of 18

The women who have no children under the age of 18 are a very heterogeneous group, including recently married women who have not yet had any children but will in the future, women who have not yet had children and will not, and women whose children have grown up and left home. To attempt to take account of this heterogeneity, the sample of wives with no children has been divided into three groups by age: (1) women aged 14–29, who are primarily recently married women who will have children in the future; (2) women aged 30–44, who are to a large extent women who have been and will remain childless, although it also includes some women who have recently married and women whose children have all left home; and (3) women aged 45–59, who are primarily women whose children have grown up and left home.

From the point of view of the concern here with family composition and family formation in relation to labor force activity, this division of the nonmothers is quite germane. These three groups of nonmothers are three additional family status groups in our cross section of the total population of wives. In addition, this classification, particularly when considered in relation to duration of marriage and children ever born, permits us to examine further the dynamics of work experience through the family life cycle.

Results of the multiple classification analyses of the employment of these nonmothers are presented in Table 5-8. In each case, color, education, and income adequacy are included as explanatory variables. For the two younger groups of women, those under the age of 45, the duration of marriage is included. I will compare the pattern by color, education, and income adequacy among the three age groups and then look at the effects of duration of marriage and children ever born. The proportion of women 14–29 who are employed is .549; that for women 30–44 is .538; and for the oldest group, .360.

Education

Again the dummy variable analysis indicates that education is related to employment in a roughly linear manner, and again, for economy of presen-

TABLE 5-8

Multiple Classification Analysis of the Probability of Being Employed in Relation to Color, Education, Income Adequacy, Marriage Duration, and Children Ever Born, for Husband-Present Women Aged 14–59 with No Own Children Under the Age of 18: United States, 1960

	Age 14–29			Age 30–44			Age 45–59		
Color	*N*	Gross	Net	*N*	Gross	Net	*N*	Gross	Net
Black	149	−.140	−.068	334	.237	.293	491	.045	.035
Nonblack	1598	.013	.006	1987	−.040	−.049	5996	−.004	−.003
Education									
less than 5	23	—[a]	—	87	−.262	−.354	339	−.112	−.163
5–6	32	—	—	112	.007	−.079	474	−.069	−.101
7	32	—	—	135	−.115	−.158	484	−.075	−.098
8	76	−.207	−.212	310	−.070	−.101	1419	−.051	−.065
9–10	257	−.137	−.137	422	−.019	−.026	1111	.006	.007
11	144	−.133	−.125	153	−.048	−.057	336	.075	.087
12	797	.043	.035	809	.057	.088	1445	.043	.062
13–15	242	.120	.129	184	.087	.127	591	.046	.079
16	121	.186	.193	71	.054	.107	201	.152	.198
17+	23	—	—	38	.225	.269	87	.330	.339
Income adequacy									
.39 or less	131	−.175	−.118	143	.008	−.039	403	.074	.120
.40–0.79	275	−.055	−.011	189	.018	.011	679	024	.064
.80–1.19	315	.009	.030	262	.020	.027	793	.066	.093
1.20–1.59	373	.024	.021	484	.041	.052	1118	.025	.038
1.60–1.99	333	.045	.030	452	.007	.024	1076	.013	.018
2.00–2.89	244	.053	−.008	532	−.015	−.016	1426	−.022	−.041
2.90+	76	−.023	−.089	259	−.094	−.120	992	−.110	−.170

Year first married									
Before 1935	—	—	—	234	−.078	−.023			
1935–1944	—	—	—	1100	−.003	.008			
1945–1949	46	.037	.110	466	.001	−.019			
1950–1954	239	.028	.045	308	.050	.015			
1955	110	.023	.035	39	.078	.045			
1956	141	.046	.044	32	.056	.039			
1957	189	.032	.028	43	−.049	−.075			
1958	276	.008	−.001	44	.076	.074			
1959–1960	746	−.035	−.041	55	−.010	−.013			
Children ever born									
0							1784	.049	.031
1							1490	.007	.006
2							1566	.004	.014
3							787	−.018	−.009
4							387	−.076	−.070
5							221	−.170	−.097
6+							252	−.134	−.116
Grand mean		.549			.538			.360	
N		1747			2321			6487	

[a]—: less than 50 cases.

tation, I will summarize the relationship with a single regression coefficient. When education is coded in single years of schooling, the slope of employment on education is .048 for wives 14–29; .024 for wives 30–44; and .021 for wives 43–59. These slopes compare to slopes of .10, .12, .25, and .30 for the four groups of women with children. The employment of the youngest group of childless women is much more responsive to variation in education than is that for any of the other six family status categories, while that of the other groups of childless women is about as responsive as the employment of the women with children over age 6.

Why should the employment of young women with no children be more responsive to differences in education than that of any other category of women? I might suggest several reasons.

Young women with education have a set of credentials which provides them with access to jobs. Young women with less education do not have these credentials. In the case of older women, both education and experience provide access. Perhaps "maturity" is also helpful in obtaining employment in the case of older women. Thus the young woman with little education and no work experience is severely discriminated against in the job market. We are hypothesizing that the greater slope for younger women results from the excessive depression of the employment rate of poorly educated wives, rather than the unusually high employability of young well-educated women in comparison to older well-educated women. One might want to argue that the young well-educated woman may be favored over the older well-educated woman because of her greater sexual attractiveness. A younger woman would be favored in the competition for jobs such as airline stewardesses, Playboy Club bunnies, and perhaps certain office positions.

In addition, at the younger ages there is a large disparity between actual husband's income for those husbands who are in "careers"—the husbands of women with much education. Thus, in order to consume at a level appropriate to the long-run social position and income, young, well-educated wives work, while young, less well-educated wives are less likely to work.

While we do not pretend to fully understand these differentials, it is clear that a full understanding would involve several kinds of considerations in addition to those already considered.

1. Women in the three different universes are selected in different ways with respect to past and probable future fertility.

2. Women at different education levels within each universe have had varying marital histories—age at marriage, first birth interval, and fertility experiences. Thus their opportunities for obtaining employment experiences earlier in their lives vary.

Income Adequacy

Income adequacy and family income minus wife's earning are very closely correlated for childless couples because most childless couples comprise two-person families; thus the denominator of the income adequacy measure is the same for most such couples. For the two younger categories of women with no children, the effect of income adequacy on employment takes the form of an inverted U. I can think of no compelling explanation for this pattern. The effect for the 45–59 group is fairly strong in the expected negative direction.

Children Ever Born

For women 45–59 with no children currently at home, having had no children increases the probability of employment by three percentage points above the grand mean. Having had one, two, or three children makes very little difference—the employment rates of each of these three categories are within a percentage point of the grand mean. The differences between four, five, and six or more children ever born are greater.

The inference I draw from this is that the effect of earlier work experience persists through time. Women who have had their opportunity to work interrupted for long periods or for several periods for raising children are less likely to work for two reasons: (1) simple persistence operating through habit and a family standard of living adapted to one income, and (2) the lower level of employability and suspected employability associated with less employment experience.

These data indicate that the differential in employment between zero and three-child wives is only four percentage points. After three children, the rate of current employment is quite depressed. Evidently the impediment to working which childbearing and rearing imposes comes only after four children.

Marriage Duration

The most common way of leaving the universe of 14–29-year-old women who are married and have no children is by having a child. The longer it has been since marriage without the birth of the first child, the less likely it is that there will be a first birth. Data for the marriage cohorts of 1935–1939 show that 78% of all women who eventually went on to have babies had had their first birth by 48 months after marriage. For more recent cohorts, the experience is incomplete. Seventy-nine percent of all women in the 1950–1954 marriage cohort had had a first birth within 48 months after marriage. Based on previous cohort experience, perhaps half of the remaining 21% will go on to eventually have a child, almost all of them by 84 months after marriage. The childless women who have been married for longer than 5 or 6 years are fairly unlikely to go on to have a child. Those who have been married for 2, 3, or 4 years without a child are likely to be intentionally postponing the birth of a child, many in order to work. Thus, the group of childless women with longer marriage duration is selective of the subfecund and sterile, as well as of the women with a strong commitment to work, in lieu of having a child. Such women are, of course, included in the short duration of marriage women as well, but make up a considerably smaller proportion of them. The expectation that I have for this effect of the duration of marriage variable is that it will have a relatively small negative effect at the short durations of, say, less than 2 years, that it will rise in the 2-, 3-, and 4- year intervals, and then remain at about the same level for durations beyond.

Some women, realizing that they are subfecund, may begin to work at increasing marriage durations. There is no reason to think that women who are working in the first place and then realize that they are sterile or unlikely to have children would stop working. Other women who have been working and postponing their first birth for several years will leave the work force and have a child (thus leaving our universe). The major selective process that is operating is that the women who are not working at all (those who are not inclined to work and do little to postpone a first birth) remove themselves from the universe of nonmothers by becoming pregnant and bearing a child. This happens more or less gradually in the first 3 years of marriage.

The observed pattern for childless women aged 14–29 corresponds quite closely to these expectations. The net deviations rise to 4 years marriage duration (i.e., married 1959–1960 to 1956). After about 4 years marriage duration the net deviations are approximately constant at about four percentage points.

A confounding influence in these comparisons of marriage duration groups within the 14–29 age range is the fact that age is positively correlated with employment within this range. The proportions of these nonmothers who are employed, by age, are:

14–29	34.0%
20–24	59.1
25–29	62.5

The age effect could be due to duration of marriage. However, as we argued earlier, age is correlated with work experience and presumed employability.

Young women seem to be discriminated against in the labor market. Their unemployment rates are considerably higher than those of older women. The effect of age within the broader age groupings should be taken into account before the effect of duration of marriage can be assessed.

For women in the 30–34 age group, the pattern is much more irregular. The irregularity is probably due to the small number of cases in the short duration of marriage categories. There is, if anything, a decline in the probability of employment as duration of marriage decreases. This would be consistent with the idea that another dimension to economic pressure of a family, apart from the current income in relation to family composition, is the couple's debt and asset levels. Childless couples married for a long time, particularly when the wife has been working regularly, are able to accumulate assets and avoid debt. When this occurs, the need for the wife's income is less. Again the decline with duration of marriage may simply be due to the decline in the proportion employed as age increases, and the correlation of age and marriage duration.

TABLE 5-9

Percentage of Husband-Present Women Who Are Employed, by Education, Family Income Less Wife's Earnings, Presence of Children and Color: United States, 1960[a]

Wife's education and family income less wife's earnings	No children under 18		With one or more children under 6		With children under 18, none under 6	
	White	Nonwhite	White	Nonwhite	White	Nonwhite
No high school						
Under $2000	16.6	32.0	14.3	24.3	27.8	36.9
$2000–3999	20.6	40.2	15.7	26.3	31.8	43.4
$4000–5999	25.3	37.1	14.8	23.5	31.9	39.8
$6000–7999	22.2	36.0	12.1	23.0	28.1	37.8
$8000 or more	17.3	31.6	11.5	25.5	23.4	38.9
High school						
Under $2000	36.8	47.6	22.6	26.6	45.8	51.2
$2000–3999	41.2	51.2	21.9	27.8	45.5	51.4
$4000–5999	47.2	50.6	18.2	26.8	43.6	49.3
$6000–7999	42.0	50.7	13.1	26.5	37.7	49.1
$8000 or more	28.2	47.1	9.8	26.4	26.7	44.5
College						
Under $2000	54.6	64.7	33.3	49.1	60.7	72.2
$2000–3999	52.7	67.0	31.2	46.1	59.4	72.9
$4000–5999	58.0	69.5	26.4	46.9	58.9	68.3
$6000–7999	53.1	70.8	18.4	38.7	51.9	70.2
$8000 or more	32.8	54.9	10.7	31.0	29.4	53.8

[a]From U. S. Bureau of the Census (1964). *Families*, PC(2) 4A, Table 42.

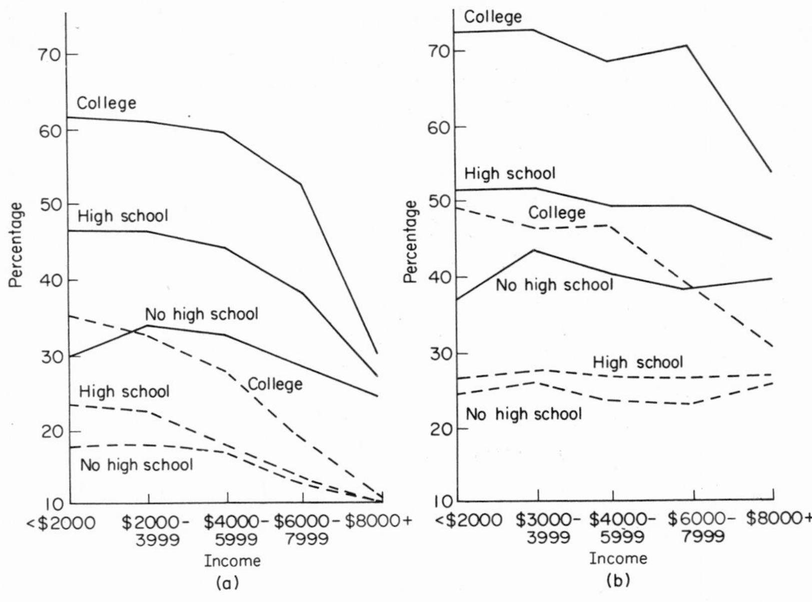

Figure 5-3. *Percentage of husband-present women with children under 18 who are employed, by education, family income minus wife's earnings, and age of youngest child: United States, 1960. (---) Women with children under 6; (—) women with children 6–17, but none under 6.*

Interaction of Education and Family Economic Pressure

In the analyses just reported, income adequacy and education are assumed to operate additively in their effect on employment. Is that a justifiable assumption? Do the departures from additivity shed any light on the process by which wives sort themselves into or out of the labor force?

Table 5-9 shows employment rates by family income minus wife's earnings, education, color, and child status. Figure 5-3 plots these relationships for the two categories of mothers. As we have already pointed out, women with no children under 18 are a very heterogeneous category, including young women who have not yet had children, women in the reproductive years who have no children and will have none, and women whose children have grown up and left home. In particular, childless women with low family income net of wife's earnings include couples who are retired, the wife of which is likely to be unable to work for physical reasons, in fairly high proportions. The age distribution of women with no children under 18 is quite different than that for women with children. In addition, the income needs are different at any given age for a couple with no children to support than for a family with children. If there were an age control, the subgroups would be more homogeneous. The necessary data have not been published. I will, therefore, confine my attention to women with children.

For both groups of women, the negative slopes are greater, the higher the level of education. Alternatively, we could say that the effect of education is substantially greater the lower the income of the husband. Among women with youngest child 6–17, there is a 30 point differential in employment between the extreme education levels at very low husband's income, and about a 6 point differential at husband's income $8000 and over. Among mothers of preschool-age children, these differentials are 19 and 1 percentage points respectively.

Using data from the 1/1000 sample, the interaction between income adequacy and employment within education categories can be seen. The greater the educational level, the greater the slope of employment on income adequacy. As a convenient summary we show below the slopes of employment on income adequacy for women with children.

Education level	b^a
9 years	−1.45
9–11 years	−4.35
12 years	−5.25
13–15 years	−7.52
16+ years	−10.12
Total	−6.60

[a] IA scores of 2.9 and over are given a value of 4.0.

This leads to the conclusion that the effect of education is to a great extent one of employability and earning potential. Women with low levels of education are less likely to be able to find jobs, and those who can find jobs often do not find it profitable or worthwhile to work because their earnings are so small. Thus, at low levels of education, the response of employment to family economic need is severely constrained by the inability to secure any job and/or the low earnings of available jobs.

This argument ignores the matter of tastes and accustomed consumption patterns determining the need for income. If women with high levels of education and their families have, *ceteris paribus*, more expensive tastes for consumption goods, they may be led to work in larger proportions in order to make up for a lower husband's income that is inadequate to permit a satisfactory consumption level. The less well-educated woman with a husband earning the same income may be "satisfied" with that income. The differences attributed to employability and earning potential would then be overstated. Part of the effect of education would reflect differences acceptable in standard of living. I would tend to think that this latter argument is less important than the former.

The observed pattern seems to be inconsistent with the idea that significant proportions of "upper middle class" wives work to find self-fulfillment and to escape the boredom of the home. If this were the case, we might expect a significantly larger proportion of college-educated wives of higher income husbands to be in the labor force, if the probability of having a job in which self-fulfillment is possible increases with education. One might expect that "self-fulfillment" and a reduced sense of boredom might be found in employment as a social worker, teacher, or perhaps in certain clerical and sales occupations. It does not, however, seem likely that significant proportions of women working on assembly lines, as waitresses, or in most other occupations available to women with less than a high school education are escaping the boredom of housework or finding fulfillment in their work.

Conclusion

In this chapter we have examined "interactions" among family status, family income adequacy, and education as they operate to affect the labor force activity of American wives. We argued earlier that these interactions are relevant both to the theory of the labor force participation of wives, and to policy questions related to the employment of women.

The importance of including family status, or stage in the family life cycle, as a variable in any model of the employment of wives is clear. Not only does this family variable exert an influence on employment, independent of the "economic" variables, education and income adequacy, but more importantly the stage in the family life cycle conditions and constrains the effects of the economic variables on employment.

We have also argued that the measured family status variables used in this analysis have both a contemporary and a historical component to their effect on employment status. The married woman who is 35 years of age and has never borne a child differs from the woman of the same age with three children in two important ways: She is free of child care responsibilities, and she has had a considerable period of time in which to gain labor force experience, and to establish herself in a secure, satisfactory job. Further research on the labor force activity of married women ought to attempt to sort out further some of these effects of history from characteristics of the current family status. In one attempt to do this, in an earlier chapter, I tried to measure the effect of early- or late-marriage, and of the length of the

TABLE 5-10

Percentage Distribution of Married Women under Age 60, with Nonfarm Residence, by Stage in the Family Life Cycle: United States, 1960

	N (thousands)	Distribution of all wives	Distribution of wives with no children under 6
With children under age 18			
Youngest aged			
0–2	8355	25.7	
3–5	4107	12.6	
6–11	5372	16.5	26.8
12–17	4133	12.7	20.6
With no child under age 18			
Wife aged			
14–29	1747	5.4	8.7
30–44	2321	7.1	11.6
45–59	6487	19.9	32.3
Total		100.0 (32,522)	100.0 (20,060)

first birth interval on current employment status after controlling for current family status, education, age, and income adequacy. In each case I was unable to isolate any appreciable effect.

About two-thirds of all married women under the age of 60 have own children under the age of 18 in the household. One-third do not (Table 5-10). As a rough index, somewhat more than 40% of the population of such women are in the three life cycle stages in which reproduction is concentrated (women with children under 6, and childless women under age 30). We know from other sources that about 8% of all married women under age 45 were pregnant at any given point in time during the period around 1965. (Unpublished data from the 1965 National Fertility Study.)

It has been common to divide the population of married women by "life cycle" for labor force analysis. Some analysts have divided the population into women with children under 18 and those without. Among those without children under 18, about one woman in six is under age 30 and thus likely to go on and have children. About three in five are over age 44, and thus generally persons whose children have grown up and left home. The remaining one-fifth are women aged 30–34, who are primarily women who have been married for some time and who have had no children. Some are old enough to have had their children grow up and leave home, and a few are only recently married.

For some purposes it has been the practice of researchers and data collection agencies to distinguish between married women who have preschool-age children and all other married women. While the first group is relatively homogeneous, the latter group consists of 47% with children, the youngest of whom is 6–17, and 53% with no children. They are divided as follows.

Youngest child 6–11	26.8%
Youngest child 12–17	20.6
No children, women aged 14–29	8.7
No children, women aged 30–44	11.6
No children, women aged 45–59	32.3
	100.0%

To the extent that the upper age limit is raised, we would find a larger fraction in that last category.

Clearly women in any residual group, such as those without children under age 6 comprise a very heterogeneous group of women with widely varying labor force propensities. Our analysis in this chapter suggests further that the various determinants of employment operate in quite different ways depending on life cycle stage. Thus, if the universe of married women is to be divided for purposes of analysis, it would seem wise to make the division into a set of explicitly defined life cycle stages, and to avoid the assumption that the only group of women with a unique set of labor force constraints is the group with preschool-age children.

6

The Earnings of Wives

While there have been numerous analyses of the labor force participation of married women, there have been few if any studies focussing on the earnings of married women, or the significance of their earnings as a component of family income. H. Miller (1966) refers at several points to the significance of changing patterns of employment of married women to the understanding of changes in the distribution of income. He does not, however, present even the most cursory description of the contributions of wives to family income. Miller's 1950 census monograph, *The Income of the American People* (1955), observed: "The working wife has become such a characteristic feature of the American economy that no discussion of family income would be complete without consideration of the factors that influence the labor force participation of married women [p. 86]." Almost nothing, however, is said about the income of employed women.

In their detailed study of income and welfare in the United States, Morgan *et al.* (1962) include a discussion of the determinants of family income, including the wife's contribution. The volume reports separate multivariate analyses of each of the various components of family income, but does not include any discussion of the relationships among the various components, or the relative size of the components under different family circumstances.

The amount of the wife's contribution to family income is an outcome of a process consisting of two conceptually distinguishable parts: (1) the process by which wives sort themselves into or out of the labor force, and (2) the process which determines the amount of money that working women earn. This latter process may be divided into two parts: the determinants of the amount of market work a woman supplies (hours per week and weeks per year, or hours per year) and the rate of pay that she receives per hour worked (Morgan *et al.*, 1962, Chap. 3). Thus, in order to understand the differential contributions of wives to family income among several categories of families (high income versus low income, white versus black, city versus suburban, etc.), it is necessary to examine differentials in rates of employment, differentials in the amount of time worked, and differentials in earnings per unit of time worked.

The differentials in employment of American wives are well-documented. In brief, the probability of employment is greater, the greater the level of family economic need, and the greater the employability and earning capacity as indexed by educational attainment (Cain, 1966: 91ff; Bowen and Finegan, 1969, Chap. 5). Black women, *ceteris paribus*, have higher rates of employment than white women (Bowen and Finegan, 1969, Chap. 5). Finally, the probability of employment is lower the greater a woman's familial responsibilities (indexed by age of youngest child and number of children in the family).

Some analysis of the determinants of hours worked has also been reported. In general, the same factors that increase the probability of employment (high family economic pressure, high education, and minimal familial responsibilities), also increase the conditional probability of working full time (Morgan *et al.*, 1962, Chap.11).

Morgan *et al.* (1962) report an analysis of the determinants of hourly earnings of working wives.[1] They find that higher hourly earnings are associated with high education, number of years employed, residence in large central cities, and the absence of any physical handicap. Older women earn more than younger women, and occupation exerts an effect on hourly earnings independent of education.

In this chapter I will examine two separate questions: (1) What is the magnitude of wife's contribution to family income, both absolutely and relatively? (2) What characteristics of women with work experience in 1959 influence the amount of their earnings? Here I shall report the results of a multivariate analysis of the earnings of wives in relation to many of the same characteristics with which I examined variation in employment in earlier chapters.

[1]Their hourly earnings measure is obtained by dividing an hours worked in 1959 figure (obtained from questions on "usual hours worked" and weeks worked) into total earnings. It is thus subject to a good deal of potential measurement error.

TABLE 6-1

Median Earnings in 1959 by Major Occupation Group, by Sex, and Whether or Not Worked Full Year[a]

	Median male earnings ($)		Median female earnings ($)	
Major occupation group	All	Full year	All	Full year
Total	4624	4897	2255	3118
Professional, technical and kindred	6622	7124	3625	4186
Farm and farm managers	2174	2458	825	916
Managers, officials and proprietors	6651	6926	3339	3800
Clerical workers	4787	5206	3014	3546
Sales workers	4983	5639	1502	2370
Craftsmen, foremen and kindred workers	5239	5699	2908	3555
Operatives	4302	4897	2320	2911
Private household workers	1058	2075	684	922
Service workers	3323	4012	1384	2102
Farm laborers	1070	1919	600	821
Laborers	2949	4018	1896	2863
Occupation not reported	4124	4940	2192	3086

[a]From U.S. Bureau of the Census (1963). *Occupational characteristics* PC(2) 7A, Table 29.

In Chapter 7 I will turn attention to black–white differences in the earnings of wives, and in their contribution to family income. Much of the analysis reported in this chapter, therefore, will refer to white women only.

The Earnings of American Wives—An Overview

Since more than a decade has elapsed since the 1960 census, and considerable increases, both real and inflationary, in incomes have occurred, we show for reference in Table 6-1 the median earnings of men and women for the major occupation groups, and in Table 6-2 the median female earnings for some of the detailed occupations that employ substantial numbers of women. The median earnings of professional men working full year in 1959 was about $7000, while for professional women it was slightly more than $4000. The comparable figures for operatives were $5000 and $3000. Female private household workers working 50–52 weeks in 1959 earned somewhat less than $1000, while other service workers earned slightly more than $2000. Overall, the cost of living has risen by about 20% between 1959 and 1968 (U.S. Department of Labor, Bureau of Labor Statistics, 1970).

Overall, 44% of wives made some contribution to family income in 1959

TABLE 6-2

Median Earnings of Female Workers, by Occupation and Whether Worked Full Year[a]

	All ($)	Full year ($)
Teachers		
Elementary	4024	4559
Secondary	4408	4931
Librarians	3673	4146
Nurses—Professional	3187	3830
Bookkeepers	2978	3414
Cashiers	1975	2835
Secretaries	3365	3812
Telephone operators	3211	3599
Typists	2786	3420
Sales—Retail trade	1474	2307
Laundry operatives	1615	2016
Operatives—Manufacturing	2443	3011
Attendents, hospital and other institutions	1830	2407
Cooks, not private household	1345	1959
Practical nurses	1848	2505[b]
Waitresses	1010	1836[c]

[a]From U.S. Bureau of the Census (1963). *Occupational characteristics*, PC(2) 7A, Table 16.

[b]Includes midwives.

[c]Includes bartenders and counter workers.

TABLE 6-3

Income of Married Women, by Age[a]

		Of those with income			Of all women
Age	Percentage with income	Median income	Percentage less than $1000	Percentage $3000 or over	Percentage $3000 or over
14–24	51.6	$1338	43.6	18.4	9.4
25–34	39.3	1576	40.0	25.4	10.0
35–44	43.9	1817	35.2	28.4	12.6
45–54	46.4	1997	31.7	31.6	14.7
55–64	41.5	1294	45.5	23.6	9.8
Total under 65	43.8	1663[b]	38.0	26.4	11.6

[a]From U.S. Bureau of the Census (1963). Subject Report, *Marital status*, PC(2) 4E, Table 6.

[b]Approximate, not directly available in source.

(Table 6-3). Twelve percent contributed \$3000 or more, while for 17% the contribution was between \$1 and \$999. Of the wives with some income, 38% received less than \$1000 (three-fifths of them less than \$500), while 26% received \$3000 or more. Only 1 working wife in 20 earned \$5000 or more.

The median income received by wives increases with age from \$1338 tor wives under 25 to \$1997 for those 45–54. The proportion of wives with very low earnings (under \$1000) decreases from 42% to 32% in this age range, while the proportion earning \$3000 and over increases from 18% to 32%. Women 55–64 are only slightly less likely to work than women 45–54, but their earnings are considerably lower (medians: \$1294 versus \$1997). Nearly half of the oldest group of women earn less than \$1000. The effect of age here is in part due to age differences in family status. Younger women who are more likely to have younger children are somewhat more likely to work fewer weeks per year. There is little age variation in the proportion working full time, except that women under 25 are more likely to be full-time workers than any of the older ages. These differentials by age in hours worked and weeks worked are shown in Table 6-4. Also, older women are likely to have longer tenure in their jobs, and thus are likely to be earning more (U.S. Bureau of Labor Statistics, 1967, Table 4). (We have no really clear evidence on the effect of tenure on earnings of women, however.) The very low earnings of wives aged 55–64 is an anomaly. It is clearly not due to differences in weeks and hours worked, since there is rather little variation by age.

These income figures are gross incomes. Various studies have shown that

TABLE 6-4

Hours Worked and Weeks Worked by Wives of Household Heads, by Age: United States, 1960[a]

	Age				
	Under 25	25–34	35–44	45–54	55–64
Of women working in 1959:					
Percentage working 50–52 weeks	26.4	33.3	42.0	46.7	45.8
Percentage working more than 26 weeks	54.2	60.3	70.2	76.0	74.7
Percentage of currently employed working 35 or more hours	78.4	69.8	69.2	71.0	67.8

[a] From U.S. Bureau of the Census (1963). *Employment status and work experience*, PC(2) 6A, Tables 13 and 18.

there are substantial costs associated with employment, including transportation, taxes, clothing, purchase of lunches, the substitution of more expensive prepared foods for foods prepared in the home, and the purchase of other time-saving equipment and paid household help. By some estimates, the net benefit of the wife's income to the family may be reduced by as much as one-third to one-half, depending on the need for paying for child care (Addiss, 1963, pp. 219–223; Clover, 1962). The differential between gross and net income undoubtedly varies with the husband's income (and the family's marginal tax rate), the occupation in which the woman is engaged, and a variety of other factors. In any event, it seems fair to say that while there are some women who make substantial contributions to family income, the contributions of many women are rather small and make only a marginal difference to the family's overall economic position.

Annual earnings are equal to the product of an hourly wage times the average hours worked per week times weeks worked per year. Individual characteristics such as education may influence annual earnings through any one of these three channels. It may, further, be useful to think of individual characteristics such as education or age as influencing any or all of the three components of annual earnings both directly and indirectly through the process of sorting individuals into occupational groupings.

Unfortunately it is not possible with 1960 census data to make the decomposition of annual earnings into the three components—hours per week, weeks per year, and hourly earnings. The only information that we have with reference to 1959 is total yearly earnings and the number of weeks worked. Hours worked per week is measured with reference to the week prior to the census enumeration, and not to the year 1959. We have chosen not to assume that the situation last week would accurately reflect the average situation last year for individual women. Our empirical analysis will show earnings variation in relation to a variety of individual characteristics. It will then show the extent to which a particular variable exerts its influence directly on weekly earnings or whether the influence operates via the number of weeks worked per year. Similarly, we will show the degree to which variation in annual earnings or weeks worked comes about as a result of the differential pattern of sorting individual women into major occupational groups, or whether it is due also, in part, to differential earnings within occupations.

In this chapter we will present results for the aggregate of all women except blacks. In the next chapter we will present similar results for black wives, along with some discussion of differentials in earnings between blacks and nonblacks. For simplicity, we will refer to the women under discussion in this chapter as white women, even though nonwhite wives other than blacks are also included.

TABLE 6-5

Multiple Classification Analysis of the Earnings in 1959 of White Husband-Present, Nonfarm Women[a]

		Net deviations	
	N	Excluding weeks worked	Including weeks worked
Income adequacy			
.0– .3	576	29	−94
.4– .7	1270	−233	−256
.8–1.1	2365	−125	−142
1.2–1.5	2993	−70	−62
1.6–1.9	2091	50	53
2.0–2.8	1764	144	184
2.9+	702	606	658
Education			
Less than 9	2308	−404	−317
9–11	2689	−161	−144
12	4585	61	−9
13–15	1343	246	239
16+	837	898	1000
Age			
14–19	336	−1378	−474
20–24	1529	−580	−190
25–29	1348	−422	−132
30–34	1460	−76	5
35–39	1770	150	71
40–44	1703	272	78
45–49	1612	345	90
50–54	1183	356	111
55–59	820	396	104
Children ever born			
None	2863	600	233
1	2684	23	35
2	2980	−180	−75
3	1692	−294	−127
4	788	−445	−247
5+	754	−527	−166
Weeks worked			
1–13	1991	−164	
14–26	1687	−105	
27–39	1543	−291	
40–47	1186	307	
48–49	596	570	
50–52	4758	1003	
Grand mean $2190		Sample size 11,761	

[a]Analysis includes only women with some earnings.

There were 11,761 white women with earnings in our sample of husband-present women under the age of 60 who were not residents of farms. These women worked an average of 35.9 weeks in 1959 and earned an average of $2190. The standard deviations of weeks worked and earnings were 16.9 weeks and $1784, respectively. The results of the multivariate analysis of earnings are shown in Table 6-5.

Interdependence of Employment and Earnings

In one sense the dichotomization of the problem of the work patterns of women into the factors that influence employment and those that influence earnings of women who are employed is an inadequate way of conceptualizing these processes. In a way, employment and earnings are two outputs of the same process. Women with a given set of characteristics may opt to be in or not in the labor force depending on the earnings which they are able to obtain by working. This minimal earnings level may vary depending on the woman's characteristics. So, for example, it may be that a woman with only a grade school education would be willing to enter the work force at an hourly wage of $1.25, while a woman with a high school degree would, generally, require an hourly rate of $2.00. Similarly, the woman living under considerable economic pressure may have a lower price to induce her into the labor force than the woman living under less economic need.

Despite this obvious inadequacy of specifying the process, I have been unable to discover any reasonable alternative to the separate consideration of employment decisions and earnings levels.

The Annual Earnings of Wives: Multivariate Analysis

A person's earnings depend on a variety of individual characteristics, as well as characteristics of the labor market in which he is seeking work. Greater education ought to be associated with higher productivity and, thus, higher earnings. Similarly, age may be correlated with work experience and job tenure, which are in turn correlated with productivity and earnings. In this section we examine a variation of the earnings of married women in relation to a variety of individual characteristics, as well as to region and size of place.

Our procedure will be much like that used in earlier chapters in the analysis of employment differentials. Variation in annual earnings will be analyzed by means of a multiple classification analysis. The basic set of independent variables includes education, age, income adequacy, and the number of children ever born to the woman. Other variables are added one at a time in order to measure their effects net of the effects of these basic variables.

In each case, two separate regression models are reported—the first without the inclusion of weeks worked, and the second with weeks worked included. The first model shows differential annual earnings and the second shows the degree to which observed differentials arise out of variation in weeks worked.

After reporting results for the entire universe of husband-present women under age 60 with some earnings during 1959, we will present results for women under age 60 with one or more own children in order to show the effects of the family composition variables on earnings.

Education

The greater the level of education, the greater the annual earnings of married women. There is about a $250 differential between the less than 9 and 9 to 11 categories and the 9 to 11 and 12 categories, and less than a $200 differential between 12 and 13 to 15 years of education. The differential between having some college education and being a college graduate is about $650.

When weeks worked is added to the regression, the relationship changes only very slightly, with earnings of the college graduates increasing by about $100 and those of the high school and lower groups decreasing by about $100. College graduate women are disproportionately school teachers who work less than full year. This fact tends to decrease their annual earnings.

It would be desirable to make comparisons of education differentials in earnings between men and women. I do not have readily available data for men that are comparable to those just reported for women. The data in Table 6-6 compare the education-age specific median incomes for men and women. There are many other inadequacies with these comparisons, including the fact that women are more likely to be voluntarily part-year workers.

Without exception, age–education specific median earnings are higher for men than for women, and with only a few exceptions the dollar increment between successive education levels is greater for men than for women (Table 6-6). These exceptions occur at the youngest age interval shown in the table, 25–29, and for the education interval 16 to 17+. In most cases the male increment in income for an additional level of education is more than twice the female increment. It seems likely that this conclusion, that increments in education have a higher return for men than for women, would hold if a valid comparison could be made. Unfortunately, it cannot be made with immediately accessible data. It would be interesting to decompose these

TABLE 6-6

Median Income, by Age, Education, and Sex[a]

Education	25–29 Median income	25–29 Difference	30–34 Median income	30–34 Difference	35–44 Median income	35–44 Difference	45–54 Median income	45–54 Difference
Men								
None	1536	508	1738	675	1710	832	1983	480
1–4	2044	891	2413	1077	2542	1206	2463	1356
5–7	2935	748	3490	803	3748	793	3819	790
8	3683	481	4293	646	4541	697	4609	635
9–11	4164	581	4939	513	5238	610	5244	562
12	4745	77	5452	603	5848	924	5806	966
13–15	4822	655	6055	1310	6772	1897	6772	2177
16	5477	−417	7365	−115	8669	422	8949	878
17+	5060		7250		9091		9827	
Total	4416		5223		5465		5091	
Women								
None	737	120	820	63	802	118	836	83
1–4	857	95	883	222	920	378	919	471
5–7	952	257	1105	346	1298	404	1390	450
8	1209	187	1451	171	1702	174	1840	266
9–11	1396	750	1622	561	1876	484	2106	506
12	2146	164	2183	54	2360	278	2612	399
13–15	2310	895	2237	531	2638	593	3011	1010
16	3205	575	2768	1268	3231	1389	4021	1344
17+	3780		4036		4620		5365	
Total	1850		1841		2037		2191	

[a]From U.S. Bureau of the Census (1964). *Educational attainment*, PC(2) 5B, Tables 6 and 7.

differentials into a component attributable to occupational segregation and a differential attributable to occupation-specific earnings.

Age

When weeks worked is not included in the analysis, there is a sharp upward gradient of annual earnings from 14–19 through 45–49, after which earnings remain almost constant. Women aged 14–19 earn about $1300 below the mean, while those 20–29 are about $400 to $600 below the mean. The women aged 40–59 are earning at about $300 above the grand mean. However, when weeks worked per year is added into the analysis, the age relationship is greatly attenuated, so that there is only about a $200 difference between the annual earnings of women aged 25–29 and 55–59, and the earnings of 14- to 19-year-old women are only $500 below the grand mean. Age is associated with family status, particularly age of youngest child. Women under age 30 or so are disproportionately mothers of pre-school-age children, who tend to work fewer weeks per year.

A recent Special Labor Force Report presented job tenure data by age, race, and sex. Job tenure in this case refers to continuity of employment for a single employer. For white women, median job tenure increases with age from less than half a year for women under age 20 to nearly 12 years for women 55–59. For men, tenure increases with age at nearly twice the rate that it does for women. Clearly women at every age have shorter tenure, and undoubtedly less work experience than men. Unfortunately, no data are presented relating earnings to tenure for either men or women.

One way of indirectly getting at the impact of job tenure and career lines is to examine the age variation of earnings of women with minimal familial interference with employment (see Condran and Condran, 1971). Specifically, let us select married women with no children present, and no children ever born, in the age range 25–39. We select these women because most childless women under age 25 will go on to have children, while those over 40 grew up prior to World War II, and are thus members of cohorts whose labor force involvement was less common, and perhaps less regular than the later cohorts. How do their earnings vary with age?

Among men there is a regular upward progression of earnings with age in the age range 25–29 through 35–44, *at every education level* (Table 6-7).

TABLE 6-7

Mean Earnings of Married Women Who Have No Own Children under 18 and Who Have Never Had a Baby, by Education and Age[a]

Age	Less than 9	9–11	12	13–15	16+
Total, all women with earnings					
20–24	1455	2195	2529	2596	2903
25–29	1546	2656	2880	2751	3453
30–34	2458	2305	2999	3444	4056
35–39	1878	2266	3181	3397	3909
40–44	2082	2542	3027	4057	4490
Worked 50–52 weeks					
20–24	2483	3597	3108	3358	3576
25–29	2200	3067	3448	3690	4209
30–34	3092	3141	3682	3848	4218
35–39	2639	2749	3866	4454	5667
40–44	2733	3019	3675	4595	5113

[a]From 1/1000 tabulations.

There is a greater increase in education for men with high levels of education than for those with low education levels, but even for men with 5 to 7 years of schooling there is an \$800 differential in earnings between ages 25–29 and 35–44.

For childless women, there is some tendency for earnings to increase with age, but the increase is by no means as pronounced as it is for men. For example, the earnings of childless women with 12 years of education differ by \$100 between ages 25–29 and 30–34, and by a similar amount between 30–34 and 35–39. The earnings of full-year workers show about twice that differential over each of the two age intervals. Our estimates for females are based on a relatively small sample, and are thus subject to greater sampling unreliability than are the figures for males. We are also attempting to make cohort comparisons from cross-sectional data.

Income Adequacy

There is a positive gradient of earnings in relation to income adequacy. Women in families with an IA score of .4–.7 earn about \$200 below the mean, while those with scores in the 2.0–2.8 range earn about \$200 above the mean. There is a marked jump in earnings between the 2.0–2.8 and 2.9 and over categories, with the latter group earning about \$600 above the grand mean. These differentials cannot be attributed in any significant way to differential weeks worked. When weeks worked is included, the relationship is strengthened slightly. We will withhold further discussion and interpretation of this relationship to a later section of this chapter.

Children Ever Born

The effect of the number of children ever born to the woman might have an effect on earnings of working women for several reasons:

1. Women who have borne several children are likely to have less work experience and less job tenure than women who have borne fewer children.
2. The women who have borne few or no children may have a greater commitment to a career than those who have borne several, and may thus be earning more. This may operate either via job tenure and work experience, via a greater level of specialized training, or via the fact that the more able women (i.e., those with greater earning potential) are selected into the career pattern and thus restrict their fertility.
3. The effect of children ever born on earnings may be operating via the correlation between the presence of children in the family affecting either the amount of time worked or the hourly wage. The only control we have introduced that would take this effect out is the age of the woman. We will

report subsequently on the effects of age of youngest child and number of children on earnings.

Women who have never borne a child earn about $600 above the mean in 1959. More than half of this differential can be attributed to differential weeks worked. There is a negative, almost linear gradient of earnings from one child onward, with mothers of five or more children ever born earning $500 less than the average. Again, much of this differential can be attributed to a differential in weeks worked. After weeks worked is controlled, mothers of four or five children earn $150 to $250 less than mothers of only one child.

Age at First Marriage

We reasoned, but failed to verify empirically, that the older the age at which a woman marries, the greater her current employment probability. The underlying argument was that women with later ages at marriage would, other things being equal, have more work experience and a greater commitment to the work role. The same reasoning might be applied to the earnings of working women. There is no reason to modify our expectations regarding earnings even though the hypothesis with respect to employment was not sustained, since the forces affecting sorting into or out of the labor force may differ from those that affect the earnings of women in the work force.

The addition of age at marriage to the array of variables already discussed shows that age at marriage has virtually no net effect on the earnings of married women. One interesting finding is that while women marrying at age thirty and over earn about $100 below average, this results from a lower level of weeks worked. When weeks worked is controlled, their earnings are about $150 above the mean (Table 6-8).

TABLE 6-8

Net Effects[a] of Age at Marriage on the 1959 Earnings of White Married Women, Age 14–59

Age at first marriage		N	Net deviations: Excluding weeks worked	Net deviations: Including weeks worked
Less than 18 years		1913	61	40
18–20 years		4076	15	−39
21–24 years		3502	28	10
25–29 years		1455	−142	−39
30 or more years		815	−88	128
Grand mean	$2190			
Number of cases	11,761			

[a]Net of the effects of income adequacy, education, age and children ever born.

TABLE 6-9

Net Effects[a] of Marital History on the 1959 Earnings of White Married Women, Age 14–59

Marital history		*N*	Net deviations: Excluding weeks worked	Net deviations: Including weeks worked
Husband and wife married once		9210	−15	−23
Wife married once, husband more than once		821	86	85
Husband married once wife more than once		787	39	66
Both married more than once		943	46	97
Grand mean	$2190			
Number of cases	11,761			

[a]Net of the effects of income adequacy, education, age, and children ever born.

Marital History

There are only very small differences in the earnings of wives in relation to our marital history variable. Wives in families where both spouses are in their first marriage earn about $50 to $100 less than wives who have themselves or whose husbands have been married more than once (Table 6-9).

Regional Differences in Earnings

Women residing in the Western region earn about $100 more than average. Despite the fact that they work fewer weeks per year, Western women earn somewhat more. When we control on weeks worked, their earnings rise to about $150 above the mean. The average earnings of women in the other three regions are very little different from one another (Table 6-10).

Size of Place

We have classified size of place into five categories—outside urbanized area, in urbanized area less than 100,000, urbanized area 100,000–249,999, urbanized area 250,000–499,999, and urbanized area 500,000 and more. There is a positive relationship between earnings and size of place net of compositional factors. Some, but by no means all, of the

TABLE 6-10

Net Effects[a] of Region on the 1959 Earnings of White Married Women, Age 14–59

Region	N	Net deviations: Excluding weeks worked	Net deviations: Including weeks worked
Northeast	3130	–10	–4
North Central	3375	–62	–44
South	3092	–0	–58
West	2164	111	158
Grand mean $2190			
Number of cases 11,761			

[a]Net of the effects of income adequacy, education, age, and children ever born.

differential may be attributed to a differential in weeks worked. Women in the largest urbanized areas earn an average of $400 more than women in small UA's or in areas outside UA's. Why might this earning differential exist (see Table 6-11)?

1. Conditions of supply and demand may differ between large and small UA's, such that there is more competition among employers for a scarce labor supply.
2. If living costs differ among areas by size of place, then the real earnings differential may be zero, even though there are differences in money earnings.

TABLE 6-11

Net Effects[a] of Size of Urbanized Area on the 1959 Earnings of White Married Women, Age 14–59

Size of urbanized area	N	Net deviations: Excluding weeks worked	Net deviations: Including weeks worked
Not in urbanized area	4143	–198	–142
Urbanized area			
Under 100,000	643	–168	–166
100,000–249,999	1442	–78	–70
250,000–499,999	809	23	70
500,000 or more	4724	217	156
Grand mean $2190			
Number of cases 11,761			

[a]Net of the effects of income adequacy, education, age, and children ever born.

3. The process of sorting of persons into occupations may differ between areas by size of place, such that the occupations in which persons with a given education level are employed are less desirable ones in small areas.

Family Status

In order to assess the effects of age of youngest child and number of children on earnings, we have run a set of regressions for the universe of married women with one or more own children under 18. The results of this set of regressions are shown in Table 6-12.

Age of Youngest Child

Women with children under the age of 3 earn about $280 below the mean for women with children, while those with children 12–17 and none younger earn about $280 above the mean. The two groups of women with youngest children aged 3 to 5 and 6 to 11 earn about $75 to $80 above the mean. Most of this differential is eliminated when weeks worked is included in the regression. Women with younger children work fewer weeks, and thus earn less, while those with older children work more than the average number of

TABLE 6-12

Net Effects[a] of Age of Youngest Own Child and Number of Own Children under 18 on the Earnings of White Married Women with Children[b]

		Net deviations	
	N	Excluding weeks worked	Including weeks worked
Age of youngest own child			
0–2	1984	−279	57
3–5	1064	8	−14
6–11	1918	8	−59
12–17	1881	282	7
Number of children under 18			
1	2944	174	69
2	2190	−42	−15
3	1032	−206	−84
4 or more	681	−305	−124
Grand mean $1887			
Sample size 6847			

[a]Analysis includes only women with some earnings.
[b]Net of the effects of age, education, and income adequacy.

weeks. When weeks worked is controlled, women with children 0 to 2 earn about $50 more than the average, while those with youngest child 6 to 11 earn about $60 below the average. The higher earnings of the women with the youngest children may reflect a higher incentive needed to induce such women into the work force. It may also reflect a higher commitment to work, *ceteris paribus*, on the part of working mothers of small children, which is also reflected in higher earnings.

Number of Children under 18

The greater the number of children, the lower the annual earnings of American mothers. Mothers of one own child under 18 earn $174 more than the mean of $1887, while those with four or more children are $305 below the mean. Much of the differential is due to a differential in weeks worked. After weeks worked is controlled, the women with one child earn about $70 above the mean, while women with four or more children earn $124 less than the mean.

Weekly Wage

The slope of annual earnings on weeks worked represents the weekly wage rate. To the extent to which the relationship is linear, persons working different numbers of weeks are earning the same weekly rate. Departures from linearity may reflect differences in hours worked per week among the different levels of weeks worked, or they may reflect differences in hourly earnings. Since neither component is measured, we cannot make this decomposition empirically. We might expect, however, that if part-year workers are "marginal" workers, their hours worked might be fewer and their hourly wage lower. On the other hand, full-year workers are stable workers, who are trained for and experienced in their jobs and thus more efficient. Their hours worked per week and their hourly wage ought to be higher.

We show in Fig. 6-1 the partial relationship between weeks worked and annual earnings. The points are plotted at the midpoints of the weeks worked categories and may be somewhat in error. The plot is remarkably linear with the only discontinuity worth mentioning between those who worked 48–49 and 50–52 weeks in 1959. Women who worked 50–52 weeks in 1959 earned nearly $300 more than their expected value based on a projection of the plot from less than 13 to 48–49 weeks. Evidently the full-year workers are either working more hours or earning a higher hourly wage than those working fewer weeks. We may think of this $300 differential as the value of the kind of continuous commitment to employment—the value of nonmarginality.

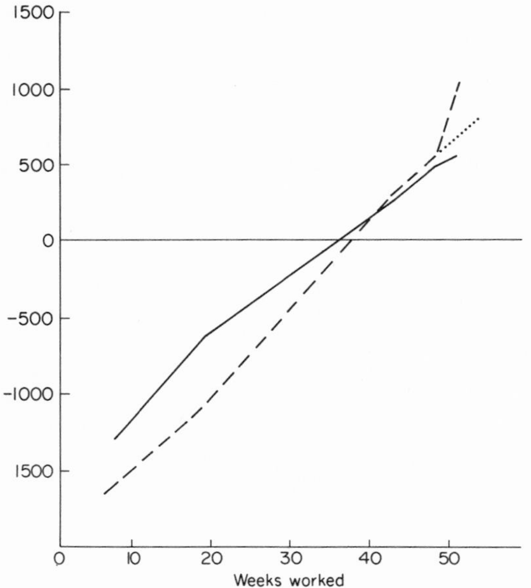

Figure 6-1. *Effects of Weeks worked on earnings. (---): Net; (——): gross.*

Marginality is used here not only in the sense of the woman treating employment as a secondary activity and continually entering and leaving the work force in response to familial demands on her time, but also employers using women as marginal workers by hiring and firing in response to seasonal or other temporary variation in the need for employees. We have no empirical evidence that would permit us to assess the relative magnitude of marginality choice as opposed to imposed marginality. The meaning of the relationship between weekly wage and marginality is thus ambiguous. The higher wage of full-year workers may reflect their productivity due to their greater commitment to the work role and greater job tenure and work experience, or it may reflect the low rate at which marginal workers can be induced into the work force. On the other hand, labor force turnover and marginality may be due, in part, to the lower rate at which women workers are paid and their marginal position in the work force.

Wife's Income as a Component of Family Income

We have examined the variation in wives' earnings in relation to a number of individual and areal characteristics. Our attention now shifts to wife's income as a component of family income—both absolutely and relatively. In much of this analysis we will rely on published data.

Table 6-13 shows mean incomes of wives with income. Overall, wives with income have a mean income of $2112. The amount of income received by wives increases with husband's income from a mean of about $1500 for wives of husbands earning $1–999 to $2400 for wives of men earning $7000 or more. The gradient is approximately linear and rather steep in the range $1–999 to $5000–5999, but beyond $6000 there is rather little variability in mean income.

About 12% of all wives and 26% of all working wives received incomes of $3000 or more, while 38% of all wives with income received less than $1000 (Table 6-14). These proportions vary considerably in relation to husband's income. For example, 54% of wives with income whose husbands earned less than $1000 themselves also earned less than $1000, while only one in six earned $3000 or more. The comparable figures for working wives of men receiving incomes of $5000–5999 are: earning less than $1000, 33%; earning more than $2999, 32%.

Married men with no income in the age range under consideration here probably consist primarily of men who are disabled, either physically or mentally, and unable to work. To the extent that husbands with no income are disabled, one might suspect that they and their wives are a more representative sample in terms of educational attainment of the total population of wives than men who earn, say, $1000 per year. Total disability may fall disproportionately on the low status segments of the population, but long-term unemployment and very low earnings are probably even more disproportionately low status phenomena.

In addition, some of the husbands with no income are enrolled in school (and receive no income during the entire year). We would expect their wives to be relatively high earners for two reasons: if they were not, the man could not afford to be in school, and men who are in school and earning no income are likely to have better educated wives than men earning, say, $1000.

Data on educational attainment and school enrollment (for persons under age 35) and on weeks worked are available in the 1960 census, and one could examine certain characteristics and activities of men with no income from them. In 1970, the census included questions on disability (including its duration), making it possible to describe the extent to which husbands with low incomes are disabled. At the present time, however, we can do little more than speculate.

Why should working wives of relatively high income husbands have higher incomes than those of lower income husbands? We know that earnings are closely related to education. High income men tend to be well-educated, and well-educated men tend to be married to well-educated women. Consequently, we would expect some positive correlation between the earnings

TABLE 6-13

Average Wife's Contribution to Family Income by Age and Husband's Income[a]

Husband's income ($)	N (Thousands)	Percentage	Proportion of wives with income	Mean income of wife (per income recipient) ($)
None	614	1.6	44.8	2424
1–999	1941	5.2	51.0	1542
1000–1999	2736	7.3	50.3	1625
2000–2999	3463	9.3	49.5	1752
3000–3999	4493	12.0	48.7	1994
4000–4999	5471	14.6	47.3	2192
5000–5999	5895	15.8	44.3	2312
6000–6999	4192	11.2	40.8	2356
7000–9999	5350	14.3	35.9	2365
10,000–14,999	2006	5.4	31.2	2412
15,000 or more	1245	3.3	32.1	2613
Total	37,406	100.0	43.8	2112

Husband's income ($)	Wife under 25		Wife 25–44		Wife 45–64	
	Proportion of wives with income	Mean income of wife (per income recipient) ($)	Proportion of wives with income	Mean income of wife (per income recipient) ($)	Proportion of wives with income	Mean income of wife (per income recipient) ($)
None	44.4	1814	46.2	2448	44.0	2522
1–999	53.2	1308	49.2	1647	51.3	1541
1000–1999	57.6	1461	49.0	1669	48.5	1667
2000–2999	54.8	1512	49.0	1790	47.3	1855
3000–3999	54.3	1678	48.2	2021	46.4	2159
4000–4999	52.2	1843	47.0	2191	45.4	2387
5000–5999	48.3	1929	43.6	2256	44.2	2573
6000–6999	44.1	1954	39.3	2262	43.0	2648
7000–9999	40.4	1994	33.6	2220	40.2	2672
10,000–14,999	39.0	2300	27.8	2180	36.4	2713
15,000 or more	41.3	2123	27.3	2322	37.2	2869
Total	51.6	1702	41.7	2116	44.5	2266

[a] From U.S. Bureau of the Census (1964). *Sources and structure of family income*, PC(2) 4C, Table 17.

TABLE 6-14

Proportion of Wives Receiving $3000 or More and Proportion Receiving Less Than $1000, by Age and Husband's Income[a]

Husband's income ($)	Total under 65	Under 25	25–44	45–64
	Proportion of wives with income earning $3000 or more			
None	30.5	20.3	31.6	31.8
1–999	15.8	11.9	17.7	15.8
1000–1999	16.1	12.8	16.7	17.1
2000–2999	16.5	12.2	17.0	18.7
3000–3999	22.6	16.7	23.3	25.6
4000–4999	28.8	21.9	29.1	31.9
5000–5999	31.8	24.8	31.2	35.9
6000–6999	33.0	26.5	31.6	37.7
7000–9999	32.8	26.9	30.6	37.6
10,000–14,999	32.2	31.6	28.8	36.5
15,000 or more	33.3	27.5	29.0	37.1
	Proportion of wives with income receiving less than $1000			
None	28.6	41.1	27.5	27.2
1–999	54.3	57.8	50.1	55.9
1000–1999	48.2	48.7	45.6	49.8
2000–2999	41.9	35.9	39.5	42.4
3000–3999	35.3	42.2	33.9	33.2
4000–4999	32.6	39.5	32.5	29.2
5000–5999	32.9	39.1	34.0	28.2
6000–6999	34.3	40.2	36.1	29.1
7000–9999	37.5	40.0	40.5	32.1
10,000–14,999	42.3	38.0	46.1	37.7
15,000 or more	43.5	42.1	48.6	39.4
	Percentage of all wives earning $3000 or more			
None	13.7	9.0	14.7	13.9
1–999	8.1	6.2	8.9	8.1
1000–1999	8.1	7.4	8.3	8.4
2000–2999	8.1	6.7	8.2	8.8
3000–3999	11.0	9.0	11.2	11.9
4000–4999	13.6	11.6	13.8	14.4
5000–5999	14.1	12.1	13.7	15.9
6000–6999	13.5	11.6	12.4	16.2
7000–9999	11.8	10.9	10.3	15.0
10,000–14,999	10.1	12.3	8.0	13.3
15,000 or more	10.7	11.4	7.9	13.8

[a]From U.S. Bureau of the Census (1964). *Sources and structure of family income*, PC(2) 4C, Table 17.

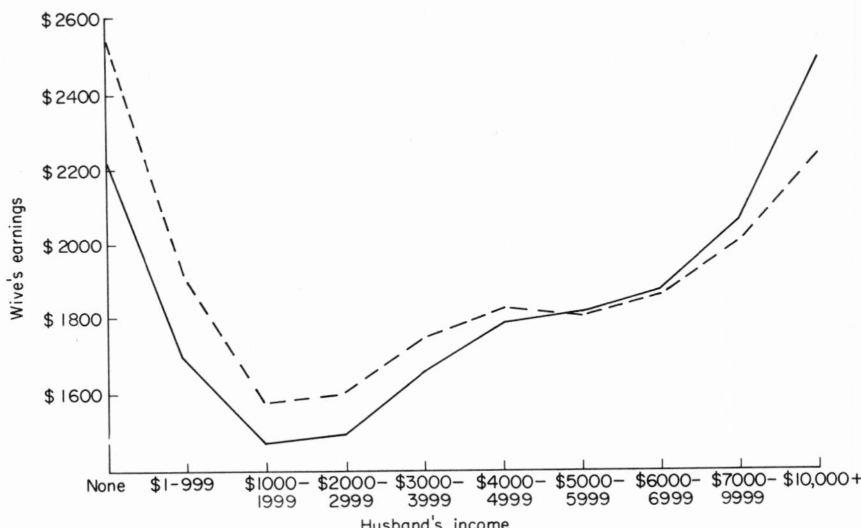

Figure 6-2. *Mean earnings of wives by income of husband, showing effect of standardizing for education composition (nonblack wives with children under 18 only). (—): Crude mean; (——): standard mean.*

of wives and husbands. Over and above the superior qualifications of wives of relatively high income men, they may also have access to higher paying jobs as a result of greater social interaction, both of themselves and their husbands, with persons who are aware of, and in many cases control, the better paying jobs.

A comparison of earnings of wives in relation to income of husband, standardizing for compositional differences in education, is shown in Fig. 6-2.[2] While education accounts for some portion of the difference in earnings, the upward gradient is still present even after a control on education is introduced. There is, for example, a $574 difference between the earnings of wives of men with $2000–2999 and those of wives of men receiving $7000–9999. When education is controlled, the differential drops to $401. More than two-thirds of the differential remains.

[2]The standardized figures were computed as follows:

$$Y_j = \sum_{i=1}^{5} P_i Y_{ij}$$

where Y_j is the standardized income for the jth husband's income group, P_i is the proportion of all earners in the ith education level, and Y_{ij} is the mean earnings of women in the ith education and jth husband income group.

Wives of low-income husbands have a greater incentive to work, and thus may find it necessary to accept low-paying jobs. On the other hand, the wives of the relatively affluent husbands may choose to stay out of the labor force rather than accept a low-paying job. In this connection, it is appropriate to point out that we know almost nothing about the dynamics of the decision process by which women choose to enter the labor force. In the case of low-income families, it may be that a search for a job may follow the decision to enter the labor force; in the case of many middle- and high-status wives, it is likely that upon becoming aware of the availability of a job, the woman decides to enter the labor force. If this is accurate, the decision to enter or not to enter the labor force may depend on the level of remuneration. If this is the case, we have one more reason for expecting correlation between income of husband and wife. This process is further an illustration of the inadequacy of separate analysis of the employment of "secondary workers" and their earnings.

It does not appear that the greater annual income of wives of high-income husbands can be attributable to a greater number of hours worked per year. In a multivariate analysis of the probability of working full time, I found that wives of families with high husband's income were considerably less likely to work full time than are working wives of low-income husbands (see Chap. 4). Morgan *et al.* (1962, Chap. 11) report that family income less wife's earnings is inversely related to the number of hours worked per year.

Similarly, wives of high-income men are no more likely than wives of men with lower income to work 50–52 weeks (or 40 weeks or more), and somewhat more likely to have worked only 1 to 13 weeks in 1959 (see Table 6-15).

TABLE 6-15

Percentage Distribution of Weeks Worked in 1959 by Nonblack Husband-Present Women 14–59 with Earnings, in Relation to Husband's Income in 1959[a]

	Weeks worked			
Husband's income ($)	1–13	14–49	50–52	Total
None	11.5	38.0	50.5	100.0
1–999	15.2	43.6	41.2	100.0
1000–1999	19.3	43.1	37.6	100.0
2000–2999	18.9	42.5	38.6	100.0
3000–3999	17.2	41.4	41.4	100.0
4000–4999	17.5	40.7	41.8	100.0
5000–5999	17.5	42.2	40.3	100.0
6000–6999	19.6	40.3	40.1	100.0
7000–9999	20.7	40.4	38.9	100.0
10,000+	20.2	37.8	42.0	100.0

[a]From 1/1000 tabulations.

The fact that the earnings of wives do not increase with husband's income beyond \$6000 is due in part to the fact that such wives work fewer hours and fewer weeks per year.

The fact that husbands and wives live in the same community and thus in the same labor market area means that any labor market earnings advantage or disadvantage enjoyed by the husband, independent of his own characteristics, is likely to be shared by the wife. In order to estimate the magnitude of this relationship we have regressed occupation-specific female earnings on occupation-specific male earnings over 102 Standard Metropolitan Statistical Areas using data from the 1960 census. Overall, the earnings of women are higher by \$51 for every \$100 differential in male earnings (see Table 6-16). The interarea standard deviation of male earnings is \$550, which gives some idea of the quantitative importance of these relationships.

TABLE 6-16

Relationship Between Occupation-Specific Female Earnings and Occupation-Specific Male Earnings, Computed over Standard Metropolitan Statistical Areas, United States, 1960[a]

	Male earnings				
Female earnings	Total	Professionals, managers, officials, and proprietors	Craftsmen and foreman	Operatives	Laborers
Professional, technical and kindred workers	.35[b]	.35	.35	.24	.25
Teachers	.51	.36	.46	.41	.43
Clerical	.33	.38	.31	.20	.22
Bookkeepers	.33	.36	.31	.20	.22
Secretary	.43	.49	.40	.25	.27
Sales	.13	.17	.11	.06	.09
Retail sales	.15	.16	.13	.08	.10
Operatives	.54	.44	.51	.46	.50
Private household workers	.08	.10	.07	.06	.10
Service	.35	.28	.32	.25	.33
Waitress	.27	.23	.25	.19	.25
Total	.51	.46	.44	.35	.43

[a] From U.S. Bureau of the Census (1964). *Characteristics of the population*, Vol. I, various state volumes.

[b] Figures shown in tables are regression coefficients from the equation

$$I_f = a + bI_m$$

where I_f is the median earnings of females in the occupation and I_m is the median earnings of males in the occupation.

The earnings of women in professional, clerical, operative, and service occupations are more responsive to differences in male earnings than is the case for private household or sales workers.

Relative Contribution to Family Income

Thus far we have been looking at the absolute amount of the wife's contribution to family income. We now turn our attention to an examination of the relative contribution of wives to family income. Total family income can be divided into four components:

$$\text{Family Income} = \text{Husband's Earnings} + \text{Wife's Earnings} + \text{Earnings of Other Family Members} + \text{Total Nonearnings Income}$$

The wife's proportional share of total family income depends on the values of the other three components as well as on her total earnings. The greater the husband's share, the greater the other's earnings share, and the greater the nonearnings income share, the smaller the wife's share, whatever the total amount of her earnings.

Wives contributed almost 12% of aggregate income of husband–wife families in 1959, while the head (husband) contributed nearly 81%. The remaining 7% was contributed by other relatives. Two-thirds of this latter

TABLE 6-17

Percentage Distribution of Family Income among Recipients, by Size of Family Income: Husband–Wife Families, Head Ages 25–64, 1959[a]

Family income	Husband's income	Wife's income	Other's income	Total
Less than $1000	70.9	18.5	10.7	100.0
$1000–1999	81.0	13.0	6.0	100.0
$2000–2999	83.4	11.8	4.8	100.0
$3000–3999	86.0	10.3	3.7	100.0
$4000–4999	87.4	9.2	3.4	100.0
$5000–5999	88.0	8.7	3.3	100.0
$6000–6999	85.5	10.5	4.0	100.0
$7000–9999	79.0	14.7	6.3	100.0
$10,000–14,999	73.6	15.1	11.2	100.0
$15,000–24,999	79.7	9.3	11.0	100.0
$25,000 or more	90.0	5.7	3.4	100.0
Total	81.7	11.7	6.6	100.0

[a] From U.S. Bureau of the Census (1964). *Sources and structure of family income*, PC(2) 4C, Table 13.

component was the contribution of sons and daughters of the married couple living in the same household. As family income increases from less than $1000 to $6000, the proportion of aggregate family income earned by the head increases from 70.9 to 88.0 and the share of the wife's contribution declines from 18.5 to 8.7% (Table 6-17). Family incomes from $6000 to $14,999 show a declining share of husband's income and an increasing wife's share (from 86% to 73%). Family incomes of $15,000 or more consist of 90% husband's income.

These data suggest that the very low-income families include many working wives, and are actually disproportionately families with unemployed, low-earning, or not-in-the-labor-force husbands. As family income increases, the husband's income share gradually increases, the proportion of husbands with income increases, and the proportion of wives with income gradually declines. A higher proportion of families with family income of less than $6000 than of higher-income families include only one earner, and the one earner is almost always the husband. As we reach a family income of $6000 or so, increasingly we have families consisting of two earners—the husband and the wife. Apart from those families receiving less than $1000 in income, families with incomes of $10,000 to $14,999 show the lowest proportion of aggregate income received by the head (73.6%).

The proportion of families with two or more earners increases from 36% for families with incomes of less than $2000 to 69% of families with incomes of $10,000 to $14,999 (see Table 6-18).

With published census data we can also examine the distribution of husband–wife families by relative size of wife's contribution to family income. These data are summarized in Table 6-19. The universe here is all husband–wife families in which the husband received some income in 1959. Sixty-two percent of all such families had no income contributed by the wife. In 15% of the families, the wife's contribution amounted to less than 20% of total family income, while in 10% of the families the wife contributed 40% or more. In the remaining 14% of the families, the wife contributed between 20 and 39% of family income.

Considering only those families in which both spouses have incomes, we find that in about 40% of the cases the wife's contribution was less than one-fifth of family income (Table 6–19, lower panel). In an additional 36% the wife contributed between 20 and 40% of family income, and in the remaining 26% she contributed more than 40%. The wife is relatively more likely to contribute a substantial *proportion* of family income in families with a total income of less than $2000 than in families with an income of $2000 to $5999. In about 45% of all families with incomes between $8000 and $15,000, the wife's contribution amounts to 20 to 39% of family income, and in an additional 25% of families the wife's contribution exceeds 40%.

TABLE 6-18

Percentage Distribution of Husband–Wife Families by Number of Earners in Relation to Size of Family Income: Urban Population[a]

Family income	Number of earners 0	1	2 or more	Total
Less than $1000	45.0	39.2	15.7	100.0
$2000–2999	20.2	53.2	26.6	100.0
$3000–3999	7.0	60.4	32.5	100.0
$4000–4999	2.5	61.3	36.2	100.0
$5000–5999	1.1	59.7	39.2	100.0
$6000–7999	.6	48.6	50.7	100.0
$8000–9999	.5	34.6	64.8	100.0
$10,000–14,999	.6	30.8	68.6	100.0
$15,000 or more	1.4	48.3	50.3	100.0
Total	5.6	47.7	46.7	100.0

[a]From U.S. Bureau of the Census (1964). *Sources and structure of family income*, PC(2) 4C, Table 1.

TABLE 6-19

Distribution of White Husband–Wife Families by Proportion of Family Income Received by the Wife, in Relation to Size of Family Income in 1959: United States, 1960[a]

Family income	Percentage of family income earned by wife 0	1–9	10–19	20–29	30–39	40–49	50–74	75+	Total
	All families in which head had income								
Less than $2000	79.1	5.1	3.3	2.7	2.1	2.0	2.4	3.3	100.0
$2000–3999	72.5	8.1	5.0	3.5	2.8	2.4	3.4	2.3	100.0
$4000–5999	68.2	10.0	5.8	4.4	3.9	3.5	3.4	.8	100.0
$6000–9999	55.2	8.9	6.8	7.9	9.8	7.9	3.2	.2	100.0
$10,000–14,999	50.3	7.6	7.0	10.9	12.6	9.0	2.4	.1	100.0
$15,000 or more	70.4	8.6	6.7	6.9	4.1	2.1	.9	.3	100.0
Total	62.5	8.7	6.1	6.4	6.9	5.5	3.0	.8	100.0
	All families where head and wife had income								
Less than $2000		24.6	15.8	12.8	10.1	9.4	11.7	15.7	100.0
$2000–3999		29.6	18.2	12.7	10.0	8.7	12.4	8.2	100.0
$4000–5999		31.4	18.2	13.9	12.4	10.9	10.6	2.7	100.0
$6000–7999		23.2	17.0	17.4	18.8	15.2	7.7	.7	100.0
$8000–9999		15.6	12.9	18.1	25.8	21.1	6.3	.3	100.0
$10,000–14,999		15.3	14.1	22.1	25.3	18.1	4.9	.2	100.0
$15,000 or more		29.0	22.8	23.4	13.8	6.9	3.1	1.1	100.0
Total		23.2	16.3	17.2	18.4	14.6	8.0	2.2	100.0

[a]From U.S. Bureau of the Census (1964). *Sources and structure of family income*, PC(2) 4C, Table 14.

Discussion

In this chapter we have described the differential earnings of American wives and their contribution to family income in relation both to the total size of family income and to the size of husband's income. In concluding this chapter I will suggest some further issues that ought to be investigated in order to have a more complete and coherent picture of the dynamics of wives' income determination and some fruitful directions for further research on the determinants and consequences of the earning patterns of American women.

We will consider first some needed extensions of the analysis of the determinants of wives' earnings.

Labor markets vary widely in the opportunities they provide for female workers. (For a measure of the opportunities for female employment, see Bowen and Finegan, 1969, 174.) One might speculate that in areas with relatively fewer employment opportunities for women, a woman would tend to earn less than would be expected both because the high level of supply with respect to demand would tend to drive wages down, and also because many relatively well-qualified women, being unable to secure employment commensurate with their qualifications, would accept lower-paying jobs. Under such conditions, well-qualified women ought to earn less, on average, and poorly-qualified women would have difficulty finding any employment at all, and would be disproportionately unemployed or not in the labor force. Unfortunately, with 1960 census data we can do very little analysis of labor market effects on earnings of women. Several innovations in the 1970 census data will make such analyses more feasible.

In connection with the low-income population, it would be informative to compare families who succeed in crossing a poverty threshold by means of the wife's increment to family income with those in a similar circumstance who do not, in relation to such factors as weeks worked, education, location of residence, family status, age, work history, husband's income history, and a variety of other factors (Lefcowitz, 1967).

We have not been able to assess the significance of different employment patterns in terms of hours worked per week and weeks worked per year in accounting for the variation in total earnings among different socioeconomic categories of the population. The lower income of wives of low-income husbands is a result of their lower hourly wage rate and their higher level of unemployment and of seasonal employment. Counterbalancing these tendencies is their tendency, when working, to work more hours per week.

With U.S. census data it is not possible to determine the number of hours worked during the previous year. Thus it is not possible, in any precise way, to decompose income differences in hours worked and hourly earnings. A further difficulty with U.S. census data is the inability to distinguish between part-time work that is voluntary and that which is imposed by the inability to find full-time work. Thus, even to the extent that we can decompose income into the two components (hours and wages), it is impossible to determine the desired responses of wives to varying economic circumstances or to estimate in any precise way the trade-off between income and "leisure."

The United States census provides no information on job tenure or work history. Indeed, there are few studies of any sort with work histories for women. If tenure or some indication of work and occupational history were available, we could make a crude division of women into those who have long or short tenure and/or work experience and those who have progressed through what one might reasonably call a career. Perhaps more useful would be a study following a cohort of women through time. What proportion of the population are in careers; what proportion of women are sporadic entrants into the labor force; what proportion of women remain in the labor force over long periods but never experience any occupational advancement or income increase, apart from compensation for inflation? More important than what proportion of women are found in each of these circumstances are the characteristics which differentiate women with sporadic labor force involvement from those with long-term involvement or differentiate those in careers from those in dead-end positions. For example, are women in careers mainly those who are childless? Are there career patterns for women with only high school or even less education, or are careers a phenomenon of college-educated women?

Another issue which we are unable to deal with using decennial census data is the effect of specialized job training on earnings. Do women with specialized training as secretary, beautician, practical nurse, etc., earn more than similar women without the specialized training? What differentiates the women who get such training from those who do not? Are women with nonacademic training employed in jobs in which the training is relevant? Some data on the incidence of nonacademic training of selected groups of female workers have been reported by Miller (1968), but none that would permit the assessment of the effects of training on earnings.

A number of consequences of the employment and earnings of wives are also deserving of further research.

1. Do consumption patterns vary within a total family income level, depending on whether the income is received entirely by the husband or by the husband and wife, and depending on the proportion received by the wife? For families in which the wife works to earn extra money for the family,

rather than out of sheer economic necessity, it would be interesting to investigate precisely how the consumption pattern differs from that of comparable families with the same husband's income but with the wife not employed.

Closely related to consumption patterns are patterns of time allocation. One might think of time allocation as related only to whether or not a women is employed and how many hours she works, and expenditures and consumption as related only to how much the women (and others in the family) earns. Such a division is not valid because expenditures of money can be substituted for expenditures of time. Thus meals can be prepared at home (expending time) or in a restaurant (expending money). Similarly, laundry can be done at home or sent out; housecleaning can be done by family members or domestic help can be hired. Thus, working women in more affluent families who are earning more need experience less disruption in their time economy than women in less affluent families who are earning less. Expressed in another way, the monetary costs of employment may be less for less affluent women than for more affluent women, because the latter substitute expenditures of money for expenditures of time.

Also relevant to the question, time allocation is the division of labor among members of the family. How does the husband's responsibility for home maintenance vary depending on whether or not the wife works (see Blood and Wolfe, 1960, Chap. 3), and depending on her earnings and whether the family can afford to buy household services and equipment?

2. Clearly the relative position of an individual family in the income distribution is affected by whether or not the wife is employed and contributing to family income. But what are the effects of the employment of wives on the overall income distribution? Apart from raising the mean family income, are there effects on the dispersion of the income distribution —i.e., on family income inequality? Various persons have suggested that the employment of wives tends to reduce income inequality (see Miller, 1966: 22; Thompson, 1968, Appendix). Whether or not this is the case depends on which wives are working disproproportionately, and how much money they are earning. We have shown that wives of low-income husbands are more likely to be working, but that working wives of higher-income husbands have higher incomes. The outcome on income inequality is an empirical question with no obvious general solution (Sweet, 1971).

3. Numerous references can be found to a supposed adverse effect of employment and especially of relatively high income of wives on marital happiness and marital stability. This is a particularly difficult thing to study in any causal sense because: (1) Women who work may also be women who are prone to unhappy marriages and marital instability, independent

of their employment. (2) Unhappily married women may seek escape from the confines of the family and seek employment because they are unhappily married. (3) Unhappily married women may be more likely to be employed and earning relatively large amounts of income in anticipation of the time when they will need to support themselves and their dependents.

But, methodological issues aside, if it could be documented that employment is not conducive to a happy and stable marriage, it would be useful to know whether the size of the wife's income relative to the husband's has any effect on marital happiness and stability (see Blood and Wolfe, 1960, Chap. 2).

4. Does maternal employment and income have an effect on the life chances of children? Does it raise the probability of continuation in school? Does it increase occupational achievement of children? Among the poor and near poor, to what extent do the earnings of mothers of high school-age children substitute for the child's earnings in maintaining the family's income, alleviating the need for dropping out of high school? Do maternal earnings finance college education? To my knowledge the only previous concern with maternal employment on life chances has been supposed adverse effects of maternal employment on the young child's social and psychological development. Although no definitive work has been done on that issue, little evidence has been found of any measurable effect (see Nye and Hoffman, 1963, Parts 2 and 4). Perhaps a more important effect on life chances operates through maternal income, rather than maternal employment per se. To the extent mother's education has an impact on child's achievement, it may be mediated through the higher rates of employment and higher earnings that higher education make possible.

5. Various economists have suggested that one important influence on fertility is the opportunity cost of children in terms of the woman's earnings foregone. Empirically it might be interesting to attempt to measure differentials in the opportunity cost of children among various subgroups in the population. Young black women (under age 25 or so), whether they are single or married, have extremely high levels of unemployment, low rates of labor force participation, and low earnings. I have suggested elsewhere that under these conditions there will seem to be considerably less economic incentive to avoid pregnancy than there would be under more favorable market conditions. Or, stated differently, it may be that the positive incentive of greater earnings is a more effective motivation to fertility control than is the negative incentive of low income and poverty. Freedman, Coombs, and Friedman (1966: 327–344) have also suggested that the work place may be a source of information on abortion (which is often illegal, although widely available), and presumably also contraception. The specification of

cause and effect relationships among fertility, employment, and other social characteristics such as education is, to say the least, most difficult.

6. How do the employment and earnings patterns of married women vary among industrial societies? In particular, how do the patterns in the United States compare with those in Eastern Europe where the employment rates are very high, where the legal position of women *vis-à-vis* work is more favorable, and where there are a number of institutional arrangements (e.g., child care services and maternity leaves) facilitating maternal employment (see Kurzynowski, 1967; Dodge, 1966; Klein, 1965a).

7. Our discussion has proceeded as if the chain of causation runs from husband's income to wife's earnings—i.e., that the wife's decision to enter the labor force and the number of hours she elects to work are influenced by the husband's income, and that husband's income is not being influenced by the wife's earnings. In general, that seems like an accurate representation of the process. In some cases, however, the reverse may also be the case. For example, whether or not he chooses to work and the amount of time a husband who has a minor disability chooses to work may be influenced by the wife's income. Similarly for men who are between the minimum retirement age and the mandatory age, the husband's labor force decision and his earning at a high rather than a low level. Empirically, it would be difficult to who experience unemployment may be more willing to extend their job search if their wives are employed and earning a substantial sum than if they are not.

In addition, there is the question of the effect of wife's employment and earnings on the acceptance of overtime employment and on secondary employment or "moonlighting" by the husband. All things being equal, a man would be less likely to seek or accept overtime employment or secondary employment if his wife were employed than if she were not and if she is earning at a high rather than a low level. Empirically, it would be difficult to figure out when both wife's employment and husband's overtime or secondary employment were responses to some unusual financial obligation or an unusually high consumption "standard," and to identify when there was substitution of wife's for husband's income.

8. More research is needed on the "costs of working" and their variation in relation to occupation and husband's income. Some of these costs, such as the taxes on the wife's earnings, the costs of transportation to and from work, the costs of substitute child care, and the cost of uniforms and other direct expenses for working equipment, are quite easy to investigate. Other expenses may be more difficult. When a family with a working wife buys a dishwasher or other consumer durable in order to save time spent on housework, it may be regarded as improving its standard of living or as simply substituting capital equipment for labor in order to adapt to the competing

demands on the wife's time. Similarly, the family with a working wife may eat more meals in restaurants than the family without the wife in the paid labor force. Is the family "better off" or is it simply substituting purchases in the market for home production? These are only two of many very difficult questions that will need to be confronted by researchers examining the costs of employment.

Black–White Differences in Wives' Earnings and Contributions to Family Income

While much is known about black–white differentials in family income, in the incidence of poverty, and in the earnings of males, very little attention has been given to racial differentials in the income of women and, more generally, to what the Census Bureau has termed "the sources of structure of family income," i.e., the composition of family income in terms of who in the family receives it and what sort of income it is.

The largest component of family income is the earnings of household heads. Family income also consists of nonearnings income, earnings of wives, earnings of children still living in the household, and earnings of other relatives living in the family. A family's relative position in the income distribution and the adequacy of that income in meeting the family's economic needs may be significantly influenced by the presence of members of the family other than the head and their earnings. In this chapter we will focus our attention on black–white differentials in the earnings of married women and the resultant differential contributions of wives to family income. More specifically, we shall concern ourselves with four questions.

1. How do a variety of individual and residential characteristics influence the earnings of black wives?
2. How do the earnings of nonwhite wives differ from those of "comparable" white wives?
3. How do the relative or proportional contributions of wives to family income differ between white and nonwhite families?

Variation in Earnings of Black Wives

In our analysis of employment probabilities, we found substantial interaction between race and such characteristics as education, family economic pressure, and age. In this chapter we will begin with an analysis of the determinants of earnings of black wives, and a comparison of these effects with those reported in Chapter 6 for white wives. These results are summarized in Table 7-1.

Income Adequacy

The earnings of black wives show a sharp monotonic increase with income adequacy. Of those women who work, given their level of education, age, and fertility level, those wives in families with greatest economic need earn considerably less than wives in the more affluent families. The relationship is similar in direction to that for whites, but much greater in slope. For example, for black wives there is a $550 differential between the earnings of black women in the .4–.7 and the 1.2–1.5 categories. For white wives this differential is only $200. Between 1.2–1.5 and 2.0–2.8, the differentials are $500 and $200.

We will withhold our discussion of these differentials until later in this chapter.

Education

For white women, annual earnings was positively related to education, with a particularly marked increase between 13 to 15 and 16 or more years of schooling. For black women the same pattern is found. The only differences are that the slope for black wives increases with increased education in the 12 and 13 to 15 intervals, whereas for white women it does not. Also, the earnings increment associated with completion of college is considerably larger for blacks than whites ($950 versus $650). In neither the case of black nor white women can we attribute education differences in annual earnings to differences in weeks worked. For blacks as for whites, more than half of the earnings differential by education can be attributed to the sorting of persons with different levels of educational attainment into major occupation groups. (Regression results are not shown.)

Age

For white women, annual earnings increased at a decelerating rate with age. Most of the age differential was attributable to differences in weeks worked, attributable largely to differences in the presence and ages of children in the household. For black wives, there is a substantial increase in

TABLE 7-1

Multiple Classification Analysis of the Earnings in 1959 of Black Husband-Present, Nonfarm Women[a]

		Net deviations	
	N	Including weeks worked	Excluding weeks worked
Income adequacy			
.0– .3	233	−385	−360
.4– .7	381	−261	−237
.8–1.1	295	56	48
1.2–1.5	199	290	272
1.6–1.9	83	478	428
2.0–2.8	51	835	755
2.9+	14	2304	2256
Education			
Less than 9	535	−317	−289
9–11	348	−65	−65
12	252	215	155
13–15	58	647	570
16+	63	1594	1676
Age			
14–19	45	−723	−301
20–24	117	−339	−139
25–29	167	14	79
30–34	204	161	140
35–39	191	14	0
40–44	188	172	98
45–49	142	62	−76
50–54	133	−86	−136
55–59	69	70	−23
Children ever born			
None	310	215	116
1	280	56	13
2	219	−18	−7
3	133	−222	−162
4	98	−68	56
5+	216	−195	−102
Weeks worked			
1–13	208	−847	
14–26	206	−606	
27–39	175	−165	
40–47	147	288	
48–49	76	485	
50–52	444	564	

[a]Analyses includes only women with some earnings.

annual earnings between ages 14–19 and 25–29, but almost no difference in earnings by age beyond ages 25–29. When weeks worked is controlled, the differential in earnings at the younger ages is cut from $800 to about $400, and the relationship beyond ages 25–29 becomes slightly negative. All that was said earlier about the absence of a career pattern of increasing earnings for white women applies even more strongly to black women.

Children Ever Born

The relationship between children ever born and earnings is less pronounced for blacks than for whites. Black women with no children ever born earn about $200 below the grand mean. As in the case of white women, when weeks worked is controlled, the relationship is greatly attenuated. Women with fewer children ever born work more weeks per year and consequently earn more.

Region

Wives living in the Northeast and North Central regions earn about $100–150 less than average (Table 7-2). When weeks worked is taken into account, these regional differentials tend to increase—with women in the Northeast and North Central regions earning at a rate of $200 above the mean and the Southern wives earning about $150 below the mean. Evidently women in the South work more weeks and women in the two Northern regions fewer weeks than the average. Women in the West earn at the grand mean when their shorter work year is taken into account.

Of more interest than these regional differences, however, are the differentials in earnings of black women in relation to region of origin and region of current residence (Table 7-3). Women who were born in the South

TABLE 7-2

Net Effects[a] of Region of Residence on the 1959 Earnings of Nonfarm Black Married Women Age 14–59

		Net deviations	
Region	*N*	Excluding weeks worked	Including weeks worked
Northeast	222	115	214
North Central	231	162	188
South	727	−74	−130
West	76	−117	47

[a]Net of the effects of income adequacy, education, age, and children ever born.

TABLE 7-3

Net Effects[a] of Southern Origin on the 1959 Earnings of Nonfarm Black Married Women Age 14–59

Origin by residence	*N*	Net deviations	
		Exluding weeks worked	Including weeks worked
Southern origin southern residence	702	−171	−206
Southern origin, nonsouthern residence	337	109	227
Nonsouthern origin southern residence	25	−272	−206
Nonsouthern origin nonsouthern residence	192	344	382

[a]Net of the effects of income adequacy, education, age, and children ever born.

and continue to live in the South are earning about $200 below the grand mean. Women who were born in the South and are currently living in another region are earning about $200 above the grand mean, while the indigenous non-Southern black women are earning about $350 above the mean. The remaining category of Northern-born women residing in the South at the time of enumeration are earning at about the same rate as the indigenous Southern residents. Southern origin and Southern residence each exert a substantial, independent effect on earnings. The Southern-born black woman makes up rather more than half of the disadvantage in earnings associated with Southern origin by leaving the South. She is still disadvantaged by about $200. These differentials cannot be attributed to differentials in weeks worked.

Since the meaning of regional differences in earnings themselves is never clear, it is even more difficult to interpret an effect associated with a change in regional residence. Several hypotheses suggest themselves.

1. The difference between the Southern-born Northern residents and the Southern-born Southern residents may be due to the fact that migration is selective, *ceteris paribus*, of persons who are more capable of earning relatively high earnings—perhaps the more intelligent, the more ambitious, the more committed.

2. It may be that the Southern nonfarm resident is more likely to be of rural origin than the Northern nonfarm women with Southern origin. This might be the case if migration tends to proceed in a stepwise fashion—Southern farm ⟶ Southern nonfarm ⟶ Northern urban. We have no data to confirm this hypothesis.

3. With reference to the differential between indigeneous Southerners and indigenous Northerners, it may be that real income is more equal than measured income because of price difference or because of a lesser need for large expenditures on warm clothing or heating of houses, or lower housing construction costs.

4. The difference may also be due to a difference in the quality of education which gives a person with a Southern education a lower earning capacity than a person with the same number of years of schooling with a non-Southern education. The Southern-born Northern resident may or may not have received her education in the North. Thus her earnings are intermediate between the two indigenous populations, reflecting the mix of Southern and Northern education.

5. The employment opportunities available to a woman in the North are greater than in the South, meaning that a non-Southern woman is better able to translate her education into occupational opportunities and thus into earnings.

Any one of these hypotheses seems plausible. None should be regarded as valid until further research is conducted in order to test them.

Size of Place of Residence

Earnings tend to be higher for black women living in larger communities than in smaller communities, just as they are for white women (Table 7-4). The major difference in the earnings pattern is that there was a rather smooth gradient for white women from small urbanized areas to the largest urbanized areas, while the relationship for black women is more discontinuous. Women in areas of less than 250,000 earn about $200 below the mean. Those in areas of 250,000 or more earn $100–200 above the mean.

TABLE 7-4

Net Effects[a] of Size of Urbanized Area on the 1959 Earnings of Nonfarm Black Married Women Age 14–59

		Net deviations	
Size of urbanized area	*N*	Excluding weeks worked	Including weeks worked
Not in urbanized area	379	−315	−220
UA—Less than 100,000	54	−136	−109
UA—100,000–249,999	123	−304	−253
UA—250,000–499,999	75	147	56
UA—500,000 and over	625	246	186

[a]Net of the effects of income adequacy, education, age, and children ever born.

Again, as in the case of regional differences, it is difficult to interpret these differences. The explanation may lie in differences in the unmeasured characteristics of the persons themselves, in differences in the occupational opportunity structure, or in differences in the money wage that have no connection with the real wage.

Age at First Marriage

As was the case for white wives, earnings do not vary substantially by age at first marriage (Table 7-5). Women married between the ages of 21 and 29 earn about $150 more than other women. Women marrying at age 30 and above earn more than other women, but this differential is due entirely to a greater number of weeks worked.

Number of Marriages

The earnings of women in intact first marriages are about $250 below the mean, while those of women married more than once, married to a man married more than once are about $200 above the mean (Table 7-6). This differential of about $450 is reduced to less than $150 when weeks worked is controlled. The earnings of wives for the other two groups of couples where either husband or wife has been married more than once are intermediate between the intact first marriage couples and the couples in which both spouses have been married more than once.

Components of Wife's Contribution to Family Income

The mean size of a wife's annual contribution to family income in any population subgroup can be usefully decomposed into two components:

TABLE 7-5

Net Effects[a] of Age at Marriage on the 1959 Earnings of Nonfarm Black Married Women Age 14–59

		Net deviations	
Age at marriage	*N*	Excluding weeks worked	Including weeks worked
Under 18	340	−25	−75
18–20	339	−14	−32
21–24	275	113	120
25–29	171	−51	−61
30 and over	131	−66	104

[a]Net of the effects of income adequacy, education, age, and children ever born.

TABLE 7-6

Net Effects[a] of Marital History on the 1959 Earnings of Nonfarm Black Married Women Age 14–59

Marital history	N	Net deviations	
		Excluding weeks worked	Including weeks worked
Husband and wife married once	852	−291	−19
Wife married once, husband married more than once	128	−41	−6
Husband married once, wife married more than once	127	56	12
Both married more than once	149	154	104

[a]Net of the effects of income adequacy, education, age, and children ever born.

Mean Contribution of Wives to Family Income	=	Proportion of Wives With Income	×	Mean Income of Wives With Income

The second component may be further decomposed:

Mean Contribution of Wives to Family Income	=	Proportion of Wives with Income	×	Mean Hourly Wage	×	Mean Weeks Worked per Year	×	Mean Hours Worked per Week

It would be instructive to make detailed comparisons of the white and nonwhite populations in terms of these components. Unfortunately, data that would permit a complete decomposition are not available in the census. Specifically, we cannot decompose income earned into hours worked and wage rates, because census income data refer to the previous year, while the only available hours data refer to the week prior to the census. We can, however, make comparisons of the white and nonwhite proportions with income, distributions of weeks worked in 1959, and distributions of hours worked during the week prior to the census.

At the time of the 1960 census, the employment rate of white wives under age 60 was 31.0%, while that of nonwhite wives was 39.5%. For wives with no children, the color differential was rather small (48.6 versus 42.6, or 14%), while for mothers, the nonwhite rate exceeds the white by more than a third (34.2 and 25.5). The differential is even greater for mothers of preschool-age children where the nonwhite rate exceeds the white by 66% (27.7 and 16.7). The relative figures for proportions with income in 1959 are of approximately the same magnitude as these on current employment.

TABLE 7-7

Mean Number of Weeks Worked by Black and Nonblack Wives Working in 1959 in Relation to Family Status[a]

	Black	*Nonblack*
Husband present with children under 18	31.3	32.4
Youngest 0–2	26.5	24.6
3–5	33.6	32.1
6–11	35.8	34.3
12–17	33.6	38.8
No children under 18	37.5	39.9
Age 14–29	35.5	40.5
30–44	37.1	41.3
45–59	38.6	40.1

[a]From 1/1000 tabulations.

Table 7-7 shows the distribution of the black and nonblack married women by weeks worked. Black women with work experience in 1959 worked somewhat fewer weeks than their white counterparts. Among wives with children, black women worked an average of about one week fewer in 1959 than white women. Actually, for mothers of children under the age of 12, black mothers worked slightly more weeks than white mothers, while for women with older children, the differential favors the nonblacks. Among wives with no children under age 18, blacks worked about 2.5 fewer weeks than whites.

White wives are more likely to work a full year or a very small portion of the year, while the black distribution is more heavily concentrated in the middle ranges (Table 7-8). The lack of concentration at the low end of the scale probably reflects the greater economic needs of black families, while the lack of concentration at the upper end reflects the disadvantaged position on the labor market—discrimination and lower levels of education—

TABLE 7-8

Distribution by Weeks Worked of White and Nonwhite Urban Wives[a]

	Nonwhite	White
Less than 26	30.0	31.2
27–49	30.5	27.8
50–52	39.5	41.0
Total	100.0	100.0

[a]From 1/1000 tabulations.

and the irregular patterns of employment in industries in which black women are concentrated. Even well-educated black women may be disadvantaged in terms of weeks worked as a result of their heavy concentration in school teaching.

Employed black women are much more likely to be working part time than are employed white women. Overall, 35% of the nonwhite and 27% of the white married women under age 60 are employed part time (less than 35 hours). The color differential for wives with children is much smaller than that for wives with none (Table 7-9). In an earlier chapter we showed that this differential can be attributed to a substantially higher proportion of black part-time workers who, although currently working part time, desire full-time employment.

Morgan *et al.* (1962) report that the differential in hourly earnings between white and nonwhite wives is $.30 ($1.46 versus $1.16). When adjusted for differential composition with respect to education, husband's income, age, occupation, work experience, and several other characteristics, the differential is reduced to $.11. Nonwhite wives worked 283 fewer hours per year than white wives. When adjusted for a variety of relevant characteristics, the differential increases slightly to 309 hours. These figures would suggest that the average aggregate contribution to family income of white wives with income would be $2009, while for nonwhite wives it would be $1268. Apart from this Survey Research Center study, I know of no data on color differences in wage rates or full-time annual salaries.

Differentials in Wife's Earnings

With available data it is considerably easier to compare the outcome of these three component processes than the processes themselves. How do the annual earnings of black wives compare with those of nonblack wives?

A substantially higher proportion of nonwhite than white wives received

TABLE 7-9

Percentage of Employed Wives Working Part Time, by Family Status and Color[a]

	Nonwhite	White
Total	35.1	26.6
With children under 18	34.4	20.1
Without children under 18	35.7	31.7

[a]From 1/1000 tabulations.

income in 1959 (52% versus 43%). Wide differentials favoring nonwhite wives exist in the age groups 25–44 and 45–64, but among wives under age 25, nonwhite wives were less likely to have received income. This probably reflects both a particularly disadvantaged labor market position of young nonwhite women and also shorter interval between marriage and the birth of the first child, including the greater rate of illegitimate births (Sweet, 1968; U.S. Census Bureau, 1968).

Overall, nonwhite wives with income had a median income of $928 in

TABLE 7-10

Income Distributions for White and Nonwhite Wives, by Age (Percentage Distribution)[a]

	Under 65		Under 25		25–44		45–64	
	All wives	Wives with income	All wives	Wives with income	All wives	Wives with income	All wives	Wives with income
White								
None	56.9		48.0		59.5		56.1	
$1–499	9.9	23.0	13.6	26.2	9.4	23.2	9.3	21.2
$500–999	5.7	13.2	8.0	15.4	5.2	12.8	5.9	13.4
$1000–1499	4.4	10.2	6.1	11.7	4.1	10.1	4.2	9.6
$1500–1999	3.6	8.4	4.9	9.4	3.4	8.4	3.6	8.2
$2000–2999	7.5	17.4	9.4	18.1	7.0	17.2	7.6	17.3
$3000–4999	9.5	22.0	9.4	18.1	9.4	23.2	9.7	22.1
$5000 or more	2.5	5.8	.6	1.2	2.1	5.2	3.6	8.2
Total	100.0	100.0	100.0	100.1	100.1	100.1	100.0	100.0
$3000 or more	12.0	27.8	10.0	19.3	11.5	28.4	13.3	30.3
Less than $1000	72.5	36.2	69.6	41.6	74.1	36.0	71.3	34.6
Median		$1714		$1357		$1732		$1854
Nonwhite								
None	47.6		52.5		46.3		47.6	
$1–499	17.7	33.7	21.4	45.1	16.1	30.0	18.8	35.9
$500–999	10.0	19.0	9.0	18.9	9.5	17.7	11.3	21.6
$1000–1499	6.3	12.0	5.4	11.4	6.5	12.1	6.3	12.0
$1500–1999	4.3	8.2	3.4	7.2	4.7	8.8	4.0	7.6
$2000–2999	6.4	12.2	4.4	9.3	7.3	13.6	5.6	10.7
$3000–4999	6.4	12.2	3.6	7.6	7.9	14.7	5.0	9.5
$5000 or more	1.4	2.7	.3	.6	1.6	3.0	1.4	2.7
Total	100.1	100.0	100.0	100.1	99.9	99.9	100.0	100.0
$3000 or more	7.8	14.9	3.9	8.2	9.5	17.7	6.4	12.2
Less than $1000	75.3	52.7	82.9	64.0	71.9	47.7	77.7	57.5
Median		$ 928		$ 630		$1095		$ 826

[a] From U.S. Bureau of the Census (1964). *Sources and structure of family income*, PC(2) 4C, Table 17.

comparison to the white median of \$1714 (Table 7-10). About 8% of all nonwhite wives, and 12% of all white wives, earned more than \$3000 in 1959. Among wives with income, 15% of the nonwhite and 28% of the white wives received more than \$3000. The nonwhite wives are heavily concentrated at the low end of the distribution. Of nonwhite wives with income, 53% received less than \$1000 in 1959, and 34% received less than \$500. The comparable figures for white wives are 36% and 23%.

Sixty-four percent of the nonwhite wives under 25 received less than \$1000 in income, while for white wives the figure is 41%. In the age range 25–44, the nonwhite distribution is closer to that of white wives than in either the younger or the older age groups. The earnings of white wives increase with age, while for nonwhite wives, women 45–64 earn less than younger women, being much more likely to earn less than \$1000 and much less likely to earn more than \$3000 than nonwhite women 25–44.

There are at least four classes of factors operating on our components (hourly wage, weeks worked per year, and hours worked per week) which may contribute to the differential.

1. The nonwhite population has less education than the white population. Education is quite clearly related to earnings via its providing access to better-paying employment opportunities. In terms of our components of annual earnings, lower education is associated with hourly earnings, shorter work weeks, and fewer weeks per year.

At every education level, black wives earn less per year than nonblack wives (Table 7-11). Differentials are wider, both absolutely and relatively, for women with less than 9 years of schooling than for women with more education. Black women in the lowest education category earned only 54% of the money that comparably educated white women earn or, in dollar terms, they earn an average \$820 less per year per woman. College-educated black wives have earnings that are nearly equal to those of white women (98%, or \$78 difference).

Composition by education level accounts for only a small part of the black–white differential in earnings. If we apply the black education-specific earnings to the white education composition, the earnings differential is reduced from \$886 to \$655. (For women with children, the effect of standardizing on education reduces the differential from \$599 to \$372 while for women with no children the differential is reduced from \$1056 to \$863.)

2. However, whatever the level of educational attainment, the nonwhite population may be less effective in translating education into occupational opportunities. That is, at any educational level there may be a higher proportion of nonwhites than whites in occupations that are less than commensurate with the educational level.

TABLE 7-11

Comparisons of Black and Nonblack Earnings of Husband-Present Women in Relation to Education (Wife under Age 60)[a]

	Black			Nonblack			Absolute difference (nonblack–black)		Relative difference (black/nonblack)	
Education	*N*	Percentage with earnings	Earnings per earner ($)	*N*	Percentage with earnings	Earnings per earner ($)	Percentage with earnings	Earnings per earner ($)	Percentage with earnings	Earnings per earner ($)
0–8 years	1111	.51	966	6762	.35	1786	−.16	820	1.44	.54
9–11 years	730	.52	1365	7010	.42	2009	−.10	644	1.23	.68
12 years	489	.56	1671	11241	.48	2390	−.08	719	1.16	.70
13–15 years	115	.54	2348	3165	.48	2653	−.06	305	1.19	.88
16+ years	74	.88	3437	1824	.54	3515	−.34	78	1.62	.98
Total	2519	.53	1387	30002	.43	2273	−.10	886	1.22	.61

[a]From 1/1000 tabulations.

If black education is inferior in some sense to white education, it might produce a lower efficiency of conversion of education into occupational level, and thus lower income. Probably more important than inferior quality education is labor market discrimination. A black woman with similar qualifications has more difficult access than a white woman to the more desirable jobs, and she is less likely to move up in the occupational hierarchy as she gains work experience. The inferior occupational options available to black women affect their earnings not only via lower hourly earnings, but also via higher levels of unemployment and job turnover, which may reduce weeks worked per year and hours worked per week.

While no formal attempt will be made here to quantitatively decompose educational differences into the differentials in the translation of education into occupation and the differential in occupation-specific earnings, we show in Table 7-12 some selected measures of the occupational distributions of various educational levels for all women and nonwhite women. It is quite clear that nonwhite women at all levels of education short of college are concentrated in substantial proportions in lower occupation groups than their white counterparts.

Among high school graduates, for example, 59% of the nonwhite and only 26% of the total are found in operative, service, and laborer occupations. There are undoubtedly also differences within these broad classes—e.g., within service occupations, nonwhite women are concentrated in private household service.

The age patterns are particularly interesting with respect to the black–white differential. Notice that almost 80% of all nonwhite women 20–24 within 12 years of education, in comparison with 23% of all such white women, are in operative, service and laborer occupations. For older women the proportions are more similar to one another: 27% total and 59% nonwhite. Whether this is a pattern unique to the period around 1960 or evidence of a long-term difficulty that young black women have had in entering the labor force is not known.

3. The occupation-specific hourly income and/or the occupation-specific hours or weeks worked may be less for black women than for white women. We will make no attempt to examine this question.

4. Nonwhite women may be concentrated geographically in areas where employment opportunities are scarce relative to the supply of potential workers. This may have several consequences: it may drive down wages of women in relatively low paying jobs; it may reduce rates of employment of women with relatively low earning capacity; and it may result in the employment of black women in jobs that are below their skill level as indexed by education. We cannot investigate these effects with available data.

TABLE 7-12

Selected Occupational Measures by Education, Age, and Color: Females, 1960[a]

Age	Total	Nonwhite
Education—8 years	*Percentage employed in service and laborer occupations*	
25 and older	35.7	68.9
22–24	38.8	72.2
30–34	37.0	66.8
35–44	34.0	67.7
45–54	33.3	70.5
Education—12 years	*Percentage employed in operatives, service and laborer occupations*	
25 and older	26.1	59.1
22–24	23.0	78.7
30–34	27.4	58.9
35–44	27.7	58.8
45–54	24.1	63.7
Education— 13–15 years	*Percentage employed in professional and managerial occupations*	
25 and older	36.5	22.8
22–24	35.3	16.5
30–34	34.1	21.0
35–44	31.5	19.8
45–54	38.7	26.5
Education—16 years	*Percentage employed in professional and managerial occupations*	
25 and older	73.6	75.3
22–24	77.7	77.9
30–34	72.1	74.5
35–44	71.9	75.7
45–54	74.9	75.9

[a] From U.S. Bureau of the Census (1964). *Educational attainment*, PC(2) 5B, Table 8.

Income Differential in Relation to Husband's Income

How do incomes received by black and white wives compare in relation to husband's income?

The greater the income of the husband, the lower the probability that the wife received income. For nonwhite wives, the pattern is basically similar to the white, except that the slope is much less steep (Table 7-13). Middle- and high-income nonwhite husbands are more likely to have working wives than are white husbands with the same income level. The difference amounts to about two percentage points at $3000–$3999 and reaches a maximum of about 11 percentage points at incomes of $7000–$7999 (white 36%, nonwhite 47%).

Consistent with previously reported findings is the result that nonwhite wives under the age of 25 are less likely to have had income than are white wives. This differential is eliminated at husband's incomes of $5000 or more. Nonwhite women 25–44 and 45–64 are considerably more likely to have had income in 1959 than their white counterparts at every husband's income level. The differences range from three percentage points to about 14 percentage points. The widest differentials are found among women 25–44 married to men with $5000 or more of income.

Table 7-13 also makes comparisons between the average income of white and nonwhite wives in relation to husband's income and age. Overall, nonwhite wives with income receive an average of $669 less than their white counterparts. At low levels of husband's income, nonwhite wives earn considerably less than white wives. For example, nonwhite wives of men earning $2000–$2999 earn an average of $634 less than white wives. Expressed in relative terms, the nonwhite wives receive only 69% as much income as white wives (Table 7–13, panel 3). As husband's income increases, the ratio of nonwhite to white income increases. At husband's income level $6000–$6999, the average income of nonwhite wives exceeds that of white wives by 14%, or $318. The same general pattern of an increasing ratio of nonwhite to white incomes of wives as husband's income increases is present for each age group.

The relative pattern of income just described indicates that a nonwhite family with a low-earning and/or irregularly employed husband is probably much less likely to succeed in achieving an adequate income level as a result of contribution of the wife. The nonwhite family is more likely to use that strategy (i.e., the proportion of wife's income is greater), but less likely to succeed.

How can we "explain" the lower income of nonwhite wives in families with great economic need?

1. Nonwhite wives are likely to have less education and thus lower earning potential than their white counterparts. But at any given low husband's income level, it might not be unreasonable to expect that both the husband and his wife will be *better educated* if the couple is black than if they are white. This might be the case simply because black men earn less, given their education, than do white men. It takes more education, on the average, to achieve

TABLE 7-13. *White–Nonwhite Comparisons of Earnings of Wives in Relation to Husband's Income: United States, 1960*[a]

	White				Nonwhite				Average per recipient	
Husband's income ($)	*N* (thousands)	Percentage	Proportion of wives with income	Average income per recipient ($)	*N*	Percentage	Proportion of wives with income	Average income per recipient ($)	Absolute differential	Relative differential
Wife under age 65										
None	517	1.5	.44	2606	97	3.1	.48	1521	1085	.58
Less than 1000	1461	4.3	.49	1798	480	15.2	.56	845	953	.47
1000–1999	2237	6.5	.49	1789	498	15.7	.57	974	815	.54
2000–2999	2880	8.4	.49	1868	583	18.4	.54	1234	634	.66
3000–3999	3963	11.6	.48	2042	530	16.8	.51	1651	391	.81
4000–4999	5032	14.7	.47	2205	480	13.9	.50	2052	153	.93
5000–5999	5601	16.4	.44	2313	294	9.3	.50	2296	17	.99
6000–6999	4073	11.9	.40	2345	119	3.8	.50	2663	−318	1.14
7000–9999	5258	15.4	.36	2356	92	2.9	.48	2744	−388	1.16
10,000–14,999	1986	5.8	.31	2403	20	.6	.40	3210	−807	1.34
15,000 +	1235	3.6	.32	2611	10	.3	.37	2856	−245	1.09
Total	34,243	100.0	.43	2 179	3163	100.0	.52	1512	667	.69
Wife under age 25										
None			.46	1897			.38	1440	457	.76
Less than 1000			.54	1494			.50	687	807	.46
1000–1999			.59	1576			.49	815	761	.52
2000–2999			.56	1584			.47	1022	562	.65
3000–3999			.55	1707			.46	1330	377	.78
4000–4999			.52	1858			.47	1561	297	.84
5000–5999			.48	1938			.47	1727	211	.89
6000–6999			.44	1958			.46	1872	86	.96
7000–9999			.40	2004			.47	1753	251	.87
10,000–14,999			.39	2295			.34	2525	−230	1.10
15,000 +			.41	2172			.65	1338	834	.62

None	.45	2633	.49	1686	947	.64
Less than 1000	.47	2024	.56	900	1124	.44
1000–1999	.46	1958	.58	1010	948	.52
2000–2999	.47	1964	.56	1271	693	.65
3000–3999	.48	2079	.52	1710	369	.82
4000–4999	.46	2195	.52	2154	41	.98
5000–5999	.43	2247	.52	2383	−136	1.06
6000–6999	.39	2244	.51	2677	−433	1.19
7000–9999	.33	2206	.48	2754	−548	1.25
10,000–14,999	.28	2162	.40	3227	−1065	1.49
15,000+	.27	2316	.35	2762	−446	1.19
Total	.40	2 174	.54	1664	510	.77
Wife aged 45–64						
None	.43	2717	.48	1387	1330	.51
Less than 1,000	.50	1761	.57	838	923	.48
1000–1999	.47	1787	.55	991	796	.55
2000–2999	.46	1948	.54	1276	672	.66
3000–3999	.46	2213	.51	1667	546	.75
4000–4999	.45	2419	.47	1958	461	.81
5000–5999	.44	2589	.45	2216	373	.86
6000–6999	.43	2644	.49	2844	−200	1.08
7000–9999	.40	2668	.47	2952	−284	1.11
10,000–14,999	.36	2708	.42	3260	−552	1.20
15,000+	.37	2868	.37	3330	−462	1.16
Total	.44	2349	.52	1389	960	.59

[a] From U.S. Bureau of the Census (1964). *Sources and structure of family income*, PC(2) 4C, Table 17.

TABLE 7-14

Education Distribution of Husband-Present Women with Earnings in 1959, by Income of Husband and Race[a]

	Husband's income										
Education	None	$1–999	$1000–1999	$2000–2999	$3000–3999	$4000–4999	$5000–5999	$6000–6999	$7000–9999	$10,000+	Total
					Nonblack						
Less than 9 years	37.6	34.9	30.4	30.0	27.7	20.4	15.5	13.7	9.2	5.8	19.6
9–11 years	21.6	24.0	25.7	25.6	23.1	25.1	24.2	21.8	20.3	11.8	23.0
12 years	25.3	25.5	28.8	31.4	36.6	40.3	43.2	44.9	42.2	39.5	38.9
13–15 years	10.5	9.9	8.6	8.6	8.6	10.0	11.4	11.3	16.3	20.1	11.4
16+ years	4.9	5.7	6.5	4.4	4.0	4.2	5.6	8.3	12.0	22.8	7.1
Total	99.9	100.0	100.0	100.0	100.0	100.0	99.9	100.0	100.0	100.0	100.0
					Black						
Less than 9 years	51.8	61.0	54.1	48.4	41.3	28.1	23.2	29.7	20.6	40.0	43.4
9–11 years	25.9	26.8	26.2	27.8	24.5	34.6	27.2	18.9	23.5	40.0	27.4
12 years	7.4	8.5	14.0	17.2	24.0	25.9	32.0	29.7	35.3	—	19.8
13–15 years	7.4	1.8	3.0	3.4	3.4	5.9	11.2	8.1	2.9	20.0	4.5
16+ years	7.4	1.8	2.6	3.1	6.7	5.4	6.4	13.5	17.6	—	4.8
Total	99.9	99.9	99.9	99.9	99.9	99.9	100.0	99.9	99.9	100.0	99.9

[a]From 1/1000 tabulations.

a given level of income if one is black rather than white. The data (in Table 7-14) show that this is not the case. Black women with earnings who are married to men with low earnings are much more likely than white women to have less than 9 years of education, and much less likely to have 12 or more years of schooling. Part of the differential in earnings of wives of low-income men is due to lower black education.

2. Black women face racial discrimination that denies them access to the same employment opportunities available to white women with similar levels of education. At low levels of education, earnings are considerably lower for nonwhites than whites. This, we have shown, is due in part to differential ability to translate education into occupation.

3. Poorly educated nonwhite wives of low-earning husbands are concentrated in relatively few urban areas, while their white counterparts are more diffused through the entire society. This competition for limited low-skill opportunities may result in a lower level of wages and higher level of unemployment (i.e., fewer weeks worked) in areas of high nonwhite population concentration.

4. Within any urban area the residences of nonwhite families are disproportionately in the central city and in the center of the central city. White families are more diffused through the area. To the extent that employment opportunities for persons with few marketable skills are diffused throughout the area, the white population would have greater spatial access to opportunities for which there were relatively fewer competitors.

The explanation for the relatively greater earnings of black wives of men earning over $6000 per year is complex. Here we shall suggest several possible factors and present suggestive evidence for them, but we shall not attempt to sort out their effects.

1. Since black men are disadvantaged in terms of education-specific earnings, it is not inconceivable that wives of black men earning $6000–$8000 actually are better educated than their white counterparts. That is, suppose that a black man earning $6000 has a mean educational attainment that is two years greater than a white man with similar earnings. Their wives may also have 2 years or so more education and thus greater earnings.

Table 7–14, however, shows that at every husband's income level, including $6000 and over, black wives with income are more likely than white wives to have less than 9 years of education. For example, 30% of the black wives and 14% of the nonblack wives of men earning $6000–$6999 have 8 or fewer years of education. At the other end of the distribution, persons with college education, the black proportions are considerably lower than the white for husband's income less than $3000, but in the range $3000–$6999 there is rather little difference. We would conclude that we cannot

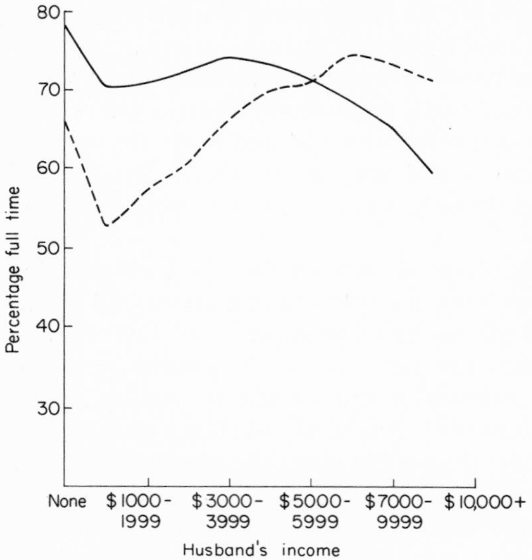

Figure 7-1. *Proportion of wives working full time by husband's income for white and nonwhite wives. From U.S. Bureau of the Census (1963) "Persons by Family Characteristics," Tables 10a, 11, (---): Nonwhite; (—) white.*

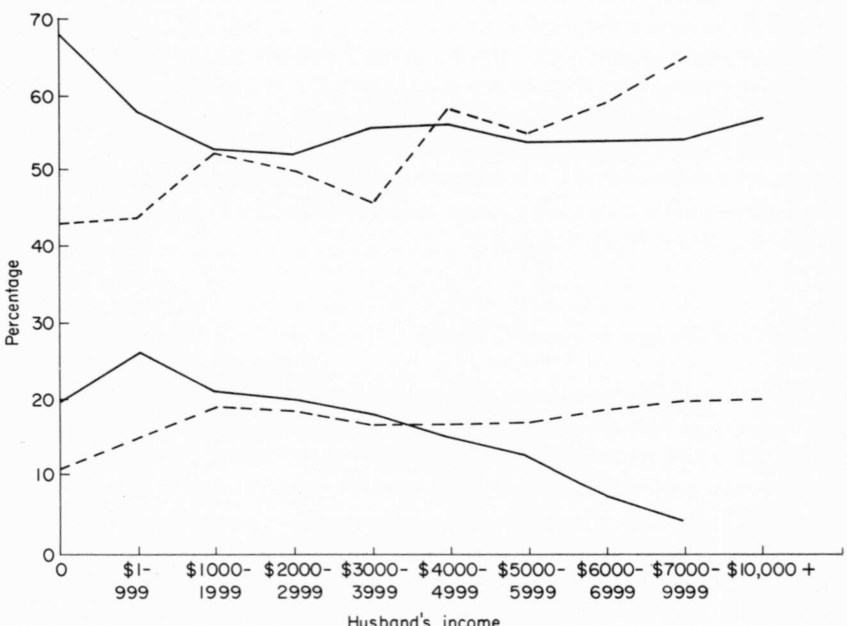

Figure 7-2. *Weeks worked by husband's income for black (---) and nonblack (—) wives. From 1/1000 tabulations. Upper curves: Percentage working 40 or more weeks in 1959 (percentage of those working at all). Lower curves: Percentage working 1–13 weeks.*

explain the superior earnings of black wives of men earning $6000 or more in terms of their greater educational achievement.

2. Employed wives of black men with relatively high incomes work more hours per week and more weeks per year than their white counterparts. Both weeks worked and hours worked decline with husband's income for white women, but increase with husband's income for black women. See Figs. 7-1 and 7-2. The same pattern holds at each age, except for women under age 18.

3. One possible reason for item (2) above might be that black wives of men with high incomes may have lower fertility levels than their white counterparts. A 1960 study showed that this is likely (Whelpton *et al.* 1966: 324). In addition to working more hours per year, the lower-fertility nonwhite women may have greater work experience and job tenure.

4. Apart from differentials in fertility, it is likely that black men earning $6000 or more are somewhat older than white men. They are probably considerably more likely to be in their thirties and forties than in their twenties. Thus their wives are less likely to have preschool-age children, and more likely to work full time and full year. Even if the black family does have preschool-age children, the wives are more likely to be employed and probably more likely to be employed full time.

5. Nonwhite men earning high incomes are likely to live in areas where potential earnings for well-educated women are relatively high. They are probably under-represented in the South, in small towns, and in rural areas.

6. Finally, it is possible that we are being deceived by the lack of correspondence between the black and nonwhite population. "Other nonwhite" wives of men earning large incomes may be, in large proportion, members of other nonwhite races.

Relative Contribution to Family Income

The relative size of the wife's contribution to family income is dependent on a variety of factors. The larger the proportion of wives working, the greater the wife's contribution. Nonwhite wives are more likely to be working than white wives, with particularly wide differentials for mothers of young children, the well educated, and wives of relatively high-income husbands. Similarly, the greater the income of working wives, the greater their contribution to family income. On the average, black women earn only about two-thirds the income of white women, although when education is controlled, the differential is reduced somewhat.

In terms of relative contribution of wives to family income, the greater the income of the husband, the less the wife's contribution, given the ab-

TABLE 7-15

Median Income by Education, Color, and Sex, for Population 25 and Older in 1960[a]

	Female		Male		Female/Male		Nonwhite/Total	
Education	Total ($)	Non-white ($)	Total ($)	Non-white ($)	Total	Non-white	Male	Female
None	687	624	1438	1053	.48	.59	.73	.91
1–4 years	733	667	1839	1554	.40	.43	.84	.91
5–7 years	897	799	3066	2358	.29	.34	.77	.89
8 years	1120	970	3892	2911	.29	.33	.75	.87
9–11 years	1616	1196	4846	3270	.33	.37	.67	.74
12 years	2184	1732	5441	3741	.40	.46	.69	.79
13–15 years	2408	2166	5978	4039	.40	.54	.68	.90
16 years	3322	3403	7388	4447	.45	.77	.60	1.02
17+ years	4664	4402	7971	5465	.66	.80	.69	.94

[a]From U.S. Bureau of the Census (1964). *Educational attainment*, PC(2) 5B, Tables 6 and 7.

solute dollar contribution. Similarly, the greater the contribution of other family members, the lower the wife's relative contribution. Nonwhite women may be more likely to make large relative contributions to family income than white women simply because their husbands' incomes are lower than the white women's.

Table 7-15 shows the median incomes of men and women in relation to color and education, and the ratio of the nonwhite to total median incomes within each education–sex category. Clearly the total earnings of nonwhite women are closer to those for all women than is the case for men. The ratios are concentrated in the range .68–.75 for men, while for women only one of the ratios falls below .75, and they are concentrated around .90. One might expect, therefore, that nonwhite wives would tend to make a higher relative contribution to family income than white wives if the education of spouse is held constant.

But the relationship between the education of husbands and wives also differs between the white and nonwhite populations. If we divide education into the eight categories shown in Table 7-16, we find that for white married couples (married *once*, between 1950 and 1960), 25% of the wives are in a higher education category than their husbands, while for nonwhites the corresponding figure is 38%. (In 36% and 25%, respectively, the husband is in a higher category than the wife.) Looked at in another way, nonwhite wives in every education category are less likely than white wives to have husbands with as much or more education than they have themselves. The differentials are particularly pronounced at education levels of 12 years or more

TABLE 7-16

Percentage of Wives with Husbands in the Same or Higher Education Category as Themselves: Husband-Present Couples Married Once, 1950–1960 Marriage Cohorts: by Education[a]

Wife's education	White	Nonwhite
0–4 years	100.0	100.0
5–7 years	89.6	83.3
8 years	83.8	69.0
9–11 years	80.4	68.4
12 years	73.3	53.7
13–15 years	70.4	42.3
16 years	72.0	46.0
17+ years	57.4	45.1

[a]From U.S. Bureau of the Census (1964), *Marital status*, PC(2) 4E, Table 11.

Thus, if we randomly select a working wife, the probability is higher if she is nonwhite than if she is white that her husband has inferior education. We would therefore expect that, given her education level, she will earn a higher share of family income if she is nonwhite than if she is white.

Income contribution of other relatives depends on their presence in the family, the proportion of such other persons with income, and the average income per other relative with income. While I was unable to find any data which show the proportion of husband–wife families that include "other" adult relatives, it is possible to compute the mean number of other relatives by family income and color (Table 7-17). At every family income level, nonwhite families have a greater average number of other relatives. This is true both of children over age 17 and relatives other than children. Particularly great is the differential for families with incomes of $6000 or more, where there is in nonwhite families an average of considerably more than one-half of an other relative per family.

It is impossible to conclude what this means causally. Families with other adults are more likely to have more earners, and hence higher family incomes. Families with higher incomes can also afford to take in other relatives who are unable to support themselves adequately. Whatever the causal ordering, we can conclude quite clearly that the greater number of other relatives among black families is at least in part responsible for their greater contribution to family income.

Overall, nonwhite wives contribute a considerably larger share of aggre-

TABLE 7-17

Mean Number of Adult "Other Relatives" per Husband–Wife Family, by Family Income[a]

Family income	Total	Nonwhite
Mean number of children 18 and over		
Less than $2000	.109	.177
$2000–3999	.113	.185
$4000–5999	.110	.213
$6000–7999	.114	.294
$8000 +	.286	.414
Mean number of "other relatives" per husband–wife family, excluding children 18 and over		
Less than $2000	.030	.069
$2000–3999	.036	.092
$4000–5999	.037	.134
$6000–7999	.048	.212
$8000 +	.094	.450

[a] From U.S. Bureau of the Census (1964). *Persons by family characteristics*, PC(2) 4B, Table 12-B.

gate family income than white wives (17% versus 12%) (see Table 7-18). In addition, other relatives contribute a larger proportion of nonwhite than white family income (12% versus 7%). As a result, the husband's contribution is 71% in nonwhite and 80% in white, husband–wife families.

At every family income level except the lowest, the wife's contribution makes up a larger share of total income. Particularly pronounced is the differential in the family income range $6000–$14,999, where the nonwhite wife's share is 7–8% greater than the white wife's.

Perhaps the most dramatic differential appearing in Table 7-18 is the size of the contribution of "other" nonwhite family members in the middle and upper income brackets. In the family income range $6000 to $6999, for example, 10% of the nonwhite and 4% of the white family income is con-contributed by "others." Further disaggregation reveals that these differentials result both from greater contributions from children and from other relatives.

At every level of husband's income, nonwhite families are more likely to have two or more earners. The differentials are particularly wide at husband's income in excess of $6000. Nonwhite families, similarly, are more likely to have three or more earners (14% for nonwhites, 10% for whites), although,

TABLE 7-18

Proportion of Family Income Earned by Various Family Members by Size of Family Income for Husband–Wife Families, Head 25–64 years of Age: For Total and Nonwhite Population[a]

	Total population				Nonwhite population			
Family income ($)	Head	Wife	Others	Total	Head	Wife	Others	Total
Less than 1000	70.9	18.5	10.7	100.0	75.7	17.2	7.1	100.0
1000–1999	81.0	13.0	6.0	100.0	77.0	15.8	7.1	100.0
2000–2999	83.4	11.8	4.8	100.0	82.0	12.5	5.6	100.0
3000–3999	86.0	10.3	3.7	100.0	82.6	12.2	5.1	100.0
4000–4999	87.4	9.2	3.4	100.0	81.9	12.1	6.0	100.0
5000–5999	88.0	8.7	3.3	100.0	79.5	13.8	6.7	100.0
6000–6999	85.5	10.5	4.0	100.0	72.0	18.5	9.5	100.0
7000–9999	79.0	14.7	6.3	100.0	62.9	23.5	13.6	100.0
10,000–14,999	73.6	15.1	11.2	100.0	54.7	22.6	22.7	100.0
15,000–24,999	79.7	9.3	11.0	100.0	55.3	15.1	29.5	100.0
25,000 +	90.9	5.7	3.4	100.0	79.4	8.9	11.6	100.0
Total	81.7	11.7	6.6	100.0	72.2	16.9	10.8	100.0

[a] From U.S. Bureau of the Census (1964). *Sources and structure of family income*, PC(2) 4C, Table 13.

TABLE 7-19

Husband–Wife Families by Number of Earners, by Husband's Income and Color [a]

	White			Nonwhite		
	Number of earners			Number of earners		
Husband's income	1	2	3 or more	1	2	3 or more
Less than $1000	52.1	38.5	9.4	39.3	43.7	17.0
$1000–1999	50.3	40.7	8.9	38.1	46.7	15.2
$2000–2999	47.1	43.1	9.8	40.1	46.8	13.1
$3000–3999	46.1	43.9	10.0	42.6	45.1	12.2
$4000–4999	46.9	43.0	10.1	42.3	45.3	12.4
$5000–5999	49.3	40.6	10.0	42.3	45.6	12.1
$6000–6999	52.8	37.5	9.7	42.6	45.6	12.0
$7000–9999	57.7	33.0	9.2	45.8	42.0	12.2
$10,000–14,999	64.5	27.8	7.6	54.6	36.2	9.2
$15,000+	69.8	24.3	6.0	59.3	31.4	9.3
Total	51.8	38.7	9.5	41.1	45.3	13.5

[a] From U.S. Bureau of Census (1964). *Sources and structure of family income*, PC(2) 4C, Table 21.

except at the very low income levels, the differentials are not great (Table 7-19).

Given the generally low earning capacity of nonwhite husbands, if a nonwhite family is to achieve a relatively high family income, contributions of two or more family members will be required. Table 7-20 shows the extent to which this is the case. Forty-two percent of the nonwhite families with incomes of $2000–2999 have two or more earners, while for white families, the comparable figure is only 22.5%. At the higher family income levels, nonwhite families are also much more likely to have two or more earners. Seventy percent of nonwhite families with incomes of $6000–7999, as compared with 49% of white families, have two or more earners.

We might look alternatively at the relative contributions of husbands and wives to family income when both spouses have incomes. In numerous discussions of the power structure of the family and of the so-called "matriarchal" family that is supposedly more prevalent among blacks and among the lower classes, the relative earnings of husbands and wives are regarded as a key indicator of power within the family, or of the degree to which the wife is economically dependent on her husband. Only couples in which the wife had earnings in 1959 are included in these comparisons. The relative income measure is the ratio of wife's earnings to husband's total income. It might have been better to have related wife's earnings to husband's earnings, but for various reasons it was not feasible. The results would not differ sub-

TABLE 7-20

Husband–Wife Families by Number of Earners by Family Income and Color[a]

	White				Nonwhite			
	Number of earners				Number of earners			
Family income ($)	0	1	2+	Total	0	1	2+	Total
Less than 2000	50.1	37.5	12.4	100.0	25.1	46.0	28.8	100.0
2000–2999	24.2	53.2	22.5	100.0	4.7	52.8	42.5	100.0
3000–3999	8.2	62.2	29.6	100.0	1.5	51.8	46.8	100.0
4000–4999	2.7	63.0	34.3	100.0	.4	49.2	50.3	100.0
5000–5999	1.2	61.2	37.6	100.0	.2	41.4	58.3	100.0
6000–7999	.7	50.1	49.3	100.0	.2	23.0	76.9	100.0
8000–9999	.5	35.7	63.8	100.0	.1	12.0	87.8	100.0
10,000–14.999	.7	31.5	67.8	100.0	.1	8.9	91.0	100.0
15,000 +	1.5	48.8	49.8	100.0	.4	20.0	79.6	100.0
Total	5.6	48.4	46.0	100.0	5.0	40.1	54.8	100.0

[a] From U.S. Bureau of Census (1964). *Sources and structures of family income*, PC(2) 4C, Table 4.

TABLE 7-21

Distribution of Nonwhite Husband–Wife Families by the Proportion of Family Income Received by the Wife

	.1–19.99	20.00–39.99	40.00–59.99	60.00–79.99	80.00–99.99	100.00–150.00	150.01+	Total
Black	29.1	21.1	16.2	9.4	6.0	9.3	9.0	100.0
Other	29.4	18.7	16.9	12.7	7.4	7.8	7.2	100.0

stantially from those reported here. Table 7-21 presents the distribution of this ratio for black and white wives.

The distributions are remarkably similar for the black and white populations. Among couples in which the wife had some income, 18.3% of the white and 15.0% of the black wives earned more than their husbands. Counterbalancing that differential is the lower black percentage earning between .60 and .99 of their husband's income—15% versus 20%. A higher proportion of black wives received income in 1959, but their relative income with respect to that of their husbands is distributed very similarly to that of white wives. The probability that a black women who worked full year earned more than her husband was .27, while for white wives it was .23. It does not appear that black wives are substantially more "powerful," or intact black families more matriarchal, in terms of the relative earnings of husbands and wives.

Working Wives and Family Income Inequality

To summarize the overall effect of differential employment and differential earnings of wives on the inequality or dissimilarity of the income distributions of the black and white populations, we have used the gini coefficient (Duncan *et al.*, 1960; H. Miller, 1966). Income distributions were divided into 25 \$1000-intervals to \$25,000, and a terminal interval of \$25,000+, and gini coefficients were computed,[1] comparing the black and nonblack distributions. Three separate income measures were used.

1. Husband's income
2. Family income minus wife's earnings
3. Total family income

Differences between (2) and (3) reflect the effect of differential wife's earnings, while differences between (1) and (2) reflect the effect of differen-

[1]A value of \$35,000 was used for the category \$25,000 and over. Other reasonable values were tried and produced no major change in results.

TABLE 7-22

Black–White Income Inequality by Family Status for Three Income Measures (Gini Coefficients)[a]

Family status	Husband's income	Family income minus wife's earnings	Family income
Husband–wife families with one or more children under 18			
Youngest 0–2	56.2	48.8	45.9
3–5	61.6	55.7	50.2
6–11	60.4	56.1	51.4
12–17	54.0	49.2	50.9
Total	58.2	52.5	49.6
Husband–wife families with no children under 18			
Wife 14–29	38.1	26.2	36.9
30–44	49.2	41.0	44.8
45–59	50.0	46.2	47.6
Total	46.0	40.5	43.5
Husband–wife families			
Wife under age 60	54.3	47.4	47.3

[a] From 1/1000 tabulations.

tial contributions of other income recipients (and wife's nonearnings income) on income inequality between blacks and nonblacks.

Overall, the gini coefficient for husband's income is 54.3 in comparison to a coefficient of 47.3 for total income (Table 7-22). Quite clearly, then, family income is less inequitably distributed than is husband's income. When family income is compared with family income minus wife's earnings, the differential is very small, 47.3 versus 47.4, indicating that the effect of differential employment and earnings patterns of wives make an insignificant difference to the inequality of distribution of income.

However, if we disaggregate the population into two categories, those couples with children and those with none, we discover that the aggregate pattern presented above results from differential patterns within these two groups. For both categories, income inequality is substantially reduced by virtue of the greater contribution of other family members. For childless couples (i.e., those with no children present), the racial inequality *increases* as a result of contributions by wives to family income, while for couples with children, inequality *decreases* somewhat. The effect of income of other relatives is greater, however, than that of income of wives.

Further disaggregation of couples in relation to age of youngest own child reveals that the wife's contribution in the case of couples with youngest own child aged 12–17 tends to increase inequality, just as it does for childless couples.

The effect of wife's earnings on the inequality of family income between the races is small because, despite the higher rate of employment of black wives, their earnings are, on average, considerably lower. Thus, a higher proportion of black families move up in the income distribution from where they would be in the absence of wife's income; however, the distance which they move in the distribution is smaller, on average, than is the distance moved by white families with employed wives.

Appendix

A Note on the Exclusion of Farm Women from the Sample

I have excluded women residing on farms from the sample because there seems to be a considerable ambiguity in applying the employment status definitions to them. In particular, there seems to be a large amount of unpaid family labor by wives living on farms which should, if it involves more than 14 hours a week of work, be included in the employed category. It is frequently classified in the census as not in the labor force. Many such misclassified women work a large number of hours per week. This fact was evident in the early 1940s when the labor force concepts and measurements were being developed and tested, and resulted in a modification in the way the employment status question was asked. There is evidence of an improvement in classification as a result of the change.[1]

However, data from the 1960 Current Population Survey—Census Match indicate that a great deal of disagreement remains in the case of women in farm jobs. Table A-1 indicates the extent of the misclassification. A comparison of the figures in Table A-1 with those in Table A-2 indicates that the problem is much more severe in agricultural than in nonagricultural industries.

It seems reasonable to assume in this case that the Current Population

[1]See Louis J. Ducoff and Margaret J. Hagood, *Labor Force Definition and Measurement: Recent Experience in the United States*. New York: Social Science Research Council, Bulletin 56. No date.

TABLE A-1

Comparison of Census and Current Population Survey Classification of the Employment Status and Class of Worker of Women Classified as Employed in Agriculture by the Current Population Survey: United States, 1960[a]

Census classification	Current population survey classification							
	Employed in agriculture		Wage and salary workers		Self-employed		Unpaid family workers	
	N (000's)	Percentage	N (000's)	Percentage	N (000's)	Percentage	N (000's)	Percentage
Employed in agriculture	298	42	89	51	47	40	162	39
Employed in nonagriculture	55	8	13	7	19	16	23	6
Unemployed	—	—	—	—	—	—	—	—
Not in labor force	349	49	73	42	46	39	230	55
Not reported	11	2	—	—	5	4	6	1
Total matched persons	713	100	175	100	117	100	421	100

[a] From U.S. Bureau of the Census (1965). *Accuracy of data on population characteristics as measured by CPS-census match*. ER(60)5, Table 28.

Survey did a better job of applying the classification to the women, since the census put more of them into the residual category (not in the labor force) and fewer in the difficult to identify category (unpaid family worker). It is also quite probable that both the Census and the Current Population Survey misclassified additional unpaid family workers in the same manner.

TABLE A-2

Census Classification of Women Classified as Employed in Nonagricultural Industries in the Current Population Survey. Matched Women, Age 14 and Over: United States, 1960.[a]

Census Classification	N (Thousands)	Percentage
Employed in agriculture	47	.2
Employed in nonagriculture	17,016	85.6
Unemployed	268	1.3
Not in labor force	1,877	9.4
Not reported	659	3.3
Total	19,867	100.0

[a] From U.S. Bureau of the Census (1965). *Accuracy of data on population characteristics as measured by CPS-census match.* ER(60)5, Table 28.

References

Addiss, Louise.

1963 Job-related expenses of the working mother. In *Children*. Washington, D.C.: U.S. Government Printing Office.

Andrews, F., J. Morgan, and J. Sonquist.

1967 *Multiple classification analysis: A report on a computer program for multiple regression using categorical predictors*. Ann Arbor, Michigan: Institute for Social Research.

Baker, E. F.

1964 *Technology and woman's work*. New York: Columbia Univ. Press.

Bancroft, G.

1958 *The American labor force: Its growth and changing composition*, a volume in the 1950 Census Monograph Series. New York: Wiley.

Belloc, N. B.

1950 Labor force participation and employment opportunities for women, *Journal of the American Statistical Association* **45**:400–410

Blau, Z. S.

1964 Exposure to child-rearing experts: A structural interpretation of class–color differences, *American Journal of Sociology* **69**:596–608.

Blood, R.

1965 Long-range causes and consequences of the employment of married women, *Journal of Marriage and the Family* **27**:43–47.

Blood, R. and D. Wolfe.

1960 *Husbands and wives: The dynamics of married living*. New York: The Free Press.

Bogue, D. J. and E. M. Murphy

1964 The effect of classification errors upon statistical inference: A case analysis with census data, *Demography*, No. 1.

Bowen, W. G. and T. A. Finegan.

1965 Labor force participation and unemployment. In *Employment policy and the labor market*, edited by Arthur Ross, Berkeley: Univ. of California Press.

1966 Educational attainment and labor force participation. *American Economic Review* **65**:567–582.

1969 *The economics of labor force participation.* Princeton, New Jersey: Princeton Univ. Press.

Cain, G.

1966 *Married women in the labor force: An economic analysis.* Chicago: Univ. of Chicago Press.

1967 Unemployment and the labor force participation of secondary workers, *Industrial and Labor Relations Review* **20**:275–297.

Clare, J.

1957 *The relationship of non-familial activities to fertility behavior.* Unpublished Ph.D. dissertation. Ann Arbor: Department of Sociology, Univ. of Michigan.

Clover, V. T.

1962 Net income of employed wives with husband present. In *Studies in Economics and Business*. Lubbock, Texas: Department of Economics, Texas Technological College.

Condran, G. and J. G. Condran

1971 Income differentials between men and women, paper presented to the 1971 Annual Meeting of the Population Association of America.

David, M. H.

1962 Family composition and consumption. In *Contributions to economic analysis*, Vol. 25, Amsterdam: North-Holland.

Deusenberry, J.

1949 *Income, savings and the theory of consumer behavior.* Cambridge, Massachusetts: Harvard Univ. Press.

Dodge, N. T.

1966 *Women in the Soviet economy*. Baltimore, Maryland: Johns Hopkins Press.

Douglas, P.

1934 *The theory of wages.* New York: Macmillan.

Ducoff, L. J.

1957 The meaning and measurement of partial and disguised unemployment. In *The measurement and behavior of unemployment*, National Bureau of Economic Research. Princeton, New Jersey: Princeton Univ. Press.

Ducoff, L. J. and M. J. Hagood.

1957 *Labor force definition and measurement.* New York: Social Science Research Council.

Duncan, B.

1965 *Family factors and school dropout: 1920–1960*, U.S. Office of Education Co-operative Research Project No. 2258. Ann Arbor: Univ. of Michigan.

Duncan, O. D.

1964 Residential areas and differential fertility, *Eugenics Quarterly* **11**:82–89.

1967The 1970 census: Challenge and opportunity. In *Census Tract Conference Paper,* Series GE-40, No. 2. Washington, D.C.: U.S. Bureau of the Census.

Duncan, O. D., *et al.*

1960 *Metropolis and Region,* Washington: Johns Hopkins Press.

Durand, J. D.

1946 Married women in the labor force, *American Journal of Sociology* **52**:217–223.

1948 *The labor force in the United States: 1890 to 1960.* New York: Social Science Research Council.

Fichter, J. H.

1967 Career expectations of Negro women graduates, *Monthly Labor Review* **90**:36–42.

Frazier, E. F.
1939 *The Negro family in the United States*. Chicago: Univ. of Chicago Press.
Freedman, R. and L. Coombs.
1966a Childspacing and family economic position, *American Sociological Review* **13**: 631–648.
1966b Economic considerations in family growth decisions, *Population Studies* **XX**: 197–222.
Freedman, R., L. Coombs, and J. Friedman.
1966 Social correlates of fetal mortality, *Milbank Memorial Fund Quarterly* **44**:327–344.
Freedman, R., P. K. Whelpton, and A. Campbell.
1959 *Family planning, sterility, and population growth*. New York: McGraw-Hill.
Friedman, M.
1957 *A theory of the consumption function*. Princeton, New Jersey: Princeton Univ. Press.
Froeder, M.
1960 Technical note: Estimating equivalent incomes or budget costs by family type, *Monthly Labor Review* **83**:1197–1200.
Gendell, M.
1963 *Swedish working wives: A study of determinants and consequences*. Totowa, New Jersey: Bedminster Press.
1965 The influence of family-building activity on women's rate of economic activity, *World Population Conference Paper No. 32*, Belgrade.
Glick, P. C.
1955 The life cycle of the family, *Marriage and Family Living* **17**: 3–9.
1957a *American families*, A volume in the 1950 Census Monograph Series. New York: Wiley.
1957b The family cycle, *American Sociological Review*, **12**:164–174.
Hauser, P.
1954 Mobility in labor force participation. In *Labor mobility and economic opportunity*, edited by E. W. Bakke *et al.* New York: Technology Press and Wiley.
1964 The labor force, In *Handbook of modern sociology*, edited by R. Faris. Chicago: Rand McNally.
Herzog, E.
1967 Is there a "breakdown" of the Negro family? Reprinted in *The Moynihan report and the politics of controversy*, edited by L. Rainwater and W. Yancey. Cambridge, Massachusetts: M.I.T. Press.
Hoffman, L. W.
1963 The decision to work. In *The employed mother in America*, edited by F. I. Nye and L. W. Hoffman. Chicago: Rand McNally.
Jaffe, A. J. and C. D. Stewart.
1951 *Manpower resources and utilization*. New York: Wiley.
Jephcott, A. P., N. Seear, and J. H. Smith.
1962 *Married women working*, London: Allen and Unwin.
Kain, J.
1964 The effect of the ghetto on the distribution and level of nonwhite employment in urban areas. In *Proceedings of the Economic and Business Statistics Section, 1964 Meetings of the American Statistical Association. Pp. 260–269.*
Kitagawa, E.
1956 The family as a unit in the work force: A review of the literature. Paper prepared for the Committee on Labor Market Research of the Social Science Research Council.

Klein, V.

1965a *Women workers: Working hours and services*. Paris: Organization for European Co-operation and Development.

1965b *Britain's married women workers*. London: Routledge and Kegan Paul.

Korbel, J.

1963 Female labor force mobility and its simulation. In *The economics of human resources*, edited by M. Perlman. Baltimore, Maryland: Johns Hopkins Press.

Kurzynowski, A.

1967 *Continuity of employment and maternity*. Warsaw: Panstwowe Wydawnictwo Ekonomiczne.

Kyrk, H.

1947 Who works and why. *Annals of the American Academy of Political and Social Science*, **251**:44–52.

1953 *The family in the American economy*. Chicago: Univ. of Chicago Press.

Lajewski, H. C.

1959 Child care arrangements of full-time working mothers. In *Children's Bureau Publication No. 378*. Washington, D.C.: U.S. Department of Health, Education and Welfare.

Lebergott, S.

1960 Population change and the supply of labor. In *Demographic and economic change in developed areas*, National Bureau of Economic Research. Princeton, New Jersey: Princeton Univ. Press.

1964 *Manpower in economic growth: The United States' record since 1800*. New York: McGraw-Hill.

Lefcowitz, M. J.

1967 *Working wives: A way out of poverty*. Unpublished paper prepared for the Office of Economic Opportunity, Research and Plans Division, Office of Research, Plans, Programs and Evaluation.

Lewis, H.

1967 The family: Resources for change. Reprinted in *The Moynihan report and the politics of controversy*, edited by L. Rainwater and W. Yancey. Cambridge, Massachusetts: M.I.T. Press.

Long, C.

1944 *The labor force in wartime America*. New York: National Bureau of Economic Research.

1958 *The labor force under changing income and employment*, National Bureau of Economic Research. Princeton, New Jersey: Princeton Univ. Press.

Low, S. and P. G. Spindler.

1968 *Child care arrangements of working mothers in the United States*, Children's Bureau Publication No. 461. Washington, D.C.: U.S. Department of Health, Education and Welfare, Social and Rehabilitation Service, Children's Bureau, and U.S. Department of Labor, Wage and Labor Standards Administration, Women's Bureau.

Miller, A. R.

1966 Migration differentials in labor force participation: United States, 1960. *Demography* **3**:58–67.

1968. Current occupation and past training of adult workers Office of Statistical Standards, U.S. Bureau of the Budget.

Miller, H.

1955 *The income of the American people*. New York: Wiley.

1966 *Income distribution in the United States*. Washington, D.C.: U.S. Government Printing Office.

Mincer, J.

1960 Labor supply, family income, and consumption. *American Economic Review*, **50**: 574–583.

1962 Labor force participation of married women: A study of labor supply. In *Aspects of Labor Economics*, National Bureau of Economic Research. Princeton, New Jersey: Princeton Univ. Press.

1966 Labor force participation and unemployment: A review of the recent evidence. In *Prosperity and unemployment*, edited by R. A. Gordon. Berkeley: Univ. of California Press.

Morgan, J.

1965 Time, work, and welfare. In *Patterns of market behavior: Essays in honor of Philip Taft*, edited by M. J. Brennan. Providence, Rhode Island: Brown Univ. Press.

Morgan, J., M. H. David, W. J. Cohen, and H. E. Brazer.

1962 *Income and welfare in the United States.* New York: McGraw-Hill

Morgan, J., I. Sirageldin, and N. Baerwaldt.

1966 *Productive Americans: A study of how individuals contribute to economic growth*, Institute for Social Research. Ann Arbor: Univ. of Michigan.

Myrdal, A. and V. Klein.

1956 *Women's two roles: Home and work*. London: Routledge & Kegan Paul.

Namboodiri, N. K.

1964 Wife's work exprience and childspacing, *Milbank Memorial fund quarterly* **42**: 65–78.

National Manpower Council.

1957 *Womanpower*. New York: Columbia Univ. Press.

Nye, F. I. and L. W. Hoffman (Editors).

1963 *The employed mother in America*. Chicago: Rand McNally.

Oppenheimer, V. K.

1966 The interaction of demand and supply and its effect on the female labor force in the United States. Paper presented to the 1966 Meetings of the Population Association of America.

1970 *The female labor force in the United States: Demographic and economic factors governing the growth and changing composition*, Population Monograph Series No. 5. Berkeley: Univ. of California Press.

Orden, S. R. and N. M. Bradburn.

1969 Working wives and marriage happiness. *American Journal of Sociology* **74**: 392–407.

Orcutt, G., M. Greenberger, J. Korbel, and A. Rivlin.

1961 *Microanalysis of socioeconomic systems: A simulation study*. New York: Harper and Brothers.

Orshansky, M.

1965 Counting the poor: Another look at the poverty profile. *Social Security Bulletin.*

Pratt, L. and P. K. Whelpton.

1958 Extra-familial participation of wives in relation to interest in and liking for children, fertility planning and actual and desired family size. In *Social and psychological factors affecting fertility*, Vol. V. edited by P. K. Whelpton and C. V. Kiser. New York: Milbank Memorial Fund.

Ridley, J. Clare.

1959 Number of children expected in relation to non-familial activities of the wife. *Milbank Memorial Fund Quarterly* **37**:276–296.

Robinson, J. P. and P. E. Converse.

1966 66 basic tables of time budget data for the United States. Draft prepared for Survey Research Center, Institute for Social Research, University of Michigan, Ann Arbor.

Rosenfeld, C. and V. C. Perrella.

1965 Why women start and stop working: A study in mobility. *Monthly Labor Review* **88**:1077–1082. Reprinted as *Special Labor Force Report No. 59*, U.S. Department of

Labor, Bureau of Labor Statistics, Washington, D.C.: U.S. Govt. Printing Office.

Rosett, R.

1958 Working wives: An econometric study. In *Studies in household economic behavior*, edited by Thomas Dernberg. New Haven, Connecticut: Yale Univ. Press.

Schnore, L. F.

1961 Social mobility in demographic perspective. *American Sociological Review* **26**: 407–423.

Schoenberg, E. and P. Douglas.

1937 Studies in the supply curve of labor. *Journal of Political Economy* **45**: 45–79.

Smuts, R. W.

1959 *Women and work in America.* New York: Columbia Univ. Press.

Sobol, M. G.

1963 Commitment to work. In *The employed mother in America*, edited by I. Nye and L. W. Hoffman. Chicago: Rand McNally.

Social Science Research Council.

1954 Proposal for a study of labor force participation in terms of family units, Committee on Labor Market Research (quoted in E. Kitagawa).

Spock, B.

1957 *Baby and child care* (rev. ed.). New York: Pocket Books.

Stein, R. L.

1967 Reasons for nonparticipation in the labor force. *Monthly Labor Review* **90**:22–27. Reprinted as *Special Labor Force Report No. 86*, U.S. Department of Labor, Bureau of Labor Statistics. Washington, D.C.: U.S. Govt. Printing Office.

Stoetzel, J.

1948 Une étude du budget-temps de la femme dans les agglomérations urbaines. *Population* **1**.

Sweet, J. A.

1968 *Family composition and the labor force activity of married women in the United States.* Unpublished Ph.D. dissertation. Ann Arbor: Department of Sociology, Univ. of Michigan.

1971 The employment of wives and inequality of family income. *Proceedings of the social statistics section, American Statistical Association.*

Thompson, W.

1968 Internal and external factors in the development of urban economics. In *Issues in Urban Economics*, edited by H. Perloff and L. Wingo, Jr. Baltimore, Maryland: Johns Hopkins Press.

Tien, H. Y.

1966 Mobility, non-familial activity and fertility. Paper presented to the 1966 meetings of the Population Association of America.

U.S. Bureau of the Budget.

1968 Current occupation and past training of adult workers. *Statistical Evaluation Report*, No. 7. Washington, D.C.: Office of Statistical Standards.

U.S. Bureau of the Census.

1943 *U.S. census of population: 1940. Employment and family characteristics of women, The labor force (sample statistics).* Washington, D.C.: U.S. Govt. Printing Office.

1953 *U.S. census of population: 1950. Special report. Employment and personal characteristics.* P-E, No. 1A. Washington, D.C.: U.S. Govt. Printing Office.

1961 *Marriage, fertility, and childspacing: August 1959, Current Population Reports, Population Characteristics*. Series P-20, No. 108. Washington, D.C.: U.S. Govt. Printing Office.

1964 *U.S. census of population: 1960*, Vol. I, *Characteristics of the population*, Part I,

United States Summary. Washington, D.C.: U.S. Govt. Printing Office.
1963 *U.S. census of population: 1960. Subject report. Occupational characteristics*, PC(2) 7A. Washington, D.C.: U.S. Govt. Printing Office.
1963 *U.S. census of population: 1960. Subject report. Families.* PC(2) 4A. Washington D.C.: U.S. Govt. Printing Office.
1964 *U.S. census of population: 1960. Subject reports. Persons by family characteristics.* Final Report, PC(2)-4B. Washington, D.C.: U.S. Govt. Printing Office.
1964 *U.S. census of population: 1960. Subject reports. Educational attainment.* Final Report, PC(2)-5B. Washington, D.C.: U.S. Govt. Printing Office.
1963 *U.S. census of population: 1960. Subject reports. Employment status and work experience.* Final Report, PC(2)-6A. Washington, D.C.: U.S. Govt. Printing Office.
1964 *U.S. census of population: 1960. Subject reports. Labor reserve.* Final Report PC(2)-6C. Washington, D.C.: U.S. Govt. Printing Office.
1965 Accuracy of data on population characteristics as measured by CPS-census match. *Evaluation and research program of the U.S. censuses of population and housing, 1960*, Series ER 60, No. 5. Washington, D.C.: U.S. Govt. Printing Office.
no date *U.S. censuses of population and housing: 1960.* 1/1000, 1/10,000: Two national samples of the population of the United States, description and technical documentation. Washington, D.C.: U.S. Govt. Printing Office.

U.S. Department of Health, Education and Welfare, Children's Bureau, and U.S. Department of Labor, Women's Bureau.
1965 *Child care arrangements of the nation's working mothers, 1965: A preliminary report.* Washington, D.C.: U.S. Govt. Printing Office.

U.S. Department of Labor.
1967 *Manpower report of the president and a report on manpower requirements, resources, utilization and training.* Washington, D.C.: U.S. Govt. Printing Office.
1965 Educational attainment of workers. *Special Labor Force Report*, No. 53. Washington, D. C.: U.S. Govt. Printing Office.
1967 Job tenure of workers. *Special Labor Force Report*, No. 77. Washington, D.C.: U.S. Govt. Printing Office.
1966 Labor force and employment in 1965. *Special Labor Force Report*, No. 69. Washington, D.C.: U.S. Govt. Printing Office.
1965 *The Negro family: The case for national action.* Washington, D.C.: U.S. Govt. Printing Office.
1967 Work life expectancy and training needs of women. *Manpower Report* No. 12. Washington, D.C.: U.S. Govt. Printing Office.
1965 Handbook on women workers, *Women's Bureau Bulletin*, No. 290. Washington, D.C.: U.S. Govt. Printing Office.

U.S. National Office of Vital Statistics.
1958 Child spacing as measured from data enumerated in the current population survey: United States, April 1950–April 1954. *Vital Statistics Special Reports.* Selected Studies, Vol. 47, No. 3, Washington, D.C.: U.S. Govt. Printing Office.

Waldman, E.
1967 Marital and family characteristics of workers, March 1966. *Monthly Labor Review* **90**:29–36.

Watts, H. W.
1967 The iso-prop index: An approach to the determination of differential poverty income thresholds. *Journal of Human Resources* **2**:3—18.
no date The measurement of poverty. Discussion Paper, Institute for Research on Poverty. Madison, Wisconsin: Univ. of Wisconsin.

Westoff, C. F., R. G. Potter, Jr., P. Sagi, and E. G. Mishler.

1961 *Family growth in metropolitan America*. Princeton, New Jersey: Princeton Univ. Press.

Westoff, C. F., R. G. Potter, Jr., and P. Sagi.

1963 *The third child*, Princeton, New Jersey: Princeton Univ. Press.

Wilcock, R. C.

1957 The secondary labor force and the measurement of unemployment. In *The measurement and behavior of unemployment*. A conference of the Universities, National Bureau Committee for Economic Research, National Bureau of Economic Research. Princeton, New Jersey: Princeton Univ. Press.

Winsborough, H. H.

1967 Components of Negro–white income differences. Paper presented at the Population Association of America Meetings.

Yudkin, S. and A. Holme.

1963 *Working mothers and their children*. London: M. Joseph.

Zweig, F.

1952 *Women's life and labor*. London: Victor Gollzncy Ltd.

Subject Index

E

F

H

I

J

L

M

N

O

P

R

S

T

W